Hunting and
the Ivory Tower

Hunting and the Ivory Tower

Essays by Scholars Who Hunt

EDITED BY

Douglas Higbee and David Bruzina

FOREWORD BY Robert DeMott

The University of South Carolina Press

Published by the University of South Carolina Press
Columbia, South Carolina 29208

www.sc.edu/uscpress

Manufactured in the United States of America

27 26 25 24 23 22 21 20 19 18
10 9 8 7 6 5 4 3 2 1

Library of Congress Cataloging-in-Publication Data
can be found at http://catalog.loc.gov/.

ISBN: 978-1-61117-849-4 (cloth)
ISBN: 978-1-61117-850-0 (ebook)

This book was printed on recycled paper with
30 percent postconsumer waste content.

Contents

Part II

Why We Hunt: Personal Accounts

Part III

Because We Hunt: Intellectualizing Hunting

Foreword

"[Hunting] certainly makes life less highfalutin and more real."

T. H. White, *England Have My Bones*

Fifty years ago, during my first semester as a graduate student, I enrolled in a seminar on William Faulkner, a writer I'd heard of but never before encountered on the page. I'd heard that he was a difficult and demanding technician whose prose was convoluted, intricate, even impenetrable, and that it represented the zenith of American literary modernism, which is to say patently aesthetic and rarefied. I considered myself an average reader in skill, insight, and dexterity, so I feared I would be in for a trying time, given Faulkner's avant-garde stylistic difficulties. But I also heard that Faulkner had a reputation as a drunk, a bounder, and, as if it were the final condemnatory nail in his coffin, a hunter. Faulkner, the gossip went, was not in the take-no-prisoners category of He-Man Hemingway, but he was a hunter nonetheless, and that was enough for many of my seminar mates to cast a cold eye.

But it was precisely Faulkner the hunter ("a good hunter and one of the fairest and most agreeable men we ever had in our camp," John Cullen said in *Old Times in the Faulkner Country*) who appealed to me, and so I went into the course vowing to keep an open mind. Reading Faulkner in a Midwest urban university setting in the mid-1960s, recently married and trying to set a responsible course in life with my wife and first child and cut off for who knew how long from my already considerable hunting and fishing experience as a boy and young man in New England, made me value the hunt and its attributes, such as they were, more acutely than ever, though (nostalgia aside) I was never sure that I'd employ them again in a large-scale way.

If graduate school panned out as I hoped it would, I might be headed for a job somewhere in urban territory in a concrete and steel environment. That would not be my preferred venue, but it was a gambit I would have to play as it lay and be willing to accept for the sake of my family if it came to pass. Whatever job I eventually landed would have nothing to do with my outdoor avocations and everything to do with my academic abilities.

Just at the moment I was bargaining with myself over issues of capitulation, steeling myself to those eventualities and imperatives, and additionally unsure that I could ever add anything meaningful to the lit-crit discussion, I encountered the scene in chapter 6 of *Absalom, Absalom!* where Quentin Compson and his father are hunting quail in a driving rain behind two dogs, and, in their back-and-forth wayfaring behind what I supposed were quartering pointers, father and son discover Thomas Sutpen's and Ellen Coldfield Sutpen's dilapidated gravestones. The discovery added fuel to Quentin's obsessive reconstruction of the Sutpen tragedy, and it gave me a way into Faulkner's highfaluting Modernist prose labyrinth that I might otherwise have never gotten. In Faulkner, I realized, each reader becomes a hunter as well, picking up the trail and its scent, so to speak, in order to corner, if not capture, the fleeting text.

So behind Faulkner's vaunted linguistic artifice and stylistic sleight of hand, there was a backdrop of gritty physical reality to be imagined—wet, tired dogs, empty shot shells, heft of dead quail in the game bag, a man and child hunting together—that (except for Luster and the mule) resonated deeply with me and echoed similar events in my own life. For someone who had never thought much about the physical underpinnings of literature, the scene was a crossover moment between the world outside and the world inside my books, a startling moment, in other words, as sharp and compelling as the first flush of a covey of wild bobwhites.

English setters, beagles, fox hounds—my own or my uncles'—were a large part of the sporting fabric of my working-class family life in Connecticut and Vermont. Bird dogs and trailing hounds were part of an earlier education mentored by my uncles Pete and Tony Ventrella that had taken place outside school and that I admit, because of its visceral quality, often commanded more of my attention than homework. Later in the Faulkner semester, when we tackled *Go Down, Moses* and his signature outdoor tale, "The Bear," in which a hunting dog is a chief character, my enthusiasm was boundless, and I became something of a village explainer expounding on the intricacies of hunting and the dynamic of the chase to my untutored and mostly urban male and female seminar mates, whether they wanted to hear it or not.

"The Bear" and "Delta Autumn" brought out the most heated critical discussions on literature I had ever witnessed up to that point. There was much to debate: spilling blood, gun violence, racial injustice, white privilege, wilderness decline, hunting ethics, and especially Faulkner's portrayal of Ike McCaslin, whose pattern of masculine behavior featured a willful withdrawal from domestic society. Half the class judged that characterization to be romantic, even heroic, and saw Ike as an exemplar of resolute American frontier values; the other half said Faulkner was treating Ike ironically and that whatever he had learned in the big woods of the Mississippi Delta was undercut or tempered by his relative ineffectualness in social, domestic, and emotional spheres.

And though I saw validity on both sides of the debate, then as now, none of those issues, none of those controversial and emotionally charged questions, could be solved or answered to everyone's complete satisfaction. The hunter in me left that seminar with an abiding sense of how suspiciously and inaccurately the academic world viewed hunting, and yet the scholar in me admired the way the academy rigorously interrogated the subject. More to the point, I came away certain that where hunting (like every other hot-button issue) is concerned, ironies and paradoxes abound, not hard and fast conclusions. In the end, we make a separate peace according to our own lights and predilections. Rabid adherents for and against hunting, which is to say extremists of both stripes loudly occupying their high ground (moral and otherwise), are the only ones who believe they have answers to otherwise nuanced and complex problems.

In my case, to leaven sixty-plus years of regimented, lock-step college life—first as an undergraduate and graduate student, then as a professor at a public university in a rural, lightly populated quadrant of Ohio where opportunities to hunt and fish proved to be numerous and varied—I indulged in an increasingly steady but less predictable nonivory-tower diet of duck marshes and upland coverts to keep a sane perspective on the academic world. Change-up is good. "I reckon I got to light out for the Territory ahead of the rest," Huck Finn famously concludes his narrative, before his Aunt Sally can "sivilize" him. As we all know, his words have become a palimpsest, a hieroglyphic, of escape, as well as a flashpoint for critical controversy and skepticism.

But high-tailing it to unspoiled wilderness territory is less feasible for most of us than it was in Twain's time, so let's be thankful we still have the tonic of local wildness to temper our otherwise well-ordered and routine civic life and to act not just as a safety net but as a refuge and source of restoration for periods of personal dissolution, job-induced ennui, and wit's-end mania. As Jim Harrison says, "I've found that I survive only by seeking an opposite field." The fact that woods and waters are the destinations less traveled than ever before by most Americans in our increasingly urbanized, tech-savvy, wired society adds a slightly delicious outland status to these endeavors.

I can count on two hands and a foot the number of university colleagues and students in the past four decades who have shared my interest in hunting. (A former doctoral student, Mike Ryan, has an essay in this collection.) We have been a small, nearly invisible cadre of like-minded enthusiasts, many of whom would gladly risk censure by our more evolved colleagues for the indescribable pleasure of eating game. Of the men and women I've counted as outdoor companions, no one knowingly shirks home life in favor of untrammeled self-indulgence, egregious antisocial behavior, or willful domestic avoidance.

Mythic contexts sometimes blur fine distinctions and gradations, so I think it's possible to view lighting out for far fields to hunt not as a negation of work-a-day daily life, domestic, familial, and educational duties, and emotional obligations and expressions but as soulful enrichment via immersion in other, equally large, realities: marshes, swamps, fields, woods, and uplands are not a denial or erasure of home, hearth, business, and school but their necessary counterbalance. The boundaries separating the two worlds ought to be porous; we need both realms for psychic equilibrium.

Men and women in and out of the academy hunt for a thousand different reasons, but I suspect, for many of us with feet planted in both indoor and outdoor realms, it should not be a case of *either/or* but *both/and*. A reasonable appetite should not have bounds: loving the wild migratory woodcock and teal of the Atlantic Flyway and the ruffed grouse of the northern tier forests does not diminish or cancel my reverence for Picasso's *Les Demoiselles d'Avignon,* Ellen Gallagher's paintings, or the original handwritten manuscript of Steinbeck's *The Grapes of Wrath.* Sydney Lea says in *Hunting the Whole Way Home* that "making sense of the two worlds together" is not always easy. I understand that but take a mediated view so both the wild game on one side *and* the world of human agency on the other side hold similar values. To put it another way, both woods time with the boys and girls *and* face time at the hearth become equally valuable, equally enjoyable, equally satisfying and instructive. Despite pressure from the know-it-alls, to whom no grey areas exist, why must we be forced to choose between cozy homebody reality and unmediated wild inheritance?

The longed-for goal is to inhabit the elusive arena where nature and culture, wilderness and art, society and self, and even life and death intersect. It is the Holy Grail of quotidian existence. Ultimately, the far field toward which we journey is as much memory, language, and consciousness as any other manner of physical place or process. In erranding into the wild, we are always seeking our home, everywhere and at once, whether it is outside the door with a shotgun, rifle, or bow in hand or inside our study with a pen in hand.

Atavism is in our past. We are evolved, sure, but maybe not as much as we think. Within reasonable parameters, I don't think that is always already a bad thing. The hunt, especially chase-style, where sporting dogs or long-distance tracking is involved, can be all about the pursuit process. This is not to make hunting into a parlor game, as Robert F. Jones cautions in *On Killing: Meditations on the Chase,* for the overall goal is to take the life of some furred or feathered creature as responsibly as possible. But the truth is, sometimes we kill game, sometimes we don't. Sometimes we have blood on our hands, sometimes it's just sweat. We have to be prepared for either outcome. But if our dogs have had a good day of trailing or pointing or flushing or retrieving, if we have had our chances on the stalk whether we connect or not, the reason for traipsing through the woods is already fulfilled.

Unlike my uncles, who grew up during the Depression and hunted to augment family meals, few of us any longer *need* to hunt to sustain our lives, and yet being able to hunt is what we need. Few of us any longer need to hunt to put food on the table, but doing so provides plenty of reason for going afield. I hunt because I like the total ritual: the way a day out of doors has its own character and qualities; the intense physical exercise that comes from miles of walking in untutored terrain in all weather; the pleasure of following athletic bird dogs and watching their bred-in-the bone work (joyfully, I think) in an acute and almost unimaginable realm of the senses that is utterly closed to me as a human being. I appreciate the ethical obligation I feel to utilize all parts of the birds I'm fortunate enough to shoot and clean (by personal preference fewer these days than in years past): wings sent to biology research stations, feathers saved for tying fishing flies, and, because I love to cook, meat to be prepared for the table. "Eating a bird, I savor it twice," Charles Fergus says in *The Upland Equation*, "I taste the succulent flesh, and I remember how I brought it to bag."

I feel both satisfaction and gratefulness when I serve a dinner to friends (some of whom are nonhunting academics) of wood duck, ruffed grouse, or woodcock—the wildest of wild birds. These species, rooted ineluctably in their geographical *terroir,* are untouched by genetic engineering and cannot be farmed or pen raised on artificial scratch, cannot be planted for harvesting on pay-to-shoot game preserves, cannot be hunted, killed, and cleaned by anyone else but myself, cannot be bought, prepared, and cooked at whatever cost at the trendiest market or restaurant in America. That's the labor-intensive, self-sufficient bottom line, the moment of consummate appreciation, toward which hunting has led me and many others as well. "The primacy of killing," Guy de la Valdene says in *The Fragrance of Grass,* "has been replaced by a love of the process and all its intricacies." Bringing it all home from field to table plugs me into the larger motions of the currently expanding and laudable locavore movement.

Postmodern theory aside regarding the primacy of language, I want it all: the raw moment of unmediated animal encounter, insofar as it is possible for insulated humans to be exposed to and participate in such primal events, and the grammar, lexicon, language—call it what you will—conservatorial or otherwise, with which to frame and communicate the encounter, even if only approximately. Chris Camuto says it best in *Hunting from Home:* "I love language as much as landscape." Which is to say, a heart full of woods and water, a head full of books: we can both hunt and write, teach and fish, read rivers and coverts and animal sign as well as books, dissect student papers and gut and clean game, make up a course syllabus and cook a dinner of squirrel or venison or grouse, because all such activities are products of an ongoing search for the genuine, for unalloyed meaning in our lives that comes only from pursuing experience by our own hands, not vicariously or at a remove. Because each activity has reinforced and informed the other, I don't want to be forced to choose one at the expense of the other, though even having said that perhaps I have already made my choice.

Some people come out of the shadows, some come out of the closet, and some, like editors Douglas Higbee and David Bruzina and all the writers of this honest, candid, provocative collection, come out of the woods. Like William Faulkner, we do so not to abandon field and forest but to open a conversation that ushers them into our lives farther, deeper, more visibly than ever before.

Acknowledgments

We wish to thank the contributors to this volume, who patiently abided our editorial ministrations; our cheerful editor at USC Press, Linda Fogle; and friends and family, who accepted what we, empty-handed or not, brought home.

Introduction

Academics and Hunting

| DH: A Hunting Academic |

Hunting didn't grab me until well after I became an academic.

Growing up in a military family meant we moved every couple years, so I never acquired the geographical and social rootedness that seems to be one of the prerequisites to becoming a hunter. By the time we got used to a new place and new friends, it'd be time to pack up again. While my father grew up hunting and fishing in small-town Utah, he left behind those pursuits along with his Mormonism when he left for West Point in 1960, and, instead of heading out to the woods on Saturdays or attending church on Sundays, my two brothers and I grew up watching cartoons and playing sports. Probably my fondest memories of boyhood are of those countless occasions when my brothers and I and our temporary military friends—the language of baseball and football is spoken almost everywhere—would play "over the line" or three-on-three football or whatever until it got too dark to see. While it's a bit creakier these days, my shoulder still feels the pleasure of throwing something, anything.

Another portable pursuit I developed was the pleasure of reading. From Dr. Seuss to J. D. Salinger, if I wasn't playing ball, I was lost in a book. I'd spend half my summer plowing through the *Encyclopedia Brown* series or half the school night staying up reading Poe. When I was midway through college, the practical idea of medical school gave way to graduate school for English. I distinctly remember the first time I read Cleanth Brooks on Keats and Paul Fussell on British First World War poetry—their ability to elucidate linguistic complexity and the drama of history deepened the pleasure of reading.

Thus I spent my late twenties and early thirties in California learning to be an academic, that is, learning how to translate my reading experiences and political inclinations into "professional" or "objective" scholarship and pedagogy. My Ph.D. culminated in a dissertation on British First World War veteran literature. Then, blown by the winds of the academic job market, I suddenly found myself an assistant professor all the way across the country in small-town South Carolina, together with a wife and four kids. At a branch campus of the state university, a few articles, an edited essay collection, and a developing sense of how to relate to mostly underprepared students got me tenure.

Tenure takes a fair amount of effort and sacrifice, and it is nice to get. When you have it, though, after years of climbing, you start looking for other mountains. Dave Bruzina had recently arrived at our department to fill in for a few courses (initially on an adjunct basis, as academic departments increasingly tend to do). I can't recall how we hit upon the subject, but pretty soon we were talking about going hunting. Dave had been a hunter for decades and even spent a year camping on a friend's farm, whereas I had fired a .22 a few times as a kid but had never hunted.

We started with squirrels. Being relative newcomers to South Carolina and without much financial wherewithal, we hunted almost exclusively on public land. I learned where to look for squirrels, how to make myself less conspicuous, how to distinguish the sound of a squirrel rustling in the brush or the telltale flash of light in the tree leaves. I couldn't have asked for a better teacher than Dave—as capable as he was in blending into the forest and as sure a shot with a .22, he believed that no questions were stupid questions and that all mistakes (save those related to gun discipline) were forgivable. Before long I had learned to find, kill, clean, and cook squirrel.

If squirrel hunting is arithmetic, hunting deer or turkey on public land is more like algebra. You try to account for as many variables as you can—ascertain your quarry's daily pathways by preliminary scouting; factor in the weather, including wind direction; hide yourself in ground blinds made of fallen branches while keeping a shooting lane open in the direction you expect the animal to travel (on public land in South Carolina, permanent tree stands are illegal); and, especially in my case, drink enough coffee to stay alert having gotten up at 4 A.M. without leaving yourself too fidgety in the field. Still, the hilly terrain in the Sumter National Forest is rutted with gullies every fifty to seventy-five yards and scored by fallen trees. This topography, along with variable acorn densities and the always inconvenient presence of other hunters, makes still-hunting big game on public land a crapshoot. But I started hunting precisely because I wanted a new challenge. Having learned the ropes of academe fairly well, we professors benefit from occasionally putting ourselves back into the position of being a student, as we tend to forget how difficult it can be to learn not just new concepts and skills but, as with first-year college students, a new mode of being. I would consider myself a student hunter: while I have put in a fair amount of study and even passed a few tests, there is still quite a lot to learn. Probably the hardest thing about hunting for me is the need to combine active attention with passive patience. When I played contact sports while growing up, success was largely a result of buckling down and getting after it. With hunting, *carpe diem* goes only so far—you have to do your homework, blend in with your surroundings, and hope for the best.

If hunting affords an opportunity to remain a student in some sense, it is a different proposition from learning how to garden, build a website, or construct an argument. There is a certain level of physical commitment, a bit of danger, and a corresponding measure of exclusivity that go with hunting. I like getting up before anyone else in the house; I look forward to the challenge of navigating the woods in complete darkness and out of cell-phone range; I like providing my family with food in a more direct fashion than work-paycheck-bank-grocery. In short, hunting provides a means to exercise my masculinity in a world where action counts, not feelings or intentions. That ethos is not something that university teaching—or modern life generally—leaves much scope for. Hunting is not for everyone, and that's a big reason why I do it.

Hunting is not just about killing; hunting can even be said to take place without killing. But I also savor the emotional mix of potency and guilt that accompanies killing a wild animal. While death is an essential part of life, in our contemporary consumerist lives we outsource death to the marginal members of our society so that we don't have to acknowledge it. While raising live-stock on family farms was common a few generations ago, now mostly migrant workers kill animals for our meat; while a couple of generations ago the military draft was in effect, now in the name of the country soldiers do our killing overseas for us, yet they constitute less than 1 percent of our population; while we are one of the few Western nations to exercise capital punishment, murderers are executed in the name of the state behind closed doors. A central reason why I hunt is not merely to kill but to play a part in the necessary drama of death and life, with all the moral responsibility that that role entails.

| DB: An Academic Hunter |

I am sometimes discombobulated by encounters with colleagues or students who have discovered that I hunt. Perhaps because these encounters most frequently take place on campus, somehow I don't *seem* to them like a hunter. And yet, I grew up chasing insects, spiders, snakes, frogs, salamanders, crawdads, squirrels, whatever was running around the yard or the neighborhood or the railroad right of way. And I grew up helping my parents garden, harvest, pickle, cook, eat, and value homemade food. And since, to me, hunting is all about chasing creatures and making food, my hunting seems to me an inevitable outgrowth of my upbringing.

My parents weren't hunters and didn't permit toy guns in the house, but Dad had grown up on a farm and around hunters; his library included copies of Jim Corbett's *Man-Eaters of Kumaon* and Saxton T. Pope's *Hunting with the Bow and Arrow*—books I read eagerly in elementary school. As a family, we were frequent campers and kayakers, and Dad took me fishing when he could. And I had friends who were allowed to own "real" fiberglass recurve bows, who taught me to seine for minnows, to fish for farm pond bass and bluegill, and to gig frogs. And later I had friends who taught me how to cast bullets and load ammunition and shoot, how to sneak and be patient, and how to scout for turkey, rabbits, and deer. Having always loved the puzzles posed by the pursuit of elusive animals, I hunted more, and I hunted more species, until now apparently I'm a "hunter."

Becoming an "academic" has been for me a much more problematic process. The bookish son of a philosophy professor might be expected to end up with a campus office in a Humanities and Social Sciences building, but though I loved graduate school and still obsessively read, write, and argue, I've been reluctant to join the ranks of the professoriate.

To me, an "academic" is someone who contributes to the great conversation from which established truths (such as they are) emerge. My father, of course, exemplifies my notion of an academic, and I know that, like my father, academics can be distracted, detached, and difficult to communicate with, though also practical and capable and competent. They can be practiced farmers, mechanics, gardeners, or carpenters, as well as serious scholars with highly specialized research interests. However, I associate with all academics a sometimes discomfiting relentlessness of purpose—one perhaps necessary to worthwhile research but often destructive to other, perhaps richer, modes of thinking, living, and being.

In graduate school, I encountered academics of many stripes—caretakers and translators and alpha-dog obsessives, politicians and diplomats, troubleshooters and visionaries, pedantics and frauds. My growing awareness of the last challenged my interest in academia. The same naïveté that led me to study poetry and philosophy despite the poor prospects of the job market also led me to believe that American university professors should be more reasonable and sensitive and capable than those with lesser resources, training, and ability. Discovering the pettiness and dishonesty with which some academics operated left me disillusioned and uncertain. If immersion in higher learning didn't help us become better citizens and people, the whole project of being an academic—the pleasurable reading and speculation, the discovery and cross-checking of references, the argument and rhetorical flourishes—

seemed self-indulgent and selfish. I didn't want to be self-indulgent and selfish.

Fortunately, the structure of contemporary academia allowed me to inhabit a loophole. As an adjunct instructor at a state university, I could indulge my love of reading, writing, and arguing—I would have access to a library and experts and artists—while retaining my amateur status. Instead of being an academic, I would be a teacher, which seemed to me a much less objectionable identity. Adjuncts are the infantry of contemporary American higher ed. They are the grunts, who go in first and soften up the opposition and make things ready for the rest of the operation. They teach the vast majority of low-level courses at most universities. And at some institutions, entire departments—often the least valuable ones, like fine arts, music, and philosophy—are staffed entirely by adjuncts. Adjuncts, I could reassure myself, aren't really academics.

Then, unexpectedly, I was offered a job, nontenure track but nevertheless "full-time," which, with mixed feelings, I accepted. And suddenly, here I am editing a collection of essays, with my own office, my two computer monitors, my multibutton phone, and my shelves of books, all academically flavored. I've been elected to the university's Scholastic Standings and Procedures Committee. I'm calculating my chances of being promoted to Senior Instructor. My salary has doubled. I've signed an offer on my first house. And soon, my new and increased professional responsibilities will compete with my hunting in ways I've not negotiated before.

That makes me nervous. Like all worthwhile activities—reading, conversation, listening to music, cooking, arguing, editing a book, writing a poem, or playing with a pup—hunting ought not to be rushed. I feel protective of my time in the woods. I'm planning next semester's syllabi with an eye on the opening dates of public-land seasons. I'm weighing skipping a conference that's scheduled during the first weekend of deer season.

At the same time, the deeper I sink into my new role as a professional academic—as I learn about my colleagues and become party to the larger machinations by which the university spins—I find myself increasingly struck by academics' dedication, discipline, and faith and by the tenacious strength they bring to their projects. Working on this book, reading drafts and arguing with contributors and my coeditor, reading and corresponding and rereading, I feel increasingly and deeply indebted. Being an academic means contributing in meaningful ways to a great conversation, one on which I've fed parasitically all my life. I feel I owe some of my own effort in return.

| Hunting and the Academy |

As we hope our self-introductions indicate, being both a hunter and an academic is not a straightforward proposition. In fact, it would be fair to say that, generally speaking, academics and hunters regard each other with mutual suspicion. This collection of essays by academics who hunt endeavors to complicate the stereotypes constructed by both sides.

Many academics' understanding of hunting largely derives from a few glances at one of the proliferating TV shows on deer or turkey hunting, from absorbing the posturing of self-identified hunter politicians, or perhaps from reading students' first efforts at the personal essay. Consequently, outside wildlife biology departments, academics have little understanding of the complexities of hunting and have generally overlooked the ethical, ecological, and cultural ramifications of the topic. Conversely, the widely held sense that academics focus on abstract and arcane minutiae and the common pejorative use of the adjective "academic" fail to account for important work that scholars perform inside and outside the classroom.

These misperceptions can be clarified via some key statistics.

According to a 2011 survey by the U.S. Fish and Wildlife Service, 13.7 million adults—up 10 percent from the previous year—spent 282 million hours hunting big game, small game, migratory birds, and other quarry. Presumably some of these people don't qualify as hunters, just as some people who sing don't qualify as singers; nevertheless, these numbers establish that a significant portion of the population engages in hunting of some sort.[1]

According to the U.S Bureau of Labor Statistics, in 2014 there were 1.2 million professors in postsecondary education.[2] According to the National Center for Educational Statistics, about half of these people were employed full time.[3] Just as with hunters and poets, it is hard to count yourself an academic—a full participant in academic culture—if you do it only part-time. (By the way, we're not referring here to those instructors who teach a full-time load on a part-time basis.) It is impossible to determine how many of the thirteen million hunters in the United States work primarily as academics. Nine percent of hunters have five or more years of college education.[4] If working as an academic usually requires a graduate degree, then that leaves approximately one million people who could, theoretically at least, be academics who hunt.

But if there are indeed that many hunter-professors, they are remarkably invisible; our recent Google search (quotation marks included) of "academics who hunt" yielded exactly four results; a similar search for "professors who hunt" yielded fifteen results. It is probably safe to say that far fewer than a million hunters are academics. A search for "hunting" or "hunter" in the *Chronicle of Higher Education* website dredges up scores of articles related to job hunting and Hunter College—and exactly two pieces related to hunting: Charles "Eisendrath's "Shoot Me, I'm a Hunter," published in 2000, and Robert E. Brown's "Hunting, Fishing and Grading Papers in the Adirondacks," published in 1991.

The relative invisibility of academic hunters, however, does not necessarily mean they don't exist. In addition to breaking down barriers between hunters and academics, this collection aims to initiate a conversation about both hunting and academia and how they relate. What can teachers, researchers, and scholars learn from hunting? How can intellectual, even academic ways of thinking help illuminate the practices of and rationales for hunting? By the time the reader puts down this volume, we hope he or she will think this is a conversation worth having.

The Spanish philosopher José Ortega y Gasset argues in his *Meditations on Hunting* that hunting is a practice situated on the boundary between nature and culture: the hunter temporarily leaves civilization in quest of his primordial inheritance. But in the seventy-plus years since Ortega's treatise appeared, the relation between nature and culture has been complicated considerably, and recently a number of mostly nonacademic hunter-writers have begun to examine hunting in ways that have significant implications for academics working in philosophy, environmental studies, or sociology, as well as literary and cultural studies.

Several recent books focus on cultural controversies related to hunting, such as Jan E. Dizard's *Mortal Stakes*, Steven Rinella's *Meat Eater*, Forrest Wood Jr.'s *The Delights and Dilemmas of Hunting*, and James A. Swan's *In Defense of Hunting*, or on the ethics of hunting, such as Charles List's *Hunting, Fishing, and Environmental Virtue*, Allen Morris Jones's *A Quiet Place of Violence*, and Jim Posewitz's *Beyond Fair Chase*. However, we know of no books that focus directly on the complex relations between hunting and academic identity. Even the growing subgenre of "becoming a hunter"–type memoirs—which includes Lily Raff McCaulou's *Call of the Mild*, Paula Young Lee's *Deer Hunting in Paris*, and Tovar Cerulli's *The Mindful Carnivore*—focuses on the author's transition from nonhunter to hunter in broad social and cultural terms, rather than from within the specific context of academe.

| The Essays in This Collection |

In this collection, we focus less on how hunting invites consideration of the relation between nature and culture and more on the relation between hunting—as an activity situated on the *porous* boundary between nature and culture—and academe. Our contributors are academics from a variety of disciplines, each with firsthand hunting experience, whose essays—varying in style and tone from the scholarly to the personal—represent the different ways scholars engage with their avocation. Structurally, our collection is divided into three sections: the first section focuses on the often fraught relation between hunters and academic culture; the second section offers more personal accounts of hunting by academics; and the third section focuses on hunting from explicitly academic points of view, whether in terms of value theory, metaphysics, or history.

In the first section of the book, contributors from a variety of academic disciplines explore the relationships between hunters and nonhunters as experienced on campus, afield, and in the media. These essays counter misperceptions of both academics and hunters by providing accounts of how such misperceptions arise and are dispelled. Tovar Cerulli and Donald Munson offer autobiographical accounts of their careers as hunting academics and describe how their own attitudes toward hunting evolved in the context of broader cultural and academic trends. Annette Watson explains how intimate exposure to hunters, gained from fieldwork conducted among the Koyukon of the Alaskan interior, changed her thinking about hunting and animals. And Alison Acton analyzes how participating in foxhunting has affected her career as an anthropologist. Lee Foote illuminates the connection between hunting and pedagogy in an essay about his students' reactions to a "Renewable Resources" course lesson during which participants butcher and eat a white-tailed deer. And, finally, in the section's last essay, Philip Mason examines how the hit TV show *Duck Dynasty* mediates viewers' relationship with hunters and hunting and worries about the show's influence on viewers. Together these essays help map the tensions between academia and hunting, as well the ways in which the two subcultures can inform each other.

In the second section of the book, contributors address the delicate question "Why do you hunt?" In contrast to the conventional narrative—according to which a young boy learns deer hunting from a trusted mentor—these essays, informed by their writers' academic orientations, emphasize less familiar ways of becoming a hunter as well as less mainstream forms of hunting. Jeremy Lloyd describes being "called" to deer hunting as an adult and elaborates on the challenge of learning to hunt without a mentor. Gerald Thurmond connects a near-fatal fascination with hunting snakes to art and myth. And Richard Swinney extolls the excitement and moral benefits of boar hunting with a spear in contemporary Florida. Like Lloyd, J. B. Weir started hunting as an adult, but in his essay he grounds his hunting in family history and regional legend. Finally, David Bruzina questions the need for a moral defense of hunting and describes his dedication to hunting squirrel as a simple extension of his love of puzzles and food. By making transparent a variety of first-person hunting experiences, these essays both provide nonhunters with a richer understanding of the way hunting practices emerge from concrete real-world contexts and offer a complex portrait of the intellectual and emotional lives of academics.

In the last section of the book, contributors focus their scholarly lenses directly on hunting, countering the notion that hunting as an activity fails to repay close academic attention. David Henderson examines the evolution of historical arguments linking hunting in America to the development of personal virtue and describes what hunters can learn about ethics from current conservation movements. David Seligman worries about a tension between theory and practice in an analysis of the ethics of catch and release fishing. Gregory Clark extends Ortega y Gasset's analysis of hunting and argues that hunting offers hunters a revolutionary perspective on human nature and history. Michael Ryan draws on the philosophy of Edmund Burke to illuminate the sublimity of hunting. And Brian Seitz draws on Heidegger and Kurosawa and others to explain how hunters experience time. In the last essay of the book, Charles List circles back to Henderson's concerns and provides an updated argument for the connection between hunting and the development of hunters' personal virtue. Douglas Higbee's annotated bibliography in the appendix offers summary evaluations of dozens of literary and nonfictional books by academics and other intellectuals. These essays together suggest the profundity of hunting as a human activity and help dispel hunting's image as an anachronistic, purely recreational pursuit.

I

Between Academic and Hunting Cultures

Starting the Conversation

Gown and Gun

Coming Out of the Tower's Closet

When I began graduate school, I had no intention of parading around campus in camo and blaze orange. Except for members of the admissions committee who had read my application essay, no one at the University of Massachusetts knew that I hunted. It seemed best to keep it that way. Things would be simpler, my time there more pleasant. Though I expected to include hunting in my studies, there was no need to shout my hunter identity from the proverbial rooftops, inviting the condemnation that that would inevitably draw.

I had two reasons for anticipating the worst. The first was geography. Like every other hunter I know, I am keenly aware of the attitudes toward hunting that prevail where I live, work, or travel. Anywhere I spend time, I have a sense of whether the pursuit is likely to be met with approval and understanding or censure and hostility. In rural Wisconsin, I have learned, being a hunter helps you fit in. A neighbor might see you cross-country skiing in spandex pants, confirming her impression of you as another weirdo who moved up from the city. But if she later sees you hunting deer in a blaze orange vest, all may be forgiven. Now you belong. Along the central coast of California, I am told, the opposite has long been true. A colleague might respect your work and consider you a first-rate human being. But if he finds out that you spent the weekend tracking down and shooting a wild pig, he may mentally demote you to second-class citizen. Now you are alien.

My home state is a mixed bag. Rooted in traditional rural culture, Vermonters who have been here for generations tend to appreciate hunting and participate in it. More recent arrivals, often from Massachusetts, Connecticut, New York, or New Jersey, tend to be less comfortable with it. By and large, though, these two Vermonts get along and sometimes even merge. When I returned to relative omnivory after a decade as a vegan, it was not just the proximity of the woods—just thirty yards from our back porch—that led me to contemplate hunting as a potential source of food. It was also the presence and acceptability of hunting in the local culture. Yet, as a member of the newer Vermont, I was still uneasy about revealing my new pursuit to others. What would my friends, all of them nonhunters, think of me? It was with some trepidation that I submitted my first hunting essay to a regional magazine. When the piece was published, I half-wished my name weren't attached to it.

Headed to Massachusetts for graduate school, I sensed that I was entering even less friendly territory. Among other clues, reports, and impressions of which way the cultural winds were blowing there, I had learned from my uncle—a hunter who lives on Cape Cod—that antihunting sentiment predominates across much of the state, changing only as you reach the rural hill towns west of the Pioneer Valley.

My second reason for anticipating the worst was that UMass is an institution of higher learning. Like geographic areas, institutions have their own cultural norms. During my years as a liberal arts undergraduate in New York City in the early 1990s, a professor assigned an article on hunting just once. The piece condemned the pursuit outright, equating it with environmental destruction and violence against women. Had I been a hunter then, the one-sided article would have had a distinct chilling effect on my willingness to divulge the fact. It certainly would not have encouraged the kind of shared and open intellectual inquiry on which liberal arts programs pride themselves.

Though I could imagine university settings that might embrace hunting—a wildlife management program out west, for instance—my personal experience was limited to humanities and social sciences departments in northeastern states. That experience told me that hunting did not thrive in the kind of scene I was about to reenter.

Elite academic institutions, in the northeastern United States and elsewhere, have not always been hostile to hunting, of course. In seventeenth- and eighteenth-century Europe and in the minds of early English colonists, hunting and scholarship were quite compatible, both being privileges long reserved for the social elite.

As the historian Daniel Herman argues in *Hunting and the American Imagination,* circumstances in the New World did complicate the social, cultural, and religious meanings of hunting. For one thing, the continent was already inhabited by millions of other hunters. In American Indians, and in their hunting, the English perceived humanity at its most brutal and primitive. For another, commoners could hunt here. In doing so, they stepped into a kind of cultural no-man's-land between the extremes of nobility and savagery, laying claim to an element of genteel identity yet also bringing the hunt down to the level of the lower classes.

But American hunting recovered much of its status by the mid-nineteenth century. Stories of Daniel Boone, Natty Bumppo, and others had recast the backwoods hunter as a noble, heroic adventurer. Inspired by these cultural icons, growing numbers of middle- and upper-class men took up hunting as a way to escape their increasingly urban lives and to symbolically embody the kind of rugged, masculine identity valued at the time.

By the early 1900s, hunting was widely associated with prominent sportsmen and their advocacy of conservation policies and regulations designed to save wildlife populations from precipitous declines. These upper-class men—including Theodore Roosevelt and George Bird Grinnell, educated at Harvard and Yale, respectively—worked to ban for-profit "market hunting." They also promoted a chivalrous code of hunting conduct that echoed the sporting traditions of England and denigrated rural people's "pot hunting," the taking of animals merely for food.

Before long, however, the very popularity of hunting began to blemish its image. Herman notes that as hunting became more accessible—due mainly to inexpensive firearms, inexpensive automobiles, and labor laws that gave workers more time off—American men flocked to the pursuit. By 1945, a quarter of them were hunting. Many were working class.

Demographically, hunting had begun to shift away from the urban, educated elite back toward the rural commoner. Its public image soon followed. By the late twentieth century, American hunting was associated more with rednecks than with Roosevelt. Hunting no longer belonged in the rarefied realm of the academy. And critiques—by ecofeminist and animal-rights philosophers, among others—had begun in earnest.

In my first year of graduate school, my identity as a hunter remained largely separate from my identity as a scholar. The two collided only rarely, as when an anthropology professor happened to Google my name and was surprised to discover the other me. The previous winter, I had started a blog focused on hunting, a step toward realizing an odd notion I had begun entertaining: to write a book about my journey from vegan to deer hunter.

Approaching my second year, I had to choose a topic for my master's thesis. Curious to know what the pursuit meant to others who, like me, had come to it later in life, I began to research what I eventually dubbed "adult-onset hunting." Among more substantial findings, the study confirmed my sense of local attitudes. One interviewee who had grown up and attended college in the Amherst area mentioned that he avoided telling local people about his interest in hunting. He did not want to be perceived as "a bloodthirsty redneck."[1] As I began talking about hunting on campus, however, a strange thing happened. One faculty member told me how much he enjoyed venison. He said that he had grown up in a hunting family and that his elderly parents still hunted. When I stopped by another faculty member's office for a brief meeting, she expressed curiosity about my research. She said that, when she was growing up, members of her family hunted to put food on the table. Having read my completed thesis, a third faculty member exclaimed that he now wanted to try hunting. There was humor in his voice, but it seemed he was only half-joking. Something in the interviews and analysis had piqued his interest.

Halfway through my third year of grad school, my first book was published, and I began doing talks at bookstores around New England, including one not far from campus. A faculty member from my department came to the talk, asked questions, expressed genuine curiosity, and mentioned that one of her close women friends from graduate school was also a hunter.

Fellow graduate students—American, Bulgarian, Indonesian, Korean, and Latvian—responded in similar ways. They told me stories of personal connections to hunting or expressed curiosity about what the pursuit was like and why I and others engaged in it.

In short, my fellow academics did not seem opposed to hunting, my participation in it, or my study of it. What are we to make of this?

Certainly there was antihunting sentiment—and a small animal-rights group—on campus. It is possible, even probable, that some professors and students politely chose not to comment on my hunting. But I am certain that those who did speak of it were speaking honestly. They were not making up stories about their personal connections to hunting, nor were they feigning interest or acceptance.

If hunting is anathema in the ivory tower, are these people and their attitudes merely exceptions to the rule? Or is something else going on?

One day, a professor told me that he and his wife enjoy listening to country music. This was, he said, something he would not bring up with many of his colleagues. Among most of the faculty, he sensed that the genre carried too many negative connotations.

Culturally speaking, hunting and country music have more than a little in common. Both are associated with stereotypes of rubes and rednecks, of rural, white Americans as uneducated and unsophisticated. Scholars are far more likely to mention an affinity for jazz or classical than for country. Likewise, they are far more likely to mention an affinity for hiking, paddling, skiing, gardening, and even fishing than for hunting. (A similar silence can be found in environmental organizations: a staff member's online profile will often fail to mention that hunting is among his or her outdoor interests.)

Scholars might talk about and even romanticize indigenous peoples' hunting. But when it comes to contemporary rural American hunting, they are

Tovar Cerulli

more apt to tell a condescending joke or criticize its backwardness. In *A Matter of Life and Death*, Marc Boglioli notes that his doctoral fieldwork among hunters in rural Vermont was scoffed at by educated friends, while his wife's research among Inupiaq hunters in the Arctic was admired.

Slowly, it began to dawn on me. Of the four faculty members with whom I had discussed hunting, three had personal connections to it. When I broached the topic via my research or writing, they talked about it openly. Until then, however, they had not volunteered the information.

There are, of course, many and sundry details of our personal lives that we are not likely to bring up in conversation. Do my acquaintances need to know that I was a voracious reader of science fiction and fantasy literature in middle and high school and that I still browse through audiobooks in that genre if I have a long drive ahead of me? If I happen to see Tolkien or Orson Scott Card on their bookshelves, I might mention it. Otherwise, I generally do not. I am not avoiding the topic. It just seems irrelevant most of the time.

But my choice not to announce myself as a hunter on campus was not a matter of casual omission. Nor was my professor's choice not to announce himself as a fan of country music. Both silences were deliberate. Being a hunter or coming from a hunting family—like being a country-music fan—is not something one generally talks about in polite, sophisticated, scholarly company.

Perhaps the dichotomy between rural American hunting and the ivory tower is not as stark as I once supposed. Over the past half-century, perhaps hunting and other ruralisms have not been banished from certain sectors of academia after all. Rather, it may simply be that a communicative norm—an unspoken rule dictating that talking about such things is inconsistent with being a scholarly professional—has relegated hunting to the tower's closet.

Fortunately, the closet door appears to be opening.

A few months after completing my thesis on the meaningfulness of hunting to new adult participants, I was invited to discuss it at an event organized by Pioneer Valley Grows, which describes itself as "a collaborative network dedicated to enhancing the ecological and economic sustainability and vitality of the Pioneer Valley food system." The audience, composed almost entirely of nonhunters, proved quite receptive, despite the fact that many of them were associated with local academic institutions. (The valley is home not only to UMass but also to four highly regarded colleges: Smith, Hampshire, Amherst, and Mount Holyoke.)

That same year, I was invited to talk about hunting at the annual conference of the Association for Environmental Studies and Sciences. There, too, the scholars in attendance were curious and receptive. When I opened the floor for discussion, more than one spoke of personal involvement in the pursuit.

These events are but two small examples of a notable phenomenon: over the past decade, discussions of food, especially local food systems, have created an opening for talking not only about agriculture but also about hunting.

This is not entirely new. Contemporary dialogues about food can be seen as reinvigorations of earlier conversations, including those sparked by Frances Moore Lappé's 1971 book *Diet for a Small Planet*. Similarly, contemporary interest in do-it-yourself food skills, including gardening, canning, and raising back-yard chickens, can be seen as a renewal of the back-to-the-land movement of several decades ago. Then, as now, hunting was among those do-it-yourself skills. Look back to 1989, for instance, and you find a detailed *Mother Earth News* article titled "Deer Hunting for Beginners."

But there has been a shift in recent years. As documented by media reports across the United States and Canada, hunting has gotten substantially more traction, particularly among ecologically and ethically concerned adults who—like Michael Pollan pursuing a wild pig in *The Omnivore's Dilemma*—are motivated by the possibility of procuring free-range meat. New and potential hunters are reading a recent flurry of related books, including Steven Rinella's *Meat Eater*, Lily Raff McCaulou's *Call of the Mild*, Paula Young Lee's *Deer Hunting in Paris*, and my *Mindful Carnivore*. Some are forking over money to take private introductory workshops. Others are taking part in new mentored hunting programs offered by state wildlife agencies, some of which have been successfully promoted through local food co-ops.

From Massachusetts to the central coast of California, we are witnessing a popular reimagining of what it means to hunt for food. At the beginning of the twentieth century, pot hunting (and the taking of opportunistic "potshots") was often condemned. Now, at the beginning of the twenty-first century, hunting for the pot is coming back into its own.

There have been dramatic changes in circumstance, to be sure. The past century, for instance, has seen a hundredfold increase in North America's white-tailed deer population, from approximately three hundred thousand to thirty million. When the species faced potential extinction in 1900, widespread and relatively lawless hunting posed a risk. Today, hunting is closely regulated, whitetails are more numerous than ever—with overpopulations threatening biodiversity in some regions—and deer hunting is entirely sustainable.

But the recent opening of the closet door has hinged more on attention to the ethics, healthfulness, and ecology of food. What could be more natural, free-range, hormone-free, and environmentally friendly than local wild meat? What could put the individual meat-eater in more direct contact with animal and nature than hunting? These rhetorical questions point to the ways in which contemporary hunting is being shaped by concerns about animal welfare, human health, and the natural world, much as nineteenth-century hunting was shaped by that era's preoccupations with urbanization and masculine identity.

To most rural Americans, of course, it is not news that deer and other wild species can be pursued sustainably and respectfully as a source of healthy, local food. But it is news to the popular imagination.

It appears to be news to the academic imagination, as well. Every year, the crop of college and university courses on food ethics and ecology seems to grow. Every year, some of their syllabi incorporate books and articles on hunting: texts intended not simply to condemn but rather to provoke serious and open intellectual inquiry. On a number of occasions, I have received invitations to talk with classes at schools ranging from Smith and Colgate to Clemson and the University of Maine. Each time, I have been impressed by the acuity and sensitivity of students' comments and questions.

As examinations of food ecology and food ethics make hunting a more palatable and more common topic of conversation in society at large and in the ivory tower, we have a number of valuable opportunities.

We have an opportunity to cultivate more discerning assessments of hunting as a practice. If we are uncomfortable with hunting, what about it bothers us? If we are opposed to certain kinds of hunting or hunting done for certain reasons but supportive of other kinds and other reasons, what underlies these distinctions? In terms of impacts on wildlife and wildlife habitat, how does contemporary hunting compare to contemporary agricultural practices?

We also have an opportunity to encourage academics, among others, to recognize and reconsider their own antirural prejudices. For decades, prominent scholars have challenged and called on the rest of us to confront a host of bigotries and injustices constellated around race, ethnicity, class, gender, sexual orientation, and so forth. Prejudice against rural American culture has been less closely examined, in no small part because of the common (and ironic) assumption that rural people, especially rural whites, are bigoted and narrowminded.

The field of food studies reminds us that we are all utterly dependent on the land and those who work it—that we are all, in a literal sense, rooted in and sustained by the rural. This recognition, along with reconsiderations of hunting, has created an opening for honest conversations about antirural stereotypes. The humanities and social sciences can help move these conversations forward, assuming scholars are willing to approach contemporary rural communities (and their hunting) with the kind of nonjudgmental interpretive commitments long afforded to traditional hunting-and-gathering communities.

We also have an opportunity to forge stronger alliances for environmental protection and wildlife habitat conservation. As the social stigma associated with hunting is questioned in the academy and elsewhere, hunter conservationists and nonhunter environmentalists may have room to reconsider long-held assumptions about one another. We may be able to more fully acknowledge our history of common ground and collaboration, from the beginnings of the National Audubon Society in the late nineteenth century through formation of the National Wildlife Federation in 1936 and passage of the Wilderness Act in 1964 to the recent defense of Alaska's Bristol Bay against the proposed Pebble Mine. In light of this history, we may more fully recognize the formidable power of our combined political will.

In my work and my personal life alike, I am keeping an eye out for ways to make the most of these opportunities. I am also alert to further signs that the closet door is ready to be propped open.

Not long ago, we had a visit from my brother-in-law, an esteemed Cornell professor. While I prepared a venison dinner, he sat at our table, drafting a conference presentation on his laptop. As usual, he had headphones on and hummed along to background music. The surprise came when he broke into song. He was accompanying the country artist Garth Brooks, crooning "I've Got Friends in Low Places."

Becoming-Academic and Becoming-Animal

From New Jersey's Suburbia to the Alaskan Bush

In the twenty-foot open aluminum boat, just after making a sharp bend, the three of us saw the moose's head and rack emerge above the plane of the water right in front of us. The bull was swimming across the river. As the sixty-horsepower slowed to make a wide turn behind the bull, I sat cross-legged on a cushion on the bottom of the boat—a non-Native academic among my Koyukon Athabascan hosts. Behind me in the passenger seat Warren[1] took up his rifle, which had been propped up against the hull. In his early seventies, Warren said that he had grown up in many of these Yukon River villages, off the road system, but I also heard he spent his early years living full time out at camp, trapping in the late winter Alaskan Interior and hunting ducks when the snow and ice receded with the spring. This was a man who had witnessed much change in these boreal forest communities, from the time when society out in the "bush" was still seminomadic and barely engaged with the cash economy. Allen, driving the boat, was not much younger and had been raised fishing out at camp every summer until he was an adult. We were intending to have lunch at one of Warren's hunting camps, not far up this tributary of the Yukon called the Koyukuk River.

The Koyukuk, being a bit less wide than the Yukon, was thus a popular river to hunt in fall for both locals and nonlocals alike: it was easier to spot animals when driving by boat. Nevertheless, the Koyukuk is the sixth largest river in Alaska; for much of its length it is wide enough to have a steep cut-bank guide every bend and large expanses of mud on the opposite shores, where silt and driftwood accumulate out of the slower-moving shallow water. On top of the cut-bank leaned black spruce and sometimes cotton-wood, whose leaves just this week had yellowed with the season; below the cut-bank, fallen timbers presented innumerable hidden hazards for a driver who has lost sight of the main current. Many of those cut-banks have been eroding at a faster rate with the melting of permafrost—one of the reasons I have worked with these Alaska Native communities is to record their local observations of a changing ecosystem. But I have thus also been privy to their hunting practices, as it is through their hunting that these people have learned so much about their local environment—day in and day out, season after season, one generation after the next.

In this essay, I present an auto-ethnographic account not only of this journey up the river but also of the larger journey I took because of my work as an academic geographer, a journey from suburban New Jersey to life in rural Interior Alaska. A white, urbanized female who became an academic to "save" the environment, my identity and how I live my life have been transformed by what I have learned from hunter-gatherers. This essay describes this journey from the cultures of the "ivory tower" to the political and social landscape of what some have called the "redneck."

| Subsistence Ways of Life and Death |

Allen leaned over from the steering column toward Warren and said, "Wow, what do you think, Cousin?"

He asked because we weren't hunting. Well, I learned over the ten years of doing research with these Athabascan communities that these hunters never announce that they are hunting, because being presumptuous—bragging—might interfere with their luck. It was disrespectful to the nonhuman to think that humans could ever *plan* to successfully hunt. Rather, Koyukon Athabascans, like many other indigenous peoples in Alaska and worldwide, believe that animals *choose* to "give" themselves. According to this belief system, these gifts are available only to a worthy, respectful hunter.

At the moment we saw the bull swim across the river, we weren't even "going for a ride"—the phrase indirectly (and thus respectfully) referring to the act of hunting. We were actually on our way to a potlatch ceremony for an elder, a ritual that Koyukon practice to honor the passing of a community member. The Koyukon are the northwesternmost group of Native American Indians in North America; their societies have occupied this part of the boreal forest for the past seven thousand years, developing an extensive knowledge of the kinds of actions required to live sustainably within this ecosystem. An elder I had known and worked with for many years, from whom I learned about animals and the Koyukon philosophy of subsistence, had passed away a few years ago; it was now time to commemorate that life with a ceremony for a final good-bye and an opportunity for the bereaved family to present gifts to those who had helped them in their immediate crisis. A potlatch is a ceremony to affirm the social fabric of the broader culture of Koyukon—literally meaning people of

Annette Watson

the Koyukuk and Yukon Rivers. To affirm our relationships to the elder and her community, my friends Allen and Warren and I were driving a boat from the downriver Yukon village of Galena up to the Koyukuk River village of Hughes. This trip would take well over ten hours in this open boat, with the wind in our faces—though I would sometimes crouch closer to the barrels of gas to shield myself from that crisp fall wind.

While I didn't want to think about how long the trip would take, Allen of course had the time and gas calculated exactly, knowing the abilities of his motor given the current load in the boat. Boat drivers learn quickly how to avoid being the target of a search-and-rescue mission for a boat out of gas—at least when the weather held. I came to admire many of the technical skills of the "outdoorsman" I saw in these Koyukon, both men and women alike. I had been living weeks and months at a time in a variety of the Koyukon villages over the past ten years. I aimed to better understand not only their local knowledge of the ecosystem but also their "traditional" or "indigenous" knowledge, the information and ideas based on their spiritual relationships with their environment.

A potlatch ceremony for the Koyukon is not just an event for the human community; it is also an event that affirms the deep respect that the people have for the other nonhuman animals and plants where they all live. Wild local foods served at a Koyukon potlatch include moose, beaver, bear, berries, salmon, and a variety of whitefish species, though many modern foods such as macaroni salad and jello are today common fare at these gatherings. Because wild species become the food that sustains Koyukon families and their way of life, the gifting of food affirms good relationships between families as well as between neighboring villages. The sharing of traditional food at a potlatch—and traditional clothing and crafts sewn from the hides of these animals—is a sacred act.

Our plan was to go right to the potlatch in Hughes, bringing a few silver salmon with us to share. Allen and Warren had recently harvested these fish on the Yukon; since salmon have recently become scarcer near communities up the Koyukuk, the fish was a special gift to the family and their community. Our plan was to celebrate in Hughes and then, after the potlatch, look out for animals on the way back down river, camping along the way, hoping to have luck.

That was the plan: but then we saw that swimming bull.

"What do you think, Cousin? Huh?" Allen repeated. He slowed the boat so that the bow rose up out of the water, and he continued to circle us back toward the swimming bull.

| Ivory Tower Environmentalism |

I have learned through my field experience that urban society is largely disconnected from what it means to kill for one's dinner. I should know: I grew up an urbanite and became an academic.

The 1980s grade-school classrooms I attended in suburbanized northern New Jersey (largely middle-class, largely white) displayed full-size Greenpeace posters of "baby" seals: fuzzy and seemingly helpless, with watery black eyeballs that seemed to plead into the camera. The image was part of the organization's campaign to legally ban the "murder" of this animal via clubbing, a hunting method used in eastern Canada. The images of these seals and their wide dark eyes, as well as similar images of "charismatic megafauna," informed my becoming an "environmentalist" as well as an academic who focuses on environmental studies—a not uncommon experience among other academics in this and similar fields. Seeing those pleading eyes affected me—but not being a part of the photograph, I read my own fantasies into those eyes. Growing up in the suburbs of New York, I donated to the popular middle-class causes and with my friends claimed that wearing fur supported murder. I imagined rural peoples as "savage" in their defense of Second Amendment rights and their practices of hunting. I didn't know until researching my Ph.D. that the Greenpeace campaign rendered the Greenlandic indigenous community economically destitute, while the photos were from Canada. I didn't know that the method of hunting in Greenland was the quickest and therefore locally understood as the most ethical method of killing the young seal. And I didn't know that those indigenous communities also were shown to be sustainably harvesting the species—targeting seals not only provided the community with an important source of fur to both wear and trade but also served to prevent the overpopulation of that species, which would mean a slow starvation for the less fortunate.[2] I didn't know that Greenpeace had made a formal apology to those indigenous peoples. Like many of my colleagues who grew up in this era, I saw and remembered only the poster and thought it applied to all hunting and hunters.

Indeed, my experience betrays a "liberal bias" in academic understandings of human-nonhuman relationships: hunting is often depicted as a violent and/or "greedy" act by the human, seen as only negatively impacting the ecosystem. Quite a few of my academic friends have said that they do not attend my presentations because they find the pictures I show of my fieldwork to be "violent." Academic friends of mine who admire my field experience have asked me for pictures of moose or other animals for their kids—but with the caveat that they *not* be pictures "with blood" or of "dead animals." Apparently, they wanted to see an image like that of the Greenpeace poster—they wanted to see the animal being "cute."

But I didn't have any photos of "cute" animals. I had photos of animals that had given themselves to respectful hunters. I documented the prayers of thanks humans said over the bodies of moose that bled out; I documented smiling children plucking dead geese; I documented which anatomic parts were allocated to which elders and families as part of the sacred subsistence economy.

Annette Watson

My academic friends were in effect asking me to remove the human from the depiction of the human encounter with the animal. Their queasiness and their request for filters on what they showed their children belied their own biases about the human-nonhuman relationship—a relationship where *there is no immediate relationship* between the human and nonhuman. Humans and their interactions with the world were not part of their image of nature. We could view it from afar.

The historian and geographer William Cronon made a similar critique of the environmentalist: that in assuming that a place called "wilderness" existed without the human, the environmentalist had effectively erased human responsibility for taking care of the land.[3] The *New York Times Magazine* version of his argument, "The Trouble with Wilderness," elicited deep disdain and death threats from the environmental community; Cronon had argued that by loving the idea of wilderness, environmentalists perpetuate myths of a "pristine" landscape that never was. After all, indigenous peoples have occupied North America for thousands of years. And they still do—all across North America. And through the practices of their subsistence they shaped the very ecologies that urbanites today most admire, including most of our U.S. National Parks and certainly all of "wild" Alaska.

Yet this assumption of a life where humans are separated from nature is evident through the use of imagery and wordsmithing, through academic theories employed to understand human–environment relations, and through the kinds of research questions being asked about hunting and hunters. Why create historical narratives that erase the human occupation of and interaction with the landscape? Why develop whole fields of inquiry devoted only to the measurement of the "impacts" that humans have on their environment, as if every human interaction with nature were destructive? Through my ethnographic research, I learned that there is a culture of "nonforagers" as much as there is a culture of hunting, and many of these "nonforagers" occupy the so-called ivory tower, being in effect "urbanized" economically and culturally, even if their institutions are located in rural communities.

| "Becoming-Animal" and Other Dynamic Identities |

Warren clicked off the safety, pumped a round into the chamber. "Yeah," he said. Allen positioned the boat behind the bull as it swam toward the muddy bank. Allen explained to me later that he had asked what his cousin thought— whether they should shoot the bull—because it would mean a serious change of plans. If they chose to accept the gift the animal and Creator gave to them—the gift being the opportunity to harvest a bull—it would mean that we might miss the potlatch in Hughes. But at the same time, Allen explained, he had learned earlier that day that others who had just traveled the length of the Koyukuk reported seeing no moose at all. And there was not much time left to legally hunt.

But Allen was commenting not so much why they took the opportunity as much as why they received it: "We got that opportunity," said Allen, "because we were honoring that elder. We intended to go to the potlatch." We had gifts of fish in the boat. We were together carrying out a sacred social obligation, related to broader patterns of food security and resource distribution across the Koyukuk region. Through my academic research as a geographer collaborating with Alaska Natives, I have learned how subsistence hunting can be part of a deeply ethical and responsible practice of socio-ecological stewardship.

Warren stood in the boat and took aim. "Not yet," said Allen. "Let him get out of the water. . . . Not yet, Cousin," he coached. If Warren shot too early, the bull would fall in the water and the meat would not be easily—if at all— retrieved. While it was essential to time the act of shooting perfectly, waiting was also an essential action. There is a universe of actions that must take place within just a few moments, during this encounter with an animal. These are not creative actions; they are not invented by the human mind but happen in response to how that other being moves or may move. Such actions cannot, because they are so fast, be conscious. These actions—perhaps what can be called instincts?—constitute a part of the hunter's identity.

Academics who theorize social life have been struggling to understand and talk about human identity, because both stereotypes and governmental policies can assume idealized, static identities. And yet we all know that identity is "fluid." That is, we are none of us a static "mother" or "brother," "professor" or "cashier" or "lover"—or "hunter." We are different things to different people in different places under different situations. Human identity is *contextual* and said by these theorists to be created by *relating to* other humans and nonhumans. These "relational" identities are fluid because they are *practiced*— that is, our identities are *rehearsed,* not a given, not static. By this theory, then, if a hunter stops hunting, for the rest of her or his life that person is no longer a hunter—present tense. It is only the iterative practice of hunting that makes one a hunter. And because identity is based on iterative experiences, people are not "beings" as much as they "become."

In this vein, the philosophers Deleuze and Guattari wrote that indigenous subsistence users were "becoming-animal": they share identities with nonhumans through their hunting practices.[4] This form of identity is often expressed in Native arts such as stories or totems or in the sounds made in traditional songs: creations populated with human-animal hybrids. Native hunters are "becoming-animal" in the sense that, because time is so short, they must "think as" the animal they hunt, unconsciously acquiring and deploying a tremendous knowledge base about the individual animal, the species, and its ecosystem relationships.[5] The hunter shares his or her environment with the animal—and thus also feels responsible for the sustainability of the species as much as for the individual lives extinguished.

The bull looked small when it was nearly swallowed by the Koyukuk, but when it began to climb onto the shore we could see this was a massive older male. Its rack spread far away from him on either side of his head. Warren remained still, standing and taking aim, as Allen drove the boat straight toward shore.

"Wait, Warren." When the bull rose up out of the water, he began making its way across the mud and up onto the beach toward the cover of the willows. I felt tension and hope for the partners to find success once Warren pulled the trigger—because success would mean their family could eat through the winter. Success with moose was especially important this year because of the declining king salmon run, which had recently affected the food security of the downriver Yukon villages as much as those on the upper Koyukuk. This king season, just a few months before, there was no subsistence harvest—because all ninety-six villages on the Yukon River, spanning both the United States and Canada, declined to harvest kings for their subsistence. In their sense of responsibility to the declining species, these Alaska Native tribes and First Nations independently coordinated a moratorium that allowed more king salmon to spawn, efforts consciously aimed to ensure the sustainability of the species—at great sacrifice to their personal freezers. Yet these families still needed to eat.

I heard the shot, so loud on my unprotected ears that my hearing dimmed, and I saw the moose take another step forward. Food security throughout Warren's village and region would have to be made up with successes during the moose season—and many families this fall had thus far not found much success.

The bull stood there momentarily, breathing heavily, in and out. It was so cold outside, and the lungshot moose was so wet I could see smoke exit the wound with every breath. But then the bull fell and ceased all breath. Warren and I were quiet as Allen raised the outboard motor when we reached the shore. We shuffled out of the boat quickly, pulling the bow line up the bank and the bow across the mud and out of the water. I watched Warren and Allen first thank their Creator; then for an hour I quietly watched them butcher the animal.

Indeed, I had found through my fieldwork that the stereotype of the rural hunter—dumb, poor, and uncaring about the environment—was a myth created by urbanized peoples. Among these non-White rural peoples I found hunters who, although cash poor, were rich in their knowledge of the environment. They cared deeply about ecosystem health—because they understood the ways that their environment directly fed their families. Their "care" was for the species, even while they might extinguish the life of an individual animal. Those who attain their food security via the grocery store are disconnected from local ecological processes, and, while "caring" about each individual animal, they are unconscious of the violence their food systems commit to species and landscapes; I have found that urbanites do not want such intimacy. They want their pictures to stay "cute."

And yet . . . it too would be unfair for me to label all urbanites this way because the urban identities of many individuals are becoming altered in their iterations. Subsistence—the procurement of foods via hunting, gathering, or small-scale agriculture—has been called a "way of life" by Alaska Natives, but it has also been increasingly practiced across Alaska by people of many socio-economic backgrounds and from its urban centers. Many—especially in the field of regulatory biology—argue it is simply not practical for all urbanites to hunt, simply because of the sheer number of fatalities that would be caused by such a large population of hunters. The predation would be unsustainable on the local animal populations. Nevertheless there is a growing fascination in national pop culture with this "Alaskan" way of life, with media taking advantage of the popularity of its "frontier" families and its "extreme" landscapes for payoffs in their ratings. Even a recent vice presidential candidate played up a hunting identity to connect with voters, both rural and urban, who associate hunting with freedom- -to the disdain of many academics, who themselves were never hunters.

I should know, as I am one of these academics—growing up in New Jersey, I had no idea even how to make a fire. But these past ten years have affected me greatly; I know how to build a fire, and so much more. This year I built a cabin by myself—with just some help with lifting up my framed walls. I did not seek any training or professional design for the cabin but instead relied on what I've learned about living in the woods from my indigenous collaborators—and from my access to YouTube. The effort prompted even my indigenous friends to call me a "woods-woman." My Facebook posts documented my struggles to build this tiny cabin and circulated among my friends, contributing to a social discourse about the need for sustainability and self-sufficiency in the modern life. These posts are merely part of a larger pattern across the United States, where educated urbanites express disdain for the ethics of Wall Street and industrialized agriculture and criticize the imperial relationships required of global commodity chains. As a result of these dissatisfactions, urbanites are increasingly interested in "organic," "wild," and "local" foods and now constitute the largest growing constituency that takes up hunting.[6] In this era, some of these (wealthier) urbanites are seeking to become . . . something else. Just as I have.

Annette Watson

This essay juxtaposes my ethnographic account of becoming a hunter with my becoming an academic, understanding these "becomings" through the social theory of what is called "relational identities." While I describe the conclusion of the life of an individual animal, I also describe the becomings—the constantly emerging identities (simultaneously at the levels of a culture and a community and a self). These "becomings" that I describe result from practices of hunting and sharing subsistence foods. Urban dwellers—including most academics—do not share such intimacies with their local ecology. Academics do not often have the opportunity to understand what it means to be "becoming-animal" in the same way as hunters—very few academics become hunters. But urban practices are changing, as are the practices among the Koyukon, who must respond to their ever-evolving ecosystem and fluctuations in wild game populations.

Practices constitute a culture and make a person who he or she is; instead of vilifying the idea of the "hunter" in our urban imaginations, what should remain under scrutiny is the practices. Hunting can be an ethical practice; hunters learn and share knowledge about the environment, and their sense of responsibility can inspire ways to be effective environmental stewards across a continent. This is in contrast to the stereotypes of hunters as rural "hicks," small-minded, ignorant, and destructive to species and the environment.

Bringing together the world of hunters and the ivory tower is here meant to open a space where new kinds of understanding about human–environment interactions might be forged—because marginalizing hunting societies through assumptions masquerading as unbiased academic work will perpetuate the very ecological degradations that liberal urban environmentalists and academics wish to avoid.

By the time Warren and Allen quartered the bull and loaded the boat full with canvas game bags, it was night on the Koyukuk. We struggled to push the laden boat off the bar. We did not make it to the potlatch in Hughes but were able to send the fish on another boat that was completing the journey. The bull fed not only Warren and Allen but their sisters and their nephews, some of the single mothers in the village, and a few families of the community that did not have the gear necessary to practice subsistence. Some of the moose was gifted for purposes other than need. When I was gifted drymeat made from the bull I was reminded to respect not just that animal but his kind and the ecosystem that provided for him. "He is part of you now," I was told.

Out of the Closet

I was raised in a family where hunting was an accepted and enjoyable activity. It was part of my family heritage. I looked forward to hunting. I was proud of my hunting heritage, felt no guilt about it, nor was I ever made to feel any guilt about it. To some degree this changed when I began my professional career in higher education.

My formative hunting years were spent solely in the presence of my Dad. At first I would accompany him when he hunted squirrels and other small game. I remember shooting my first grey squirrel with a .410. As all young boys would, I thought it was the biggest specimen in the world and kept the salted, dried skin on my bedroom wall for many years. I also accompanied him on duck-hunting trips. My first duck was a mallard hen (again shot with a .410). I loved to go duck hunting with Dad even though it was often cold and uncomfortable. When I was twelve or thirteen my Dad gave me my first shotgun for Christmas. It was a 20-gauge Winchester Model 12 pump gun. It was full choke, and I still have it. I love that gun. I used that gun throughout my youth and hunted squirrels, rabbits, ducks, and pheasants with it. My proudest memory of early hunting with that gun occurred when I was fourteen. I was hunting with my Dad and my brother on Hogg Island, off the lower eastern shore of Virginia. That is where I shot my first Canada goose. I will never forget that. The goose seemed to be the size of a B-52! Looking back on these memories, I realize that hunting for me was as much about spending time with my Dad as it was about bringing home game. Later in my high school years I shot ducks on the Hudson River whenever I could (we lived on the river). In those days you could carry your unloaded gun through the small town where I lived and have no problems! My study hall teacher often let me out a few minutes early so I could get to hunt before dark. Because of his "understanding," I saw that he received some ducks along the way! By then I often used my grandfather's 12-gauge double-barreled L. C. Smith. Although "tight shooting," it was a bit more effective on longer shots. I hunted ducks and geese with that gun until the lead shot ban came into place in the mid 1980s. Once I started college and then graduate school, my hunting was limited to vacation times that mainly involved hunting ducks on the Hudson River with my brother and a few excursions for grouse and woodcock in New England, where I was studying.

Since the mid-1970s I have spent most of my academic career on the faculty of a liberal arts college in the middle of the Atlantic Flyway, where goose and duck hunting and other hunting (deer, quail, dove) are widely accepted. When I arrived on campus there was always a small group of students (and a very few faculty members) who regularly hunted. Regionally, waterfowl hunting was accepted. It brought much needed money to the area (through sporting goods stores, motels, guide fees, restaurants, and bars). In my early years I offered a popular goose dinner for auction in an effort to raise funds for the library. It was a good fundraiser. Yet slowly through those years, I detected an ambivalent attitude on campus toward hunting. Most students seemed accepting of it. Many faculty colleagues appeared to accept hunting in a neutral kind of way, but from some there was an undercurrent of disapproval, even disdain; the local, nationally recognized waterfowl festival was referred to by some as "art ducko."

I continued to hunt whenever possible, although of necessity I had to become involved with climbing the academic ladder, scholarship, research, grant writing, and so on, and thus my times afield were relatively few and far between. I hunted whenever I could or whenever I was invited. Most of the land around me is private property, and you need to be invited or to draw a permit to hunt. I did not make my hunting excursions obvious and rarely mentioned them to colleagues (except to the few who hunted). I recall a couple of conversations in the faculty lounge with colleagues about hunting and gun ownership. They could not understand why anyone would want to own any gun or hunt anything. I tried to explain the fulfillment hunting provided me—the oneness with nature, the skill involved in the stalk, the pride and satisfaction of a good, clean shot. It fell on deaf ears. They could not understand why anyone would want to kill something or own any gun, especially an AK-47 or a semiautomatic rifle with clip capacity of fifteen or more. Personally I have difficulty with that last concept as well, but I could not and cannot extend that to ownership of shotguns, rifles, and handguns. My colleagues could not or would not see the difference.

There was also an insinuation of "class" and academic snobbery here. It was implied that most hunters were blue collar and not on a higher academic (or intellectual) ground and that all hunters wanted to do was shoot everything they could. I tried to refute these thoughts, having known some very fine, intelligent persons who hunt and are highly respectful of all they hunt. Still, the image of "locals" in a pickup truck with two white-tailed deer in the back with their tongues hanging out is an image that many have of hunters.

When I was appointed head of a newly created Environmental Studies Program, one of my responsibilities was to bring speakers to campus. I invited many of them, representing all points of view, during the next twenty-plus years. I also was supported by the administration in building a natural history collection of regional wildlife. As I taught a course in the natural history of birds, I mainly focused the collection on birds. Much of the collection came from students who hunted and who donated their least damaged birds to the collection. I also had support from a local taxidermist who would give me a "discount rate" on any specimens that were never picked up or paid for by the person who gave them to him. Over the years a significant collection was built up. It was primarily housed in display cases in my office. Most students appreciated it and showed interest in it, but it was not rare to have a colleague visit and ask, "How could you shoot them?" I, of course, informed them that I had not shot most of them but that they were provided by students, local hunters, taxidermists, and others to help in building the natural history collection. This was absolutely true, but I realized over time that I was becoming a "closeted hunter," something I never thought I would become. I was becoming embarrassed about my hunting, and I never mentioned my hunting experiences to any colleagues.

During this period the program was given two black bears (a sow and her cub) that had been killed in automobile collisions. The college paid for their taxidermy and the building of a very nice display case for them. I was taken to task at a faculty meeting about the display, even though I explained they were not shot, were provided by the state Department of Natural Resources as support for the academic program, and so on. One colleague referred to them as the "dancing bears." The display was allowed and they are still on display, but a large hue and cry concerning them arose from both some faculty and some students. To this day the display evokes mixed emotions.

About this time some students wanted to organize a college trap and skeet club. I was asked to be the faculty adviser for the organization. There was much initial opposition to the club by the administration and faculty, but eventually it was allowed. It was difficult for some to accept that "the shooting sports" are a natural part of many college and university programs. All guns are kept in Campus Security, are removed only for designated shoots, and are returned immediately after the event. I am happy to write that the team now participates in national competition.

In 2002 I decided that I wanted to extend my hunting experiences beyond waterfowl and upland game to include big game. I contacted several outfitters in the West, and during the next several years I was fortunate enough to hunt and kill several mule and whitetail deer, pronghorn, and bison. In 2008 I went on safari in Africa (a longtime dream) and shot plains game and Cape buffalo. Upon returning, I continued to hunt big game, including elk and black and brown bears.

After shooting my elk I approached the College Public Relations Department about having a picture (of me and a very nice bull elk) placed in the alumni magazine under "Faculty Accomplishments." It was "gently denied," as it "might be upsetting to some alumni." I wonder if I had a picture of me and the chairman of the college's Board of Governors with a "trophy" rockfish (striped bass) from the Chesapeake Bay or one showing me goose hunting with him on a wealthy landowner's farm, would it have been denied?

As I neared retirement, I wanted to give a lecture in the series that I had directed for many years. As I wrote earlier, the series had a great variety of speakers—scientists, attorneys, politicians, artists, authors, and myriad others who represented a broad spectrum of environmental opinions. I realized that of the 175-plus invited speakers through the years, none had addressed hunting as such. I wanted to do so and to "come out of the closet," to let the audience know that I was not a blood killer but rather a sentient, feeling human being who enjoyed and was fulfilled by hunting.

The lecture was advertised, and I expected the usual modest attendance. I was amazed that the auditorium was filled to capacity with students, faculty, and townspeople. The lecture was titled "On Hunting." My opening focus was to try to differentiate between "hunting" and "killing." The initial visual was of me at the age of eighteen on a fishing vacation in Canada. In my right hand I held a .22 Colt Woodsman pistol, and in my left I held three ruffed grouse that I had shot on the ground. I explained that as "killing, not hunting." I then showed two visuals by one of my favorite artists, Winslow Homer. The works were "A Good Shot" (deer hunting in the Adirondacks) and "Right and Left" (sea-duck hunting off the coast of Maine). I then tried to explain how I believed that both of those works could be described as "hunting, not killing," even though they are quite dramatic in their representation.

I then briefly discussed Henry Thoreau and his often quoted (and in my opinion misinterpreted) writings about hunting. I do not believe Thoreau was as against hunting as many people believe. As he wrote, "There is a period in the history in the individual, as of the race, when the hunters are the best men. We cannot but pity the boy who has never fired a gun; he is no more humane while his education has been sadly neglected." But then he continued: "No humane being, past the thoughtless age of boyhood, will wantonly murder any creature which holds its life by the same tenure as he does."[1] Many believe that statement to be antihunting. I do not.

I believe the important word here is "wantonly." My dictionary defines "wantonly" as showing utter lack of moderation, unrestrainedly excessive, uncontrolled and gratuitous maliciousness. I do not believe that any thoughtful, feeling hunter could be described with these words. They are words that sometimes may be applied to someone in "the thoughtless age of boyhood" or to the unfortunate few adult game hogs that we all know exist. Many mature hunters today probably could have been described as wanton in their youth, especially when the goal was to "limit out." For me, and, for most hunters I know, this was a brief, transitory period that was replaced by a mature attitude, an attitude of respect, admiration, thankfulness, and reverence. Unfortunately, there are some "adult" hunters who appear never to outgrow their "boyhood" attitude. That is more than a shame, and they give hunters as a group a very bad name. In my opinion they should be seriously reprimanded or even have their licenses taken away. Mature hunters should speak out strongly against such hunters.

Aldo Leopold, author of *A Sand County Almanac,* regarded by many as the father of American environmental awareness, certainly was a hunter and accepted and encouraged hunting as an important means of game management. He wrote that he would raise his sons as hunters, yet in his essay "Conservation Esthetic" he was critical of the trophy hunter who "never grows up." In one of my favorite essays of his, "Smoky Gold," he described grouse hunting and wrote of those "luckless ones who have never stood gun empty and mouth agape, to watch the golden needles come sifting down, while the feathery rocket that knocked them off sails unscathed into the jack pines." As he later wrote, "I become aware of the dog down by the spring, pointing patiently these many minutes. I walk up, apologizing for my inattention. Up twitters a woodcock, batlike, his salmon breast soaked in October sun. Thus goes the hunt."[2] He never describes shooting at the bird. I believe he enjoyed the closeness with nature as much as (or more than) he did shooting the bird.

For the past eleven or twelve years I have primarily been involved with big-game hunting. Most of it has been good, most animals being killed with one shot. I take some pride in that fact. But in Africa I had an experience that still haunts me today and has had a profound influence on my personal feelings about hunting. Much shooting in Africa is done with shooting sticks, a pair of sticks joined in an X and used as a rifle rest. In my opinion this is not the easiest way of shooting. I was sighting on a waterbuck (using sticks), and just as I squeezed off he moved, and I made a very poor shot in his lower abdomen. He fell down and then got up and ran. As he ran a loop of intestine could be seen extending out of a hole in his lower abdomen. He vanished in the tall grass and I (and the professional hunter) could not get another shot off. We tracked that animal for several hours until dark. The head tracker believed that the animal would be killed either by poachers or by lions during the night. We resumed tracking at dawn the next morning. We found where the animal had bedded down—the grass was blood soaked. We found him near death a few hours later and immediately put him out his misery. The image of that animal with a piece of intestine extending from a hole in his abdomen has been with me since then. I still remember how much blood loss he incurred and how much pure stamina he exhibited. I have been told by many hunters, professional guides, and others that if you hunt big game long enough, you will have an experience like that. Maybe so, but it is not something I am proud of or want to repeat. So I had to make a decision. Would I stop hunting large game, or would I "get back on the bicycle"? I chose the latter, vowing to be even more careful and sure of my shots in the future. I made myself continue to hunt and from 2009 to 2012 I shot a bull elk (two shots, one directly after the other), two very nice mule deer (one shot each), and a black and brown bear (one shot each). The memory of that waterbuck is still with me, and I have learned from that experience. I passed up a shot on a brown bear in Alaska that I thought was risky. The guide did not like that, but I wanted to be sure of my shot and I told the guide that. I know now that if I take my time, take careful aim, take no chances, and am more than 99 percent sure of my shot, my waterbuck memory will continue to fade.

My lecture was followed by several questions. Most of the questions were reasonable, even respectful. The audience seemed truly interested in a topic that many knew little about. Many students appeared supportive. However, there were two questions from fellow faculty members that I tried to answer well, but I do not believe the questioners thought my answers were adequate. One asked, "What are you thinking when you aim at an animal and know that you are trying to kill it?" I answered that I always hoped to shoot cleanly and accurately and kill the animal as humanely and rapidly as possible, that I held the animal in utmost respect, both before and after the shot. The same questioner asked again, "But what are you really thinking?" I tried to explain again with the same answer and added, quoting Santiago in Hemingway's *The Old Man and the Sea* when he says, "the fish is my friend too . . . but I must kill him."[3] I do not think my answer satisfied that colleague. Another colleague asked if it would not be better just to take photographs (reminiscent of Leopold's valid criticism of trophy hunters). I said for some it probably would, but photographing a cape buffalo from the safety of a Toyota Land Cruiser is an entirely different experience from stalking one, sometimes on hands and knees, through thick grass, thorns, and mopane scrub.

Will I ever hunt large game again? I hope so, and I would like to if physically able. When I was a young boy it was important for me to fill the creel. It no longer is. I fish on some of the finest trout streams in the east, and I release 99 percent of the fish that I catch. I am now a bit "long in the tooth" and cannot slog through marshes or climb hills and mountains the way I once did. I love the field, the whistle or whirr of wings, the smell of the marsh, the rustle of alder leaves in the wind, the joy of watching a good dog work, and the humor in watching a "not so good" dog work. A heavy game pocket in a hunting coat is not as important to me as the peace and tranquility in my mind that the hunting experience provides. Without it there would be a void in my life.

For me hunting is a personal experience that has little to do with bringing home game. It is an attitude that evolves and develops after a lifetime in the field. It is a remembrance and continuity of family and memories of times past. It is the camaraderie one experiences with friends. It is a personal, philosophical fulfillment, a recognition and acceptance of a oneness and a connection with nature, of appreciation for it, of respect, reverence, and awe toward it. It is taking pride in the hunt, in the gun cradled in your arm, in a good clean shot, doing it as well as you can. For me, it is also a recognition and acceptance of one's mortality. Yes, hunting "dangerous" game can be life threatening (that is why guides and professional hunters always back you up on those hunts), but the smell of a decomposing and recycling marsh also reminds me of the continuity and cycle of life and that the hunter is part of it.

One of my favorite hunting and fishing authors is Dana Lamb. In the final essay, "Come Fall," of his last published work, *The Fishing's Only Part Of It,* he wrote: "with boundless joy the setters dash ahead to drink at springs: to read the messages on stumps and rocks, left there by fox or passing pointer. Thinking back to halcyon days on trout and salmon rivers with his harmless hooks, the hunter has but one more wish: why can't he shoot the gentle creatures of the field, the forest and the marsh with *barbless ammunition?*"[4]

I wholeheartedly concur.

The Knife, the Deer, and the Student

Academic Transformations

The blade slid along the deer's inner thigh, and the hide retracted to expose the translucent fascia enfolding perfect red muscle. With the sharp glistening Gerber in her right hand, Michelle paused as her eyes welled up with tears. As group leader, I hadn't anticipated this, and I blurted "Is everything OK?" Her response both surprised me and opened a new discussion for our group. She said, "I miss my grandpa; he would have loved this." She explained to those of us kneeling in the snow beside the handsome whitetail buck that this visceral experience had carried her back to her early childhood at the family farm where her deaf grandfather would return from the back pasture each November with his deer, moose, or geese to hang in the barn. Michelle was always there at his side, helping skin, pluck, gut, and butcher the season's wild meat. When she was nine, this tradition stopped with his death. Shortly thereafter, her parents sold the farm, moved to town and closed the door on a much-loved part of her childhood. It was one of the most poignant and heart-felt eulogies to a broken connection to the land I have ever witnessed. It was all there: the power of blood, the memory of being connected to the earth's gifts, the meaning of heritage and self-sufficiency. Braided in was the knowledge that she was needed and valued by a competent but deaf grandpa whom she idolized.

What may seem odd about Michelle's insights is that they were part of a senior class I taught at the University of Alberta.

Each November for eleven years, my students and I gathered for an outdoor deer laboratory as part of my Renewable Resources class. We met in my back yard on a Sunday morning after the opening Saturday of deer-hunting season. The goal was to talk about the meaning of the hunt and the personal and biological reasons for hunting and to make at least part of the experience real and tangible by examining and then step-by-step disassembling a wild animal. Through watching, feeling, smelling, and, later, tasting the unfolding production of human food, it became a complete sensory-emotive-cognitive-reflective experience. Students' actual participation provided a relatively rare chance to engage in the ancient and somewhat primal process of changing an intact organism into healthy usable products for humans. Importantly, the hunter's sequence was clear: (1) preparing mentally, attitudinal, and in some cases spiritually and communally; (2) collecting tools and knowledge for the hunt, including procuring the weapon, practicing skills, obtaining cultural/legal permissions, and understanding the habitat and species traits; (3) encountering, recognizing, and having a relationship with the living animal, albeit sometimes fleeting; (4) making a conscious decision and acting to end the animal's life, thereby converting its life energy to another state; (5) recovering the animal and reconciling the kill by taking responsibility for its death in the moment; (6) assuming possession and responsibility for the carcass through tagging, field preparation, and transport; (7) respectfully extracting value from as many parts of the carcass as possible (for example, hide, antlers, meat, stew bones, suet for birds, hooves for dog, tails for fly-tying, sinew for bow-making); (8) using and sharing the meat in meals and communicating the experience; (9) reflecting on the experience with a heart open to growth, change, insight, and learning; and (10) looking forward to our hunting future, which includes feeding ourselves and developing our growing relationship to the natural resources on which we depend. Interestingly, with meat purchased commercially, these ten important steps are reduced to a portion of step 8. Even though both can be delicious, wild-killed meat constitutes a very different life experience from store-bought meat.

There is, however, a background story here regarding the run-up to this lab. Why meet in my back yard instead of at the university as I initially requested? Early requests to hold this exercise on campus or even at the campus farm were met with resistance, fear of community complaints, fearful suggestions that the media might show up and university spokespersons would botch the explanation, and concerns about the graphic nature of buckets of blood on the white snow—or possibly even student protests. Each of these hit soft PR spots in the corporate portions of the university.

When I started this exercise in my early years as a pre-tenure professor, I tried to appeal to reason and address each of the dreamt-up concerns. No luck. My request was then passed up to the Safety Office, which enflamed concerns about violent protests, use of sharp knives, lead-tainted meat, and mistaken calls to the police about blood on the snow. The opposition was topped off with the objections of the University Animal Care Committee, a representative arm of the Canadian Council of Animal Care. They asked me to file an animal care protocol for my laboratory exercise. This request was a hill too far. Fortunately, I had been a member of that university committee for several years and knew to reply: "This is a legally harvested and tagged animal under the auspices of the Province of Alberta, and students will only be exposed to a carcass, something which is not living and over which you have no jurisdiction." That hushed them. I hope you will forgive my small fist pump here. Wins over intransigent administrators are rare.

In compromise mode, though, I agreed to start with a carcass and hold the lab off campus, so the university bureaucracy was sufficiently mollified. Administrators metaphorically washed their hands of the bloody topic and dropped their opposition. I didn't specify that the lab would be held in my back yard, and they didn't ask. Interestingly, no protests appeared, the police didn't come, nobody got lead poisoning, and a few interested nonhunting neighbors actually strolled over to watch, too. I invited in a few reporters over the years, and, to a person, they did some fine bits of positive coverage on the class.[1] One story garnered one mildly opposing opinion and sixteen letters of positive feedback from dozens of respondents on four different continents, including Native elders, hunters, and some nonhunters. However, the knee-jerk opposition from the university's imagination confirmed for me that the media campaigns of groups opposing hunting had achieved some success. I never encountered a single individual who strongly opposed my hunting or holding the lab; rather, the bureaucrats' and administrators' strong reactions were in *anticipation* (read fear) that an antihunting movement was ready to pounce.

The class itself, Environmental Conservation Sciences 474, Utilization of Wildlife Resources, was a very well-subscribed course of twenty-five to sixty students each year. Eventually, after fears had been sufficiently allayed, it became a curriculum requirement because it was at the core of our renewable, managed-resource program. We explored dimensions of wildlife use from subsistence users to commercial production, from prehistoric evidence to high-tech computer-based hunting. We examined trapping and spent a day on a trap line with a registered trapper, and class activities included skinning the beaver, mink, or muskrat caught that day. We pulled nets through the ice with commercial fishermen, engaged in formal debates with a well-spoken antihunter from the university's Department of Philosophy, and worked a hunters' check station on a military base. My students ranged from the Birkenstock-and-dreadlock-vegan crowd to the camo-wearing rural Alberta hunting bunch, with occasional First Nations and international students rolled in. Students from other faculties sometimes took the class as an elective, especially Native Studies and Philosophy students. It was important to maintain a large and welcoming tent to accommodate such a diverse collection of backgrounds, value sets, and experience levels.

Although I wanted students to consider whether hunting was for them, I did not intend to convert students into consumptive or extractive users of wildlife. I took a lesson from the little toys called "Chinese handcuffs." You may recall the woven straw apparatus that would bind ever tighter on your fingers as you pulled harder and harder. This rather Taoist "open palm is the firmest grip" approach was evident to students, and being open and nonjudgmental did result in some students becoming hunters. Possibly the greater effect was that many students gained some tolerance and appreciation that hunting could be "done well."

The course goal was to erase ignorance and to allow students to compare as many thoughtful perspectives on wildlife use as we could find. Everyone had come to his or her position from a basis of knowledge: to display self-knowledge and accept the emotion, morality, and sentiment involved and to know that such sentiments are personal and individual. While others have their own emotional frameworks, many of the biological, economic, and physical realities were common to all. Even antihunters could benefit from understanding the motivations and biological implications of hunter harvests from animal populations. Students were held to a rigorous standard of being factually conversant in the biological implications of harvest responses (such as density dependence, altered fecundity, habitat responses, competition, and predator-prey dynamics) but were also allowed their own intuitions or sentiments. Students were asked to go outside their own comfort zones and to listen critically to views very different from their own. They never knew when they might be asked on a test or in class to argue a point, say, "To hunt or not to hunt trophy elephants; explain the rationale for wolf control; or justify a closed season on grizzly bears."

Back to the deer exercise. Although the farm kids and hunters in the class were comfortable with dead animals, it was a profoundly moving, even shocking experience for some nonhunting urban-raised students to be suddenly faced with an 80 kg, fur-covered dead animal that had been intentionally killed by a human for food. To them, the glassy eyes, the stiffened hocks, and the delicate whiskers emanating from a somber muzzle are the stuff of urban theater sets or late-night horror movies; there is an implied malevolence.

I overcame my perverse desire to prank during this "Ah ha! moment." These students needed to ease into their introduction to a large dead animal. A professor of veterinary medicine once told me that immediately after the first vet science lab in which cattle were dehorned and castrated (with some graphic but inconsequential blood spray and splatter), 25 percent of the freshman in the class changed majors. It was just too abrupt and distant from their fanciful dreams of cuddling sick kittens and administering pills to dogs, dreams based on depictions of vet work on television and in books.

To recognize death and our role in it is to turn our hands and hearts to a deliberately killed and highly useful organism such as a deer, grouse, or rabbit. Feeling the delicately patterned feathers or tugging the cape over a rippling neck roast leaves us unable to deny that we too share this common un-alive end point. Denial is a powerful and addictive drug that lets us escape into a world of self-delusion. Hunting, like childbirth or grieving, is an antidote to this denial; all of these activities draw us back to honest introspection about the clocklike nature of life.

Processing one's own kill forces a genuine reckoning with mortality and the assumption of responsibility. It can reawaken a sense of belonging to a community of the living. The discomfort this sometimes causes may also explain the lengths to which raucous self-absorbed hunters will go to distance themselves from self-examination. The insecure may take overly long shots, lack persistence in trailing wounded game, get others to gut, process, or butcher, and give all their meat away. Some will also toss carcasses around roughly or refer to them with terms like "This SOB" or "That big bastard. . . ." These individuals' behaviors can lead to missing out on very important opportunities for personal growth and can prompt the question "What were the rewards for you in the hunt or why did you bother in the first place?" Most subsistence cultures hold game in an almost reverential regard for the role it plays in sustaining their ancestors, themselves, and their children. There is room under the big tent of hunting, however, for many different methods, styles, and motivations. What academia can and, I believe, should bring to the process of hunting is the transparency that comes from thoughtfulness and polite questioning of motives and consequences, historic and potential future repercussions, and opportunities for understanding.

Hunting, like subjects such as abortion rights, political parties, evolution, and spanking, is a hot-button topic, and discussion often serves to more deeply entrench discussants in their unexamined convictions. Academic approaches allow some logical ju-jitsu, and the students' energy and passion can be redirected to achieve common ground, compromise, mutual respect, and tolerance—that is, if the discussion doesn't go nuclear and lead to name-calling, castigation, and derision. With that explosive possibility as a backdrop, the tension in my classes was always high, and students were attentive, which encouraged learning. It is easy to get agreement on increasing sustainability, food security, the reduction of animal suffering, increases in biodiversity or natural habitat, and widespread conservation sentiment. As these are discussed, the astute antihunting students sometimes realized they were being led into a contradiction between their moral stance against killing living beings and their pragmatic conservation ethic. That is exactly the kind of conundrum and teachable moment that professors live for.

With these rather heavy concepts looming large, the class's introduction to the deer was deliberate and methodical. By design, all of the animals I used for class demonstrations over the years were neatly killed with a single bullet to neck or lungs, and carcasses were then cleanly field dressed where they fell. I made sure the body cavity was well scrubbed with snow or water and largely odor-free before returning to town. There is room for students' personal growth and engagement with rougher conditions later. Besides, on my website I had photos of the step-by-step evisceration process. I would also collect small tissue samples from the various interesting organs as well. Each sample was well washed and pinned out for examination.

The next morning in my back yard—about a three-block walk from campus—the carcass waited, chilled and positioned under a clean canvas tarpaulin. When the students arrived, they would be greeted by a warming fire in the back-yard fire pit (with Alberta at latitude 55 degrees north, Novembers are predictably cold); cups were set out, and hot chocolate was warming over the fire. My daughter(s) and dog would typically be wandering around unconcerned about the deer but quite interested in the students and hot chocolate. Here, the presence of casual mood-setting children and a well-balanced and sociable pet helped set the mood and show that their professor was not a psychopathic killer but rather a fairly normal human being to whom students could relate. The rationale for creating a pleasant, bucolic environment was the notion that true learning is best accomplished with a relaxed and comfortable openness to all possibilities. Is this a deception or a manipulation of reality on my part? Possibly, but the deeper messages about what the hunt meant to me and what it yielded needed an introductory "ramp" constructed of space and time to give students intellectual and emotional access to the messages they could self-construct. A context is essential in setting the stage for learning because the human–wildlife relationship does not distill well to simple biology, coarse utilitarianism, or the fanciful self-aggrandizing conquest of trophies. Academia is often overly sterile and thus underconnected to meaning and personal relevance. Profound understanding and personal interpretations of the profound must be nurtured through experiential learning and sharing. I sought to reduce tension-filled distractions in my back yard by making students comfortable with the setting so that they could better deal with any discomfort they felt with the processing.

Before the tarp was pulled back, we held a ten-minute discussion about respect for the animal, the well-considered intentions of the hunt, the commitment to full utilization, the permissibility of a range of reactions, the importance of openness, and the historical significance of wild meat to our ancestors. To illustrate the final point, I had students create a human time line in the alley behind my yard. The first meter of the time line represented the period during which refrigerated meat was cut by metal knives and made available for sale in stores. The two-hundred-meter gap to the end of the alley represented the part of the time line during which our ancestors' meat was processed fresh and cut with sharpened stones.

The recognition settled in that most moderns are truly disconnected from the historic need for wild meat and the skills of physical processing and the cooking of wild-killed animals. The paramount importance of respect for the animal we were about to butcher together was emphasized without my being unctuous or sanctimonious. Slang, cursing, braggadocio, and disgust were inappropriate because even though the animal was dead and would neither hear nor feel anything ever again, there is always a spirit or mood present at an animal's preparation, and that spirit is ours. By cultivating or tolerating negative attitudes, we run the risk of degrading the human spirit among ourselves and losing the ability to connect meaningfully to nature in the future.

No student was required to actively participate in pulling hide, slicing meat, or manipulating bones, but I strongly encouraged all to observe and share their thoughts and questions. Eventually, most did help a little bit. The sensationalized fear of blood was noteworthy, though, and, as a concession, I offered latex gloves but stressed that they were not really necessary. When we pulled back the tarp to access the deer, there was typically a reverential and curious hush over the class as if to say, "What now?" I always used this moment to usher in appreciation for the wondrous physical adaptations that have evolved in whitetail deer. For example, we located the seven scent glands (interdigital, tarsal, metatarsal, urogenital, supraorbital, cranial, and salivary) and discussed their respective glandular roles in animal communication and behavior for delineation, timing of breeding, dominance and its suppression, estrus timing, aggression, receptivity, trailing, olfactory warning, territories, and identification. Students often wanted to feel the hard black hooves and manipulate the feet to see their traction pads, sharp-edged cleats, dew claws for snowshoe effects, and polished upper surfaces resulting from slipping through leaves. These are wondrous enough adaptations that the carcass became a fascinating specimen that drew them in. This sense of wonder and new knowledge provided an important shunt for and distraction from any preconceived distaste for death and an essential entry into an inquiry of what, how, and ultimately, why and what if. . . .

Following Shakespeare's "pound of flesh" analogy for the human heart, it was an important ritual to lift the one-pound, intact, and well-washed heart muscle of the deer. Because a deer heart is virtually indistinguishable from a human heart in size and configuration, I invited students to actually hold and heft this remarkable organ and think about their own hearts currently hard at work inside them. I opened the heart to examine the treasures inside—valves, ventricles, auricles—and I would personalize this heart by pointing out the very left anterior descending artery (LAD), called the "widow-maker," that often clogs and deprives the outer heart muscle of blood, thus function, leading to heart attack. A faulty LAD has killed most of my male ancestors over the past four generations. This little aside is a reminder that we are not so different from other large vertebrates. These deer hearts are almost pure muscle and are perfectly edible. A quick show of hands as to who has eaten heart muscle would yield one or two responses. A second question as to who has eaten hot dogs caused 100 percent of hands to go up.

Well, hot dogs are made of heart, among other ground body parts. The question emerges whether eating these mysteriously "laundered" body parts with no real knowledge of their meat origins is a shirking of the personal responsibility for animal death. What intimate knowledge is lost by running that meat through a high-pressure grinder or strainer and inserting it into innocuous little unidentifiable tubes of protein? Isn't this a deliberate denial of responsibility through ignorance? It is disingenuous, really.

Third- and fourth-year university students are nobody's fools, and, collectively, they constitute a rich repository of reason, critique, and questioning. Given a little material, they make good connections. They recognize that their appearances, moods, and indeed their lives and the lives of their future children result from and revolve around estrogen-producing organs. Not surprisingly, the young women showed a keen interest in inspecting the intact female reproductive tracts (during years in which a doe was on the tarp). By pinning out and labeling the entire reproductive tract from ovaries to fallopian tubes to uterus to vagina, these women got a pretty good image of what they carried around inside of themselves. Sometimes we would delve into the risks associated with rapidly dividing ovarian and cervical cells, as a way of revisiting the animal/human mortality point. If the doe happened to be mature, we would also look for placental scars to count the numbers of fetal umbilical attachment points, thereby estimating the number of fetuses she had carried in previous years. Because whitetail fawns weigh about the same as human babies, the elasticity of the uterus showed it to be a remarkably flexible organ swelling from the size of a tea cup to rugby ball size during pregnancy. Who would have thought that this class would verge on discussion of the legislatable topics of sex and reproduction?

But what about the gross-out factor? Even among most sportsmen, the notion of unconfined excreta resulting from a bad shot is off-putting. However, when small swatches of the four stomach chambers (rumen, reticulum, omasum, abomasum) were washed clean of ingesta and pinned out, students were clinically interested. I did this to show their distinctively patterned lining of pebble-grain reticulate design, anemone-like projections, and book-like folds. This functional anatomy lesson brought the unseen into a very real and inspectable light and added to the fascination of the deer. It also let them think about haggis and tripe a little differently. Firm maroon livers sometimes carried scarring from parasites, thereby inviting comment on the similar repercussions caused by excessive alcohol use in mammals (OK, college students). Healthy pink lung tissue from the deer is what the smokers in the class could only wish for, and kidneys served as a pretty good index of the animal's overall health based on kidney fat. Healthy fat kidneys swaddled in layers of suet also showed the deposition places of omental fat, the exact same abdominal fat plaguing North Americans and lamented by college students on spring break. These animals offered many lessons about healthy living and the implications of unthinking existences.

In the students' syllabus, this lab was listed as "Shopping Cart on Hooves." We used the carcass as a way of channeling us back into an era that predated plastics and metallurgy. The deer carcass was a cornucopia of structural materials. We created a sewing needle from a bone splinter and a water canteen from the bladder, and rattles could be created from the hooves. I showed tanned hides from previous years' animals that could easily be converted to durable footwear and warm clothing. Other products shown were leather lacing for rope and snowshoes, brains for tanning, fat for waterproofing, sinew for sewing thread or bow-building, and teeth and antler pieces for buttons, scrapers, or ornamentation.

Finally, the students became so fully immersed in the process that the actual skinning and meat removal became a non-issue. As a simple pandering to familiarity, I would gently roll one of the tenderloins off the spine and slip it into a clear plastic vacuum bag. After I had pulled the air out with a vacuum storage sealer and passed this around for examination, it finally twigged with them that they were holding something almost identical to what a grocery store would offer. The hermetically sealed and labeled loin was familiar, while at their feet lay the animal from which it was taken moments before. It was almost possible to see the wheels turning in their frontal lobes as they made the connection and realized "Hey! This thing is *edible!*" so I would remove the other tenderloin and slice small pieces to dip in spiced olive oil before impaling them on shish kabob spears. Aromatherapy was in the air as the venison roasted over the fire pit. Most students were willing to try this delicious lean meat cooked to pink flavorfulness. It did occur to me that I had them literally eating out of my hands at this point. The path to a man's heart is through his stomach . . . but only if there aren't starving students along that path because they will scarf all the free food available!

At this point I typically handed the knives over to any willing students and coached them on how to take off the hide—here is where Michelle had her nostalgic moment. They were keen to see how to cut roasts into recognizable pieces, strip the pelvic girdle for stew meat, save the tongue, create a laced-boneless neck roast, use a thin knife to extract marrow, and learn that long bones can be smoked or slow-roasted for savory soup flavoring.

Sometimes we would make the effort to saw the antlers off if it was a buck, and I would challenge them with "Why do this?," a question sure to generate some discussion about what constitutes a "trophy." As one outdoor writer once quipped, "My trophy is a 115-pound doe raised near corn." For others, it is the largest buck they can bag for sausage meat and wall adornment. We discussed the marketing impetus behind big-antler pursuits, the oohh-ahhh phenomenon, and the notion that a hunter can actually bask in the sense of accomplishment, public accolades, and reflected glory from killing an unusually large specimen. Really, it is an old phenomenon if the Lascaux Caves are to be believed, but is it wrong and if so, why?

So I would lay out half-pound Ziploc bags of venison stew meat, chops, small roasts, and cutlets and invite students to take home a sampler of venison to cook, think about, and report back on to the class. This extended the lesson over several days and provided opportunities for reflection and reinforcement. And of course those who did this then shared their experiences with friends who were not at the butchering—thereby spreading the knowledge and eliciting external feedback. Most wanted to try their hand at cooking venison, and a surprising number of vegetarians could see their way clear to eat this organic, free-est of free-range, antibiotic-free, locally grown, and humanely killed meat. Inevitably, they wanted to trade recipes and get some recommendations so we talked cooking styles, nutrition, and treatment. Even though hot and fast to rare perfection is my preference as demonstrated with the tenderloin, most opted for the safer slow-cooking for five hours in a crock pot or stew meat with spices and veggies. The tendency to share and build connections through sharing hunted meat marks one of the ways such meat fundamentally differs from beef, pork, or chicken. Wild game that has been hunted and taken as a gift from nature, unavailable in any store and bearing the care and packaging of the hunter, is precious and rare. It brings about a generosity and willingness to share that is both timeless and a spontaneous act of gratitude.

Perennially, students rated this laboratory as one of their year's highlights, and many were greatly moved by participating in the respectful and utilization-intensive exercise. Incidentally, over the years a surprising number of my previously nonhunting students, both men and women, have taken the hunter safety course and become proficient hunters themselves. Furthermore, I am confident that many of those who didn't hunt carried a more favorable and informed set of views on the rationale of hunting and eating wild-killed foods.

So was there progress in the students' understanding of hunting and eating wild animals? First, I had to sidestep a wall of fear-based opposition at the institutional level, opposition resulting from an administration unwilling or unable to shoulder the risk of negative publicity. However, the exercise provided opportunities for students to think (engage), act (butcher), and internalize (eat) components of renewable resources in the form of hunted products. I wanted students to try their experience out on others, to learn critical thinking skills, to reflect on their decisions and then act. Isn't this the goal of a university?

ALISON ACTON

A View from the Saddle

The Provocative Mystique of Foxhunting Culture

Enigma, anathema, a cherished way of life? Foxhunting remains a politically conspicuous, contentious, and contested subject, yet relatively little social scientific research has been conducted on its culture. Consequently, it still retains a mystique, and distanced oversimplifications and misapprehensions about the nature of the culture prevail.

My nascent engagement with foxhunting has certainly piqued my curiosity. This resilient hunting culture reveals a web of complex human, animal, and spatial connections and exhibits strong and enduring bonds of community, cultural memory, flexible tradition, and ritual. These characteristics have enabled it to survive massive social and economic change and, lately, legislation outlawing its traditional practice. It also represents a sensory means of establishing a relationship with our environment, a relationship that is becoming attenuated in our increasingly virtualized world.

| Escaping the Ivory Tower |

As an academic, my work peels away the taken for granted to reveal the complex constitution of society. Notwithstanding the great sociological insights gained from other methods of analysis, my approach is best summed up by the sociologist Robert Park. "Gentlemen," he urged. "Go get the seat of your pants dirty in *real* research."[1] Evidently, he lamented the fact that the "real world" is a place that some academics eschew, preferring instead the sanctity of a closeted academic haven, a potentially expansive realm but one that can incipiently shrink into a cloister of abstruse detachment. Park realized this latent trap, encouraging his students to visit the theaters, hotels, and flophouses of 1930s

Chicago, but his approach is applicable to gaining a genuine understanding of any culture. As for me, I literally got the seat of my pants dirty in contact with the English and Irish countryside when I began to study foxhunting.

| Foxhunting: A Background |

Mounted modern foxhunting developed in the eighteenth century in England.[2] The hunt is an organized group comprising horses (known as "hunters"), humans, and hounds. The hounds search for, pursue, and *possibly* kill the fox. The huntsman works with them, with one or two assistants, known as "whipper-ins" or "whips." The rest of the mounted participants are followers known as the "field," led by a "field master." Their role has never been to hunt the fox. They participate in order to absorb the multifaceted elements that constitute the hunt and to enjoy the rural environment and equestrian activity. Additionally, an important motivation for their hunting is the bonds of community and belonging, which stretch far beyond the immediacy of the day.[3]

The fox may be a predator to be controlled, but in this culture it is important and is not merely base vermin to be eradicated. Indeed, when foxhunting grew in popularity during the eighteenth century, the animal became culturally elevated from a "disdained" and "inferior" pilferer to a worthy adversary.[4] The fox became nicknamed "Charlie" or "Old Charlie" after the eighteenth-century Whig politician Charles James Fox. The sporting artist Lionel Edwards uses the moniker "Master Charles" to refer respectfully to the fox as an adversarial partner. As he explained, "The fact remains that among the many partners of the chase, the only one who makes few errors is usually the fox . . . for no one knows better how to take advantage of each and every circumstance than 'Master Charles.'"[5] Indeed, a successful hunting day results in a pursuit of the scent of a fox; a killed fox is not necessary.

| Escaping the Cloisters: Meeting Old Charlie |

My introduction to Old Charlie occurred in Ireland, in the counties of Tipperary and Limerick. This region's beautiful, uncompromising landscape defiantly displays traces of the hardships of its history. Nineteenth-century famine walls, built by the starving population in return for welfare pittance, scar the face of the mountains that dominate much of the countryside, determining its indomitable character. These ranges stand as an immutable presence with a mutable countenance, looming powerfully over the pastures of farmland, dwarfing the churches, houses, lanes, and hedgerows and altering the landscape with each shifting mood. Although signs of economic development and downturn are evident in this region, it is clearly rural in character, and equestrianism and field sports feature strongly in the local culture.

Alison Acton

I had newly arrived in the neighborhood, and Michael, a local man, dropped by my house en route to a hunt meet to welcome me. Shaking my hand with a bone-crunching grip, he invited me to join the local Hunt cubhunting. This activity, held before the foxhunting season begins in full, introduces the "new entry," the next generation of foxhounds, to hunting. It is traditionally called cubhunting as, in addition to adult foxes, the new generation of foxes, now independent of the vixen, are hunted and dispersed. In this particular Hunt cubhunting occurs on foot before the actual season, conducted on horseback, begins. So it was that I took my first hunting footsteps, clinging to the coattails of the experts until some fragments of the morning's activity began to come together.

On my maiden outing I attempted to absorb Michael's commentary on this hunting environment. He explained how the movement of creatures provided clues to the location of the fox, told me what the actions and sounds of the hounds meant, and tried to enlighten me on the mysteries of scent and wind direction. There was so much to absorb in this new world that I just did not see until it was translated for me. Even then my perception was limited to fragments, generating more questions.

Thus, this bewildering new world piqued my academic curiosity. Its fecundity lay within realms of the sensory and corporeal, the symbolic and tangible, the present and ancient, the animal and human. To an anthropologist, this cultural package was overwhelmingly enticing, so, following Robert Park's advice, I joined in, got on a horse, and set out upon an exploration of this world. Many seasons later, I am still exploring.

| Custom and Belonging |

Each Hunt has a distinct territory, known as a Hunt Country, which is recognized within foxhunting culture as a space "belonging" to each Hunt. But the land within that territory is generally owned by private landowners, not by the hunt. Consequently, these hunting territories are owned, in a customary, negotiated, nonlegal sense, *through* hunting, as the hunt has no *right* of access. Instead it uses sections of the land with consent, at no cost, and is frequently hosted as a guest by the landowner, often receiving hospitality in the form of food and drink at the meet.

Hosts provide and Hunts acknowledge this relationship chiefly by respecting the land and taking care to cause as little damage as possible. This custom fundamentally underwrote every day of my hunting experience. These bonds, often referred to as a "golden thread" within the countryside, go beyond the hunting day or season. These hunting territories continue across the centuries through use, consent, cooperation, compromise, and a deep connection with the landscape.[6]

In foxhunting, the landscape and environment is an active element as much as the creatures that live in that landscape. It is mutable; it hosts, speaks, signals, challenges, forbids, and entertains. It dictates the multifarious engagements within a hunting locality and shapes the varieties of hunting across regions. Additionally, Hunts have a fundamental ecological connection with their territories, managing them for hunting in a way that contributes to the biodiversity of these areas.[7] This tradition of husbandry also perpetuates the dwindling skills and traditional knowledge of how to manage these equally dwindling precious habitats. Furthermore, landowners favorable to hunting often allow sections of land to be managed and used for hunting (and often shooting) at a sacrifice to economic reward. Instead of being put to plough or pasture, sections of land may be managed as scrub or wooded habitat, which contributes to the biodiversity of an increasingly undifferentiated rural environment. Research indicates that some of these wildlife havens were specifically reserved for foxhunting centuries ago.[8]

| A View from the Saddle |

Having decided to "get the seat of my pants dirty" meant only one thing: riding with the hunt. This activity introduced me to the multispecies engagement that defines the hunt. Hunting necessitates an extension beyond the human realm, for these foxhunting spaces come into being in part through the transformation of a hunting "Chaseworld," which characterizes these spaces and is shared by both the humans and the animals within the hunt.[9] These hunting landscapes are what Philo and Wilbert have termed "beastly places," where the animals are not merely placed or used but play *their* part in shaping these places.[10]

Principally, this superhuman entanglement emerged through my partnership with my hunters. Foxhunting engenders a dynamic in which rider and horse are absorbed into and extend into the environment, accumulating and generating the sounds, scents, sights, energies, temporalities, and cadence of hunting. Because foxhunting presents unpredictable challenges to horse and rider, within hunting culture the seasoned hunter is revered as a knowledgeable partner who may save you from danger and may also tutor and mentor you. Heart in mouth, I trusted the judgment of these horses as we leapt ditches and hedges. Yet this aspect of my journey from the ivory tower took on yet another dimension. I absorbed hunting conduct through my connection with these horses who "knew the ropes." Their individual personalities, their role in the hunt, their hunting attributes, sensory abilities, and knowledge were crucial to my engagement with and grasp of hunting.[11]

In my relationship with my trusted hunter, Ben, I learned that he had what

Donna Haraway refers to as an "earned authority."[12] He possessed an aptitude to read hounds, the huntsman, and the landscape and to judge space and distance in a way that was far superior to mine. This ability is important, as riding within a Hunt is far removed from the experience of the riding arena. Moving at speed in a canine-human-equine collective involves a vital transformation in the way one encounters the landscape. Roger Scruton, a professor of philosophy who also hunts, describes this spatial metamorphosis: "These peaceful, dreamy English lanes and ditches are not what they seem: they come at you with all the speed and ferocity of the turning globe and they come at you with teeth of stone."[13] So a clever hunter paired with a rider who understands the wisdom of enabling the hunter to employ its aptitude makes for good hunting teamwork.

Ben's stride to a jump or impulsion when leaping a ditch or hedge was never flawed, so I joined in with his spatial choreography, trusting his movement and absorbing his rhythm (albeit sometimes in a somewhat syncopated manner) and taking his cues in a human–equine dance. In turn, Ben consumed the terrain with a confidence that indicated that he knew I trusted him as he responded enthusiastically to my movement, mood, and voice. On landing after a challenging obstacle, I would "high five" him with a strong congratulatory slap on the neck, to which he would respond with equine gestures of exuberance and affirmation.

This embodied sensory connection with my hunters was also key to my absorption of the hunting environment. I felt, watched, listened, and learned from my mounts as their awareness resonated within me. Scruton provides an example of how this connection can operate: "The experienced hunter will prick up his ears and stare into the wood, following every sound and movement, sensing that soon he must run. He will often know before you do if hounds have left . . . the other side, and when he has caught sight of them he will watch them, carefully taking measure of the land ahead."[14] Thus, the hunter watches, smells, listens but may also read the trajectory of the hounds and anticipate the ensuing action, thinking ahead about its part in the performance. As central players in this drama, they can follow and enact the plot often better than their riders.

| Bells of the Chase |

Vital as the relationship with the hunters is, the cultural elevation of nonhumans is most evident in the role played by the hounds within "team Hunt." Foxhounds are never referred to as dogs, unless making a distinction between a dog hound and a bitch hound, and, although they are known as named individuals with personal attributes, they are also regarded collectively. They constitute a pack and are counted as couples, so, for example, three hounds would be referred to as one and a half couple.

Hounds are held in esteem as the chief narrators of the hunt, so their movements and anatomy have specialized terminology. Their utterances are referred to as speech and music, never barking. A huntsman from the early twentieth century described the nuances of the sound and movements of this key actor: "It is in those woodlands and coverts . . . that the Bells of the Chase ring out in such stirring peals. Inspiring—yea it is wondrous—as those bells of the Chase peal their carillon, whose notes gather tone by echo, as their revels of music in arresting cadence awaken the glades of woodland, and seemed to be reincarnated again and again—just as if the silky beeches—the stately ash, the hoary gnarled oak were playing their part of a loud speaker."[15] So vital to hunting is hound language that hounds are bred with their voices in mind. This became apparent to me when I visited my first Hunt Puppy Show. This is an annual event held by a Hunt, where young hounds are judged in relation to the premium characteristics required for hunting. The judges drew attention to the conformation of hounds, not just in terms of how their physique would help them read and traverse the land but also in relation to how their jowls and throat would contribute to their voice.

| The Mystique of the Elephant in the Room |

Within this foxhunting world I found a way of life that retains a mystique. This pageant of horses, humans, and hounds, heralded by hooves, horns, and "hound music," doesn't hide, but it is often hidden, flitting through large tracts of countryside. Even in rural communities where hunting is commonly practiced, most nonhunting residents' view of their local Hunt is limited to "partial sightings."[16] Indeed, when I have been with part of the field that has become separated from the main group, it has been an endeavor to rejoin it, such is its fleeting pattern of transit.

Despite its rich cultural pickings, foxhunting is a world into which few anthropologists care to venture in person. As one eminent folklorist who has participated points out, although foxhunting has been part of English culture for generations, it remains an unpopular and uncomfortable subject for research. It is, he declares, "the elephant in the room of English folklore," contending that the political controversy surrounding this culture is a major reason that it has been largely overlooked in research into traditional English customs.[17] Similarly, the anthropologist Garry Marvin suggests that one of the reasons foxhunting has been sidelined in anthropological research is that it is commonly regarded as "morally unacceptable."[18]

Foxhunting has a history of being a contested culture in three main respects: animal welfare, class conflict, and urban and rural divisions.

Donna Landry argues that changes in English social attitudes toward animal welfare and hunting are apparent in the eighteenth-century literature. She cites the shift from a tradition rooted in hunting and farming, which embraced the realities of mud, sweat, and viscera, to a pastoral aesthetic detachment.[19] The latter was associated with a metropolitan middle class and "well-to-do townsmen, remote from the agricultural process and inclined to think of animals as pets."[20] Moral censure was emerging against stag and hare hunting in the early eighteenth century; the fox, however, regarded as a "pilfering thief," did not attract the same pity until later that century.

Hunting, in various forms, was associated with the historical legacy of land theft and the appropriation of the game on that land. During the eighteenth century a process known as Enclosure appropriated land from commoners. With their customary property stolen, the most marginal commoners became part of a new immiserated urban working class.[21] The land, partitioned and drained for agriculture, provided the perfect conditions for the development of foxhunting. So, even though it was not the cause of that divestiture, foxhunting was connected to this upheaval in the imagery and class consciousness of those whose livelihood, community, and identity were bound to these landscapes.

Although foxhunting was patronized and embraced by the upper classes, even in previous eras when British society was more highly socially divided, foxhunting provided a rare means of interaction across social classes. Scruton argues that foxhunting had a role to play in ameliorating class barriers, as Hunts required consent to hunt the land: "Farmers, smallholders, tenants, vicars and even labourers would be invited to join in an activity that crucially depended on their consent."[22] Critics, however, point to the fact that this engagement never extended beyond mere presence. There is, however, evidence that contradicts this perspective. The nineteenth-century novelist Surtees, for example, declared that foxhunting "reverberates . . . through the whole of our [British] social system."[23] Whatever perspective is taken, such inclusiveness deserves to be recognized as a contemporary rarity, unacceptable in many other social contexts.

In Ireland, modern foxhunting became emblematic of colonial oppression as it was imported during British rule. Jane Ridley noted that "Hounds have always been kept in Ireland, but the Kilkenny was the first hunt club of the Anglo-Irish gentry and John Power was the first to bring the new-style fox hunting to Ireland."[24] Even though Power had been a supporter of Catholic

Emancipation, in the latter part of the nineteenth century foxhunting suffered because of its connection with British imperialism. The Land League targeted Hunts, killing hounds and burning coverts and kennels.[25] However, today foxhunting is regarded by Irish supporters as a continuation of indigenous hunting, and they absorb it as part of their own culture, embracing it in a daredevil way that foreign visitors admire with awe. Accomplished Irish hunters are also valued as a commodity for export.

Nevertheless, the Irish Green Party initiated moves to curb hunting by introducing restrictions that make it more difficult for Hunts to operate. As in England, these policies are characterized by supporters of hunting as alienated urban diktats. At a meeting of the Hunting Association of Ireland I noted angry references to "antis from Dublin," the sentiment being that the urban middle class was militating against the customs of the ordinary rural people. Yet, in a historical paradox, Irish proponents of foxhunting at this meeting and in the media drew on Ireland's colonial past as a reason for resisting threats to hunting. An article titled "Greens Must Not Be Allowed to Sabotage Our Ancient Rituals" encapsulates this perspective, warning: "Given the historic battle for the repossession of the land and our emotional relationship to it, the Greens could be picking a fight with forces they are badly underestimating."[26] Interestingly, both Irish and British foxhunting communities were regarded as having a common system of beliefs and, in the case of antihunting policies, were united, in their view, as the victims of unjust urban persecution. Paradoxically, the colonial legacy in this debate had been transposed to native threats to hunting, and the British hunting fraternity was regarded as fellow oppressed. Irish support for British foxhunters was staunch in the face of political moves to ban the sport in England and Wales.

| Political Censure |

Foxhunting remains legal in Ireland. However, the 2004 Hunting Act finally outlawed traditional forms of hunting with dogs in England and Wales. A similar law had already been passed in Scotland, in 2002, to curtail hunting with dogs.

However, if foxhunting is controversial, so is the legislation. Many critics maintain that it was motivated not solely by issues of animal welfare but was backed by many on the basis of class politics.[27] The Labour Party had traditionally been a party of the working classes, and foxhunting exemplified the vestiges of an old class war. John Prescott, the deputy prime minister, was emblematic of the Party's working-class roots. As Adam Boulton observes, "For him, hunt supporters fitted into a glib class stereotype—hunters [sic] equal toffs—so he mocked them at any opportunity."[28] Airing sentiments dubious of a representative of democracy, Prescott declared that his determination to ban foxhunting was redoubled whenever he saw the contorted faces of members of the Countryside Alliance, a pressure group that campaigned against the ban on hunting with dogs.[29] Prescott himself appeared as a token anachronism in a modernizing, rebranding Party, but his sentiments were shared and aired by many advocates of a ban. Rhetoric such as this framed the legislative debate through images of entrenched partisan alignments, as well as geographic and class divisions.

Although traditional foxhunting is banned in England and Wales, foxhunting continues, albeit in a convoluted form designed to comply with an equally convoluted law. Some provisions include a limit of two hounds, rather than a pack, to drive a fox to be shot, providing the fox has been predating certain creatures and the hunting is sanctioned by the landowner. Arbitrarily, game birds are specified as creatures where predation may warrant hunting under certain restrictions, but some types of farm stock are not. Because the Act does not qualify the position in relation to hunting with a bird of prey, theoretically it allows a whole pack to be used in conjunction with such a bird, and in 2009 the High Court ruled that searching was not hunting.[30] Searching for and following the scent of a fox accounted for much of traditional foxhunting, so, arguably, this key aspect is now allowed.

Tony Blair, Labour prime minister at the time of the ban, has since claimed that he regrets the legislation, stating that he failed to appreciate the cultural significance of hunting for rural communities. Confessing that it was "not one of [his] finest policy moments," he explained: "It is not that I particularly like hunting or have ever engaged in it or would. I didn't quite understand, and I reproach myself for this, that for a group of people in our society in the countryside this was a fundamental part of their way of life."[31] Charlie Pye-Smith pointed to this lack of understanding, maintaining that, to many, foxhunting remains an enigma in that few are effectively informed about the activity and culture. He claimed, "We would never have ended up with this unworkable piece of legislation if M.P.s who were ideologically in favour of the ban had visited the countryside, witnessed hunts at work and talked to farmers and others about alternative methods of controlling foxes."[32] Blair's repentance suggests that Pye-Smith had a point. In his retrospective Blair identified three key elements underlying these misconceptions: engagement, diversity, and understanding.

| Engagement, Diversity, Understanding |

These elements featured in my journey from the ivory tower. Regardless of its own significance, foxhunting may encompass unexpected and increasingly rare forms of behavior, the examination of which may enhance the understanding of our cultural history. After I foxhunted, the paradoxes and enigmas were replaced by a global comprehension of a culture that offers experiences that are dwindling in an increasingly alienated Western world.[33] Not to engage in the investigation of a culture because it is regarded as "morally unacceptable" amounts to ethnocentric censorship.[34] As Eric Eliason notes, "Foxhunting practice maintains moral, ecological, and skill-set resources we may need to turn to sometime in some way we cannot foresee—just as the rainforest's store of ethno-and biodiversity may offer treatments for physical and social ailments present and yet unknown."[35]

I concur that foxhunting provides cultural booty for the anthropologist, which can be used to maintain dwindling yet precious skills and knowledge. These ancient ways of engaging with the landscape are the antithesis of the increasingly alienated relationships that characterize our experiences with the world. The ability to read the land through communication with animals is passed on through deep-rooted generational knowledge.[36] The hunting homeland provides a resilient, flexible, living model of community, offering an alternative to one that overwhelmingly operates according to profit and bureaucracy. Indeed, largely because of these factors, foxhunting has proven to be a resilient, adaptable culture, surviving many factors prophesied and latterly designed to induce its end.[37]

Cultural resilience and flexibility are, in themselves, phenomena worthy of investigation, but hunting knowledge and practice, closely related to a way of life, are also sociologically and environmentally valuable. The anthropologist Hugh Brody pointed to these other rarely acknowledged benefits of foxhunting: "Perhaps the most compelling reason for leaving hunts free to hunt lies in the way the intensity of the thrill will be defended by those who can . . . save the countryside—not for foxes so much as for skylarks, cuckoos, warblers and hosts of waterborn insects. The gradual disappearance of so much life is far more dreadful, far more cruel, of much more serious import than the fate of the hunted fox."[38] Brody's observation contextualizes issues of reality, death, and cruelty; the fate of the iconic, ubiquitous fox is juxtaposed with the fate of the less visible, threatened species that benefit from field sport ecologies. In their submission to the Burns Report, commissioned prior to the Hunting Act, Stuart Harrop and D. F. Harrop argued that hunting ecosystems contributed to the UK's legal responsibility to comply with European and international environmental obligations, adding: "Little or no discussion has concerned the issue of whether or not hunting with hounds has a place in the wider preservation of ecosystems and of biodiversity. Yet the emphasis on the welfare only of a small, arbitrarily chosen selection of mammals, to the neglect of other species and the resultant failure to address comprehensive inter-species and habitat relationships, may cause the undermining of idiosyncratic, slowly evolved social mechanisms which sustain and preserve biodiversity."[39] Nor does banning foxhunting protect foxes from being deliberately killed. What the Hunting Act inhibits is the cultural practice of foxhunting. On the issue of cruelty, Lord Burns, who headed the inquiry into hunting, stated, "Naturally, people ask whether we were implying that hunting [with dogs] is cruel. . . . The short answer to that question is no."[40] The anthropologist Kaoru Fukuda also considered the cultural relativity of our perceptions toward animal cruelty. Contrasting urban pet-keeping with foxhunting, she concluded that "judgements about animal suffering are highly dependent on the types of relationship they have with animals. The contrast between fox-hunting and pet-keeping suggests that the more highly condemned activity is not necessarily the one that is more destructive to animals but is the one that is less appreciated by humans."[41]

Even if one disagrees with these perspectives, the fox as a predator will still be killed legally via a range of methods, the majority of which are more indiscriminate, less swift, and more deadly.[42] James Barrington, former executive director of the League against Cruel Sports (LACS), stated that he and other members of the League, after "a long, slow learning-curve," came to see hunting as a comparatively humane method of controlling the fox population.[43] Yet, they were forced from the organization by absolutist members for voicing this view.

Hunting seeks ecological balance, not eradication. Cooperation among landowners, hunts, and animals allows foxes to be tolerated to a degree. This is particularly a balancing act where shoots and Hunts use the same territory. Even in areas where revenue-generating shooting conflicts with hunting, Hunts are still likely to be permitted.[44] Arguably, it is in the interests of gamekeepers to keep fox numbers as low as possible so as to have minimum predation of birds, but traditionally they will endeavor not to obliterate foxes if they have a good relationship with the hunt. Furthermore, the hunting season ceases when cubs are being raised, meaning that dependent cubs will not be left to starve. Vermin control does not employ these restrictions and also frequently results in wounding. Thus, hunting provides cultural incentives and networks to accommodate and control rather than exterminate the quarry or cause a lingering death.

Contextually, there is a question of what a ban on foxhunting has actually achieved in terms of ecological diversity and animal welfare. Arguably, it has been detrimental, and, whether one agrees with hunting or not, there also is much to be learned from the ancient knowledge systems of hunting that know animals comprehensively and expertly as agents in their own right.

| Class Lines |

The perception of foxhunting as elitist prevails as an almost unquestioned fact in much academic writing and in representations used to justify a hunting ban. Drawing on images of elites and rurality, Mark Thomas claimed that the best reason for banning foxhunting was to enrage and upset the upper classes.[45] Similarly, former deputy prime minister Prescott argued that repeal of the Hunting Act would only bring "pleasure to a bunch of ruddy-faced toffee-nosed twits."[46]

Remaining in the ivory tower can lead to ill-informed judgments that reflect and perpetuate stereotypes. This can have serious consequences for the viability of and tolerance for a culture. Such characterizations of foxhunting as elitist are ubiquitous in accounts that represent the English style of mounted foxhunting unquestionably as an upper-class sport, though the authors have not participated in Hunts.[47]

The simple point is that the subject of the current social composition of Hunts remains virtually uninvestigated. As my participation broadened, I rode with a range of Hunts, and I would not characterize them as elite institutions. They included people from a spectrum of backgrounds, and, as is the case with a range of clubs, their social composition varied regionally. Similarly, James Barrington, who followed Hunts initially as a saboteur and later as an LACS observer, explained, "Hunting is the perfect vehicle for a package of prejudices that sees its proponents as rich, dim upper-class Conservatives. Yet when you visit a hunt you discover the majority of followers . . . do not fit the stereotype."[48] Hunts such as the Banwen Miners Hunt, a "working man's hunt" originating in a Welsh colliery village, are certainly not elitist in origin, nor is the internal social diversity of Hunts acknowledged.[49] Indeed, what little academic research has been conducted suggests that the political aim to attack the upper classes has hit the wrong target. Milbourne's rare piece of research, which actually investigated the social background of hunt participants, found the relationship between class and hunting to be *opposite* to the popular perception.[50]

To conclude, and with a little irony, I return to the reflections of Tony Blair and the central themes of engagement, diversity, and understanding. Foxhunting culture provides the *means* to understand our cultural diversity and entanglements with other species and the environment. Whether or not hunting remains anathema, it need not remain a mystery or an enigma.

Alison Acton

PHILIP MASON

Duck Dynasty

Hunting for Nonhunters

"I have a God-given right to pursue happiness, and happiness to me is killing things, skinning them, plucking them, and then having a good meal. What makes me happy is going out and blowing a duck's head off."

Phil Robertson, *Duck Dynasty*

In 2012, A&E created the reality TV series *Duck Dynasty* (for which I will use the abbreviation *DD*), a show centered on the small family-run duck call company Duck Commander (DC) located in West Monroe, Louisiana. The show celebrates a stereotype of Southern culture, with traditional gender roles, Christian prayer, and plenty of hunting. To the surprise of many, the show became the most-watched nonfiction cable television show, drawing nearly twelve million viewers.[1] As a result, DC is no longer an obscure company. Its products now include novelties like bobblehead figurines and costumes; kitchen items; seasoning; glassware; clothing ranging from pajamas and t-shirts to underwear; bedding and shower curtains; Christmas cards and tree ornaments; and books, including biographies, religious devotionals, and cookbooks.

To whatever degree reality shows are constructed, it is important that their mass-communicated "lessons" be analyzed. Recent reality television programs showcasing "hunting" culture in the American South (like *Hillbilly Handfishin'*, and *Swamp People*) have gained viewership through accentuating existing stereotypes, and for many viewers *DD*'s dramatized portrayals will be their closest connection to a hunting experience. As a highly visible (and highly edited) force in popular culture, *DD* has the potential to affect the general public's attitudes toward hunting and, to some extent, the American South. *DD* presents some predictably problematic messages, and it misses opportunities to promote a better dialogue between hunters and nonhunters, but it also makes visible important aspects of being a contemporary hunter that nonhunters can appreciate. In this essay, I examine how *DD* portrays hunters and hunting and worry that its images damage relations between hunters and nonhunters. To a much smaller extent, I also examine a secondary effect of the show: that it reinforces negative stereotypes of Southerners.

| *DD* and the Ignoble Hunter |

I was raised in Utah with no close family members or friends who hunted. And, like many nonhunters, I largely associated hunting with environmental exploitation, hypermasculinity, and Jeff Foxworthy jokes. My only regular interactions with hunting was listening to school peers bragging about how bloody they became butchering a deer, stumbling upon forgotten traps and shell casings while backpacking, or seeing the remnants of burnt beer cans, cigarette butts, and litter from vacated deer camps recently populated by vehicles adorned with Confederate flags and "Proud to Be a Redneck" stickers. The venison I was exposed to was desiccated, gamey mule deer steaks burnt over a fire. The harvester of the steaks described eating the meat as a burdensome chore that offset the "thrill of the kill."

Despite the strong, generally negative stereotypes that I associated with hunting—stereotypes of hunters as uneducated rednecks—I knew hunters came from a variety of classes and cultures. And I was aware that there was a hierarchy of hunters determined by quarry. For example, I knew that waterfowl hunters were considered more distinguished than those who hunted only small game and deer. I was also cognizant of the close relationship between many hunting-focused conservation groups and other environmental groups. And I recognized that there was a common bond of reverence for nature that united members of both groups, regardless of how mutually exclusive their membership appeared to be. Yet, because ignoble hunter stereotypes were more visible to me than other kinds of hunters, as a nonhunter I could only speculate what characteristics a principled hunter possessed and which morals guided him or her.

In *DD*, the Robertsons' relationship with nature is perplexing and reinforces an image of hunters and hunting like the one I absorbed as a youth. The show focuses on the lives of the backwoods-raised Robertson family and their paradoxical relationship with the natural environment and their suburban lives in McMansions. Each episode shows the family working and laughing together as they overcome a whimsical "crisis" (for example, building a lawn mower for racing, bull frog hunting illegally at the country club), which plays on exaggerated stereotypes of Southerners and hunters, and ends with a family meal (often of wild game), prayer, and a folksy proverb. In many ways, the show is a contemporary, bearded, country version of "Leave It to Beaver" presented as reality TV.

One aspect of this relationship is illustrated by the Robertsons' generally reckless attitude toward the environment, particularly a persistent war on beavers. In real life, beavers are regarded as a nuisance animal with few natural predators, and they often require intervention from humans to manage their populations. *DD* repeatedly depicts the Robertsons using extreme means—explosives and fire—in attempts to exterminate the beavers (along with Uncle Si's unwanted vehicle in one episode) in order to maintain appropriate habitats for the waterfowl they love to hunt. Without sufficient explanation of the beavers' potential destructiveness to waterfowl habitats, these episodes allow the nonhunting viewer to assume that hunters are reckless and that all wildlife is subject to human caprice. There are many similar examples of environmental hostility. In one episode, while dressed entirely in camouflage and face paint, Phil (the founder of DC and the patriarch of the family) bites into a dead duck as he begins cleaning it at his grandkids' school's career day. In a later episode, when Phil and the grandchildren are fishing, he bites into a live snake and one of the caught fish. On another occasion Uncle Si (Phil's brother) exhibits unnecessary violence by shooting a snake about a dozen times. In general, on the show, the desire to hunt is phrased in terms of something like "I'm ready to go kill something." From these actions and phrases, a viewer may perceive unnecessary violence and disrespect to nature not only as socially appropriate but also as an integral component of the hunter identity and perhaps masculinity in general.

Another way in which *DD* presents hunters in problematic ways centers on their treatment of game. For many hunters, food on the table is more satisfying when one has harvested it him- or herself. However, the Robertsons' treatment of game as food seems inconsistent to the nonhunter. Characters' comedic complaints and sarcasm while cleaning the harvest likely lead viewers to question the validity of hunters' arguments about how the hunt is less about the kill and more about the meal afterward. For example, when DC employees become jealous of Willie's imported biltong jerky and decide to make venison jerky (as they have already eaten their supply of store-bought beef jerky), they discover that only Godwin (a warehouse worker) has a dehydrator. After struggling to find his rarely used tool, they compare the smells of their jerky to that of Si's (Phil's brother and a warehouse worker) underwear. The finished product is said to be fit for only dogs to consume, so Kori (Willie's spouse) provides the DC employees with the company credit card to *buy* more jerky.

Two points emerge from this episode. First, the boys had already eaten all of the corporately processed food that DC had provided. For people suspicious of store-bought meat, dehydrated, heavily preserved meat found in any commercial jerky is anathema. Why do they not make their own? Or why do they not have a professional meat processor make it for them using their own harvests? Second and most important, no mention is given as to why their jerky smelled foul. Was the animal healthy? Was there a problem with the butchering process that caused it to spoil? Was the smell related to improper storage? Did they not know what they were doing? Or was it simply just part of the characters' script? The viewer does not know, and the nonhunter viewer is left to view wild game as undesirable and inferior to commercially processed food. On the basis of the Robertsons' actions and dialogue, nonhunter viewers may see eating wild meat as a laborious duty that lingers long after the hunt has concluded (just as I had as a nonhunter). When Miss Kay (Phil's spouse) finds fish in a freezer that has been long forgotten, and when a freezer full of meat in the warehouse has spoiled because of a power outage, there's little concern about waste. In the latter episode, the *DD* characters' only real complaint is about the arduous task of disposing of the spoils. These and similar intermittent references to burdensome spoils may lead nonhunter viewers to unfairly perceive hunters as wasteful.

In addition to depicting the *DD* family as (often) environmentally abusive and wasteful, the show presents the characters as uneducated, culturally backward, and resistant to social demands, potentially linking them in viewers' minds to "redneck" cultural stereotypes. The popular comedian Jeff Foxworthy defines the redneck as "the glorious absence of sophistication"[2] and has made a career out of listing supposed redneck attributes, including being white, wearing camouflage, distrusting formal education, speaking in simple phrases, driving trucks, exhibiting a connection to rural places, tirelessly competing, and being Christian, politically conservative, reckless, crudely honest, frugal, and ingenuously creative, etc. In an expanding trend, many recent reality television programs showcase characters embracing "redneck" culture in the American South (for example, *Hillbilly Handfishin'*, *Here Comes Honey Boo Boo*, and *Swamp People*), and many viewers proudly label themselves "rednecks." Because *DD* characters *self-identify* as rednecks and because embracing "redneckism" is a fundamental component of the *DD* franchise, the show effectively reinforces the notion that hunters and (indirectly) Southerners are rednecks.

Duck Dynasty propagates stereotypes of hunters by accentuating unnecessary violence and rash behavior, perpetuating a consumerist hunting culture, and linking hunters to problematic stereotypes. To a degree, these stereotypes line up with how hunting has been commodified in the United States, where popular hunting media allows for a connection to the crude, violent, and insensible aspects of the sport whether a given consumer hunts or not. Not only has *DD* continued to perpetuate not only gross hunter stereotypes, but also it maintains these exaggerated stereotypes regarding Southerners.

In reinforcing problematic stereotypes, *DD* has missed several opportunities to educate viewers by showcasing a variety of hunters that complicate the Jeff Foxworthy stereotype. Besides failing to present a richer spectrum of hunters, the producers of *DD* deemphasize other important aspects of hunting, for example its relationship with environmental conservation. Environmental conservation is supported by hunters and nonhunters alike, but very few nonhunters are aware that conservation is in large part funded by special taxes placed on sportsperson purchases (for example, taxes on licenses, firearms, and ammunition). Declining numbers of hunters have reduced by millions of dollars funds available for wildlife conservation and have led to fervent debate among scholars about how to offset the loss.[3] Hunters, however, are much more aware of how taxes on sportsperson equipment funds conservation, as well as of the role that Ducks Unlimited, Delta Waterfowl, and other hunter/conservation nonprofit organizations have played in environmental protection efforts. *DD* could have helped relay this information to nonhunters by presenting a perspective to offset some of the negative stereotypes of hunters

| The Hunter as Nature Guru |

Although *DD* teaches some problematic and predictable lessons surrounding the hunter and his or her sport, deeper and more important messages are embedded in the series, messages that shed light on aspects of hunting that the nonhunter might not otherwise notice. Despite the negative attitudes toward wild game as food previously described, several *DD* episodes promote eating natural wild foods and remind viewers that humans are one of many interdependent species sharing an environment, while also challenging nonhunters' perceptions of what food is and is not. For example, the "tree rat" (the common gray squirrel): many hunters view the pursuit of squirrel as uncouth and pedestrian or question the practicality of chasing this game because of its small size, and nonhunters see squirrels as cute inhabitants of local parks and yards. The Robertsons, however, are quick to showcase the squirrel's prized meat. Not only is the squirrel praised as a healthful, organic meat, but also its brains are highlighted as succulent morsels by Miss Kay. Squirrel and dumplings even provide the main dish for a Christmas dinner.

Aside from Phil, Jase (the second oldest son) appears to be the family member who most truly appreciates the health and culinary advantages of harvesting wild food. Jase acknowledges that food tastes better when it is processed by oneself. In the pilot episode, Jase emphatically states, "I don't like to eat meat from the grocery store. It makes me nervous," thereby showing that one of the greatest benefits of hunting is knowing where one's food comes from and how it arrived on the table. In another episode, he describes the meat of a catfish he has caught and says: "Appaloosa catfish only run two weeks a year.

[One] can't put a price on 'em." In other episodes, Jase comments that bullfrog legs are a "delicacy of the highest order" and "dove is the filet mignon of the sky." Through repeated comments of this kind, Jase emphasizes that the hunting experience may continue at the dinner table, long after the shot has been fired, and illustrates the pride that many hunters feel about harvesting one's own food.

Valuing wild food is only one positive aspect of *DD*'s presentation of hunting. In general, Phil maintains that "it is clean and honorable to live off the land." Despite the violence directed toward animals and the environment, being a Robertson means having a deep connection to nature and harvesting one's own food as often as possible. As the family patriarch, Phil's character ultimately wants younger generations to understand that it is best to eat the way he eats, live the way he lives, and be connected to the natural environment. Though in one episode Phil's grandkids adamantly declare they prefer Chick-fil-A to wild duck, Phil takes great pride in teaching them to harvest and process wild foods (honey, mayhaw fruit, crawfish, fish, and bullfrogs) and thus emphasizing their relationship to nature.

DD shows that characteristics of control and integrity are central to Phil's character's identity. The Ecologist Paul Shepard describes people's connection to hunting and self-sustenance this way: "Man is in part a carnivore: the male of the species is genetically programmed to pursue, attack, and kill for food. To the extent that they do not do so, they are not fully human."[4] While Shepard's language is problematically gendered, he recognizes that humans have a primordial desire to control their environment in order to survive, and contemporary writers have suggested that the connection between naturalness and hunting provides hunters with a perceived self-image of "integrity, beauty, and even stability."[5] This image of oneself provides the hunter with a sense of control (perhaps falsely) over his or her environment.[6] Although Phil has the resources to move into a nicer home, he and Miss Kay remain in their humble homestead, where he hunts game in his back yard. For Phil, the woods are simultaneously his standard of beauty and his sustenance. Moving to the suburbs, confined by concrete and Homeowner Association covenants, would (to use Phil's own term) make him a "yuppie." Removing Phil from the woods would violate his identity as a man subsisting directly on nature.

| The Gender of Hunting |

In *DD*, men bring home the meat and perhaps prepare it, and women provide opportunities for the men to hunt. This binary display of gender and hunting roles is problematic for nonhunter viewers as they may unfairly interpret these roles as resulting from misogynistic attitudes that are applicable to hunters generally. The gender differences in hunter participation among the Robertsons may be a result of their assumption that hunting is a male rite of passage. In other words, Robertson females are not actively discouraged from hunting, but because the expectation to hunt is not there, a Robertson female would have to be self-motivated to hunt if she actually wanted to pursue game.

Although none of the *DD* women hunt (and Willie's teenage daughter had never fired a shotgun prior to an episode in which Phil and Willie take her shooting), *DD* implies that if a woman does not hunt herself, she may acquire a hunting identity through three routes. The first is by proxy through her male kin who hunt: "I am married to a hunter, therefore I am a hunter." The second way she may participate in the hunting identity herself is through purchasing hunting-related commodities (such as DC cooking supplies and books) and engaging in food preparation. The most important way that *DD* women assume the hunting identity, however, is by performing domestic duties so that the Robertson men can hunt.

Admittedly, the hunter identity is very weak among the Robertson sons' wives in forms of participation and is arguably adopted by default, but for Miss Kay, the hunting identity is strong. In nearly every episode, Miss Kay is seen seducing Phil with food, often from his harvests; contrastingly, the sons' wives are never seen doing this. Miss Kay's identity stems from her ability to provide meals that bring the family together in the gathering of its ingredients, preparation (hunting, fishing), and consumption. While her attitudes toward gender are traditionally rigid, Miss Kay adopts a more fluid gender role in the kitchen because of her liberal definition of what food is. Miss Kay's connection to hunting on *DD* challenges the traditional hunting identity that is reduced to the kill and expands the hunter identity to include a feminine aspect otherwise unseen to nonhunter viewers.

While *DD* presents viewers with a complex image of gender and the hunter, ranging from Miss Kay's feminine version to the pseudo-masculine one rooted in blood culture, the show also presents viewers with an intricate message about the commercialization and commodification of hunting. The *DD* series as a whole is in many ways an infomercial for DC/BC products and, to a lesser extent, for a particular vision of the South and of Christianity. The connection *DD* establishes between one's identity as a hunter and commodities related to hunting is evidenced in popular box stores by aisle after aisle dedicated to *DD* merchandise. Jeffrey Cain has termed the connection of commercial hunting gear to one's hunter identity "blood culture."[7] Blood culture is exemplified the act of purchasing hunting commodities (such as camouflage vehicle floor mats, pink t-shirts blazed with a popular outfitter's logo, a particular firearm advertised during a hunting show, or camouflage vehicle mud flaps) in order to present oneself as a hunter. One is able to adopt the hunter identity because one has purchased the right tools (many of which emphasize violence) and has thereby engaged in the hunting experience, even if one has hunted only once or twice a year as a child and has not hunted in the past thirty. Because one has then vicariously engaged in hunting by watching *DD* and/or purchasing hunting products/paraphernalia, one presumably possesses the requisite skills to successfully hunt. In Cain's words, "buy the right gear and the authentic experience and the essence or secret of hunting will be yours."[8]

On *DD*, the Robertson sons have been quick not only to engage in blood culture but also to actively produce it in part because of how their hunter identities clash with their urbanized lives as prodigal suburban husbands and "yuppies." Although Phil created the first DC call, the company never flourished until the sons ran the company; Phil would rather be hunting than talking about hunting, making goods for hunting, or writing an essay on hunting. In contrast, the sons have become active producers of blood culture as each *DD/DC* product sold reaffirms the sons'—as well as the purchasers'—paradoxical position between the suburbs and the woods. Although they want to be in the woods, they are confronted with the physical and social barriers that come with suburban life. Put simply, the Robertson sons are legitimating their hunter identities through the same commercialized products that other contemporary hunters use.

Many contemporary hunters live in suburban environments and are able to escape to the outdoors to hunt only on weekends. But popular hunting commodities/media provide opportunities to be hunting, even if the hunt is only in the consumer's mind. Each hunting show viewed, magazine article read, or accessory purchased recreates the individual's perception of being a hunter. Many hunting products are essentially blood-culture commodities because they are not used to increase harvests or transfer knowledge but instead signal to others that one *is* a hunter and not just one who hunts. The message delivered in *DD* is not only "all things camo are good" but also "I am a hunter, even when I am not hunting."

| Conclusion |

When I moved to Mississippi to attend graduate school, I found friends who introduced me to hunting. After taking a hunter's education course (where I was the only adult pupil among a pack of twelve-year-old boys) and buying an extra-extra-large camouflage shirt to fit over my blue ski jacket, I anxiously awaited for opening day. As I sat against a cypress tree waiting for the ducks to fly in, the stillness of the forest was abruptly interrupted by the sound of my companions' shotguns. The noise froze me in place as the shots echoed like cannons across the swamp hole. After taking a few deep breaths (realizing that the sound was coming from my comrades and not a foreign army), I raised my 870 Express, looked down the barrel and put the bead in front of the head, and watched my first screaming wood duck suddenly stop and fall into the decoy spread. As I took the drake from Takota's (the golden retriever) gentle mouth, I was stupefied by the beauty of the bird and the connection I had to the environment.

It was unlike anything I had felt backcountry skiing in the Wasatch Front, climbing sandstone cliffs in Moab, or even fishing for salmon in Alaska. I saw a whole new side of hunting that was previously hidden from me and that extended far beyond my limited scope of experiences and exaggerated stereotypes. I was able to hold this magnificent bird and see the light shimmer off his feathers. I had never seen a duck look so beautiful. I felt the warmth of his blood drip on my cold hands and recognized that it was made up of the same physiological systems as I am. There was something about the colors and warmth from the blood and feathers that was so different from the cold fish I have caught. Seeing Takota eagerly jump into the cold water to retrieve the bird and fulfill some of his genetic inclinations that would have remained dormant had he been a nonhunter's indoor dog made me question to what extent I had not been truly human because I had not readily acquired my sustenance as a hunter. As an angler whose spouse does not care for most fish, I largely practiced catch and release. But there, in my hand, was tomorrow's lunch, and there was a sense of reverence for it.

One of the constant themes of *DD* is Phil's binary perspective of suburban life and country life. For Phil, the woods are honest and the civilized world is synthetic and artificial. And as his sons have married suburban wives, they have adopted comfortable suburban lifestyles that are at odds with Phil's understanding of manliness. Actively producing blood culture reaffirms the boys' roots in the woods and allows them to be a part of the woods even while they live in McMansions and relax at country clubs instead of residing in humble homes similar to the one in which they were raised. While it could be argued that the blood culture and stereotyped Southern identity presented by *DD* are merely the result of characters adhering to a script serving as a weekly infomercial for DC products, I think that *DD* is much more than its comically reductive characters. The Robertsons are performing characters, but they do so for the same reasons contemporary hunters participate in blood culture; they are negotiating contradictions between ideals of self-sufficiency and contemporary convenience.

Being a modern hunter in America is difficult because of rigid stereotypes (for example, that hunters are hyper-masculine, violent, reckless, and uneducated), limited access to huntable land, and occupations and social obligations that keep one from hunting. I have had students who upon hearing I avidly hunt are surprised because I am "too kind," "gentle," "educated," "open-minded" or even because I "dress too nice." I have heard life partners of those with whom I have hunted ask if I cry when I see a dead animal or if I "get in the way" because I am an academic and uncomfortable outside the ivory tower.

The point is, the hunter identity is so rigid and steeped in narrow stereotypes that if one is not constantly in the woods one is often told that one is not a true hunter by others and/or oneself. Much as Christians identify themselves to other Christians with the Ichthys symbol, hunters proudly display hunting status symbols. Just as some Christians question the faithfulness of others who do not publicly display their faith, those who hunt may question the sincerity of those who profess to hunt but do not display blood culture commodities. I do not fit within the narrow hunter stereotype, and thus my ability to perform masculine roles is doubted. Because I do not prominently display blood culture products, my allegiance to the chase is questioned.

As a novice hunter, I can speak to the division that often exists between hunters and nonhunters and am frustrated that *DD* did not work harder to bridge that gap and work to celebrate more positive aspects of hunting and its role in identity construction. *DD* had the opportunity to bridge differences between hunters and nonhunters and to make important aspects of hunting visible. To an extent, *DD* has done this. *DD* has showcased the deep connection that many hunters have to the environment, and it has praised the organic, healthy quality of wild game. And the show has perhaps helped nonhunters understand why blood culture is a prevalent part of the urban hunter and his or her identity.

As a relatively new participant to the sport, I am still negotiating to what extent hunting is part of my identity. *DD* has made me, and probably other viewers, question the role of hunting in one's identity. I see myself as a person who likes the outdoors, and hunting is only a subset of the larger attraction. Perhaps others see themselves as hunters first and outdoorspersons second. Within the existing stereotypes, this difference of perspective precludes me from being a hunter, but ain't I a hunter? According to *DD*'s implied message, I clearly am. From *DD*'s superficial message, which plays upon stereotypes, the answer is less clear.

DD has also reinforced the negative stereotypes of hunting and the South indirectly. To this end, it has been problematic. By glorifying redneck character roles, it has possibly only exaggerated the perceived connection between hunting and hostility to the environment. Hunters and (because of the show's location) Southerners are portrayed as being backward and as expecting women to be in the kitchen. The extent to which *DD* has portrayed an authentic hunting experience or is even "real" and not a scripted show is debatable, but it has both created opportunities to promote aspects of hunting that are invisible to nonhunters and reaffirmed negative stereotypes about hunters and Southerners.

Philip Mason

PART

II

Why We Hunt

Personal Accounts

Deer Stand

My watch tells me thirty minutes until first light. Breathing the mid-December air deep into my lungs, I exhale slowly. The cold on my face feels good, at least for now.

More than half a dozen deer stands are scattered around the woods where I've come to hunt, and from a few of them you can look out during daylight hours and see rolling hills dotted with neighboring farms. The kind I'm sitting in resembles a ski lift that doesn't go anywhere and comes with a safety bar that is supposed to keep me from falling thirty feet to the ground should I fall asleep. Though this one is stingy on views, in the distance I can make out a car's moving headlights.

Once owned by a coal company and later functioning as a Christmas tree farm, this patch of Pennsylvania forest belongs to the parents of a friend I've known since high school. Other than putting up a house and a barn, Joel's folks have left the place untouched. Somewhere on the property are three shafts belonging to the old Whiskey Run Mine, which I've looked for but never found. These days, deer haunt every acre. One year Joel's father Mike counted 140 deer grazing on a hill at the same time. I'll count myself lucky if I see just one today. One, though, is all I want.

When first light arrives, it comes quiet and still. I try to keep as motionless as possible, ready with a pair of binoculars. It's meat, not a rack, I want, and since males are overhunted I'll want to make certain any deer I spot is antlerless. I have hunted here on opening day when the crackle of gunfire greets first light for miles around—a moment when perhaps as many as a million hunters across the state are doing the same thing, and a reminder that I'm taking part in something much larger than myself. The noise helps other hunters by getting the deer to move, which increases the chance of seeing something and getting to do one's part in becoming a direct link in the food chain. But because today is not opening day, dawn is met by silence.

Deer stands, I decided the first time I used one several years ago, are mis-named. A deer *sit* is more like it because that's mostly what I do: sit and wait, sit and think while struggling to keep my mind from straying from the task before me. Hunters talk about the opportunities for watching wildlife hunting affords, which is true enough. While sitting in deer stands I have seen a fox and a mother black bear with cub and followed the movements of a yearling fawn as it passed underneath me, each one oblivious to my presence. Nuthatches and downy woodpeckers, hunters themselves, will come daringly close while work-ing a neighboring tree trunk in search of insects. And always there are squirrels weaving their way through infinite patterns of twig and branch.

Mostly, though, there is only the waiting.

This kind of waiting takes work and requires a mind at ease with contem-plative stillness and observation, which I'll admit isn't exactly my forte. It relies as well on a mind that needs to turn predatory in an instant if an opportunity comes. Despite my limited experience, it unnerves me a little knowing how quickly I am capable of making the switch.

It is often a source of wonder to me whenever I am hunting to realize I am hunting at all. I make my living as an environmental educator at a residential learning center located in the Great Smoky Mountains, where my organiza-tion's motto is "connecting people and nature." You might say I fell into this line of work, since at the time I was hired I was wholly unqualified—an English major in a roomful of biologists. If not for the desperate circumstances of my employer that summer, twenty years ago, I doubtless would not have made the cut. My job more or less consists of taking children, college students, working adults—anybody—into forests, fields, and creeks to help them consider more deeply their connection with the nonhuman world. It was all on-the-job train-ing in those early days, and it never crossed my mind that an activity such as hunting might, for some people, be another way to accomplish this. A num-ber of years would have to pass before I arrived at the conclusion that a per-son could be a responsible citizen of the natural environment by becoming a hunter.

Because I did not start until I was an adult, hunting still feels to me like a for-eign language I have only just begun to comprehend. The fathers of friends speak eagerly with me about the subject whenever it comes up in conversation, and because I have so much to learn I listen intently to whatever they have to say. Desire seems to count more than achievement in their eyes, and I find my-self a welcome new member of their tribe.

Though my own father hunted a few times in his youth, he never raised the idea with me while I was growing up, and I am certain I would have declined if he had. For most of my childhood I could not have fathomed pointing a gun at a living creature and pulling the trigger. This happened only once when I was twelve and aimed my BB gun at a chipmunk in our back yard. Watching it spin in circles when I hit it, the poor creature neither dying nor quite able to go on living, I instantly retreated indoors, unwilling and unable to bring an end to its terror. I stowed the gun in my closet and did not touch it again for a long time.

Growing up in western Pennsylvania meant being surrounded by deer hunters. The season opens on the Monday following Thanksgiving, a de facto statewide holiday when many schools remain closed until the following day. Neighbors, childhood playmates, and extended family members hunted, and on one occasion our neighbor's son-in-law hung a deer he'd shot in the branches of the maple tree outside my bedroom window. Though I wasn't afraid to wander over and peer into the empty ribcage and inspect the organs lying on the ground in a puddle of blood, I was certain I did not ever want to be the cause of something so horrific in my life.

I knew several girls who were as enthusiastic about hunting as were a larger number of boys, which helped to insulate it in my mind against toxic associations with machismo. Hunting instead seemed to have more to do with class. Schoolmates who hunted were not the sons and daughters of doctors, university professors, and coal mine executives. They were kids whose families mostly lived out in the country—the ones the rest of us referred to as rednecks. Hunting for them was a birthright in much the same way country club membership was for the privileged children of our county's wealthiest residents.

Rednecks got their meat from the woods. The rest of us got ours from the store. But every once in a while a neighbor or family friend would arrive at our door with a gift of fresh venison, and we found it strange to find ourselves eating the flesh of a creature we liked to watch descend from the woods many evenings to browse in our back yard. My sister would sniff her food and put down her fork if she thought she detected the smell of deer meat, despite our parents' assurances that it was, in fact, beef. I didn't much care for it myself. Venison tasted earthy and too close to home, and bullets and slaughter were the reason it was on our table. We did not have to know such intimate details about the poultry and pork we ate, nor did we want to. Ignorance was much preferred.

I acquired a taste for venison several years ago thanks to a friend who gave me steaks from a deer he'd shot while hunting with his father on their annual trip to the Allegheny National Forest—"deer camp," Mark always called it. Despite overcooking the meat, I savored each bite and considered how satisfying it would feel to secure food from the wild with one's own hands, no matter how much hard work and luck it would require. I'd tried gardening a few times, only to feed the mouths of caterpillars and aphids more than my own. I wondered if I ought to try hunting, which carried the possibility of filling my freezer with meat in one fell swoop.

A number of hurdles lay in my path. For starters, I was living in a national park where hunting was prohibited. Also, I didn't own any firearms, and I would have to come to grips with using lethal force against defenseless creatures. By this point in my life, a notion had crept into my way of thinking that said nature could only be harmed by humans taking anything from it. A thing of beauty, nature was to be admired, basked in, fallen in love with, but not intruded upon for one's own ends. Native Americans hunted, true, but they were *Native Americans*. Fishing was another form of hunting, and though I'd caught and eaten fish plenty of times, a twinge of guilt had always accompanied the act of harvesting creatures that were minding their own business before I came along.

I recalled a conversation I'd had with a fellow environmental educator upon returning from my sister's wedding in Alaska, when I'd confessed to him the mixed emotions I'd felt after reeling in a king salmon and watching it die. Taking something that was beautiful and untamed from the wild had left me feeling hollow inside. "If I'd gone to the grocery store instead it would still be alive," I told Steve.

"Except then something else would be dead," he said. "How is it better to eat a domesticated animal likely raised on a factory farm? Or paying someone to do your killing for you? Hunting is one of the oldest, most natural methods there is."

He was right, of course. Humans are a part of the wild, too, if they choose to be. Appropriately enough, the bumper sticker on Steve's truck at the time read: "Save the Neanderthals."

Individuals who "care about the environment," as it's often put, are not supposed to get their food from cute, furry animals they take aim at and kill, at least not according to popular wisdom. But as an environmental educator I should have known better. For one thing, hunters were the original conservationists, and since the establishment of hunting laws in the early twentieth century no game animal in North America has joined the ranks of extinct species. And so, in time, I would tack onto the mantra "reduce, reuse, recycle" another principle I would henceforth try to live by: "kill my own meat."

Blood, I realized, had been on my hands all along. Becoming vegan or choosing any path other than suicide wouldn't make a difference: I had no choice but to remain an accomplice in the death of creatures merely by taking up space on earth. Wherever I made my home, other creatures couldn't make theirs. Wherever I drove my car, asphalt had obliterated habitat for untold generations of wildlife. We humans break up the forest wherever we leave our mark, and while this benefits commensal species such as mice and deer, other creatures without the means to adapt to humankind have no place left to go.

Hunting seemed at least one way of owning up to a reality which others—rednecks included—had figured out long before me: death is a part of life, and it is impossible to avoid playing some role in it. The silver lining was having at least some say in deciding what role.

If I were pressed to muster a defense of hunters and why I decided to become one, I might cite the two hundred human deaths caused annually by automobile collisions with whitetail deer. Or point out that many woodland plant species are in decline as a result of deer overpopulation. Or appeal to the predatory instinct sealed in our DNA that calls forth a desire to carry on what our human ancestors began doing thousands of years ago. I might argue that in a hyperindividualized society such as ours we have lost sight of the common good in our veneration of individual rights and have extended the same half-baked logic to the natural world—with disastrous consequences. Or question the assumption some people make in believing that killing an animal because it has a face and a mother is worse than killing a garden vegetable because it has neither.

But the main reason I became a hunter, the one that sits deepest in my gut and feels most honest to me, is because I felt called. More and more it was what both the woods and human culture seemed to require of me. A calling, by one definition, is something one can't say no to, not because one doesn't have a choice but because choosing otherwise would mean hiding from oneself and missing the mark. Taking responsibility—what every vibrant culture depends on its members to do—is what follows: finding one's ability to respond to a new orientation toward the world, then exercising one's obligation to act. These are freighted words that can lead to cheap moralizing. But there's another aspect to being called that is seldom discussed, which is that responsibility and obligations can result in a humbling *joy*. In my case it meant seeing more clearly my dependence on the nonhuman world and discovering some measure of independence by recognizing that I did not have to acquire every mouthful of food I ate from an impersonal source. Hunting seemed the most obvious, practical, and personally satisfying way to accomplish this given my circumstances. What's more, my wife, herself a quasi-vegetarian, liked the idea.

I began taking the necessary steps to becoming a hunter by enrolling in a safety course and purchasing a rifle, orange coat, and gutting knife, and as I did so I waited for some reason—ethical, financial, or otherwise—to tell me I was heading down the wrong path. (No wonder so many low-income people living in rural areas hunt, I kept thinking while making my purchases, surprised by the how relatively inexpensive each item was, except for the rifle, though the rifle itself was a lifetime investment that would pay dividends for years to come.) But none did. And when the moment came to walk for the first time in the dark to a deer stand and climb the ladder and sit in utter stillness for hours, harvesting a deer neither that year nor the next, it felt to me like the most natural thing in the world. By mere virtue of being present in the woods, making just a little effort and sharing the same desire every other creature around me possessed—to find food—I was becoming part of the wild.

When the time came for me to pull the trigger for the first time, no longer as a boy carelessly pointing his BB gun at a chipmunk but as a man aiming a high-powered rifle at a deer that seemed to stare right through me with its big brown eyes, the questions hurtling through my mind appeared in the form of vows. Are you sure you want to take this innocent creature's life? *I am.* Will you be satisfied to know you took a life through a violent act that may never fully leave you at peace? *I will.* Do you promise to make its life valuable by eating as much of it as you can? *I do.*

Hunting isn't for everybody, and I imagined someday becoming like older hunters I've met who are content to sit in a deer stand each fall not to kill animals but only to watch them. But for now, having spent so much of my life in the woods, a place I love, I wanted to become a more active participant in it. I wanted to enter nature's economy more fully and take part in the sacramental transformation of the woods becoming part of me by carrying out an act that made me a part of it.

Two hours before sunset I'm back at it, taking watch in a deer stand different from the first. Box-like and surrounded by plywood walls, this one looks out over a meadow. Perched four feet off the ground, it's in easy view of a gas well, the community water tower, and the ubiquitous Christmas trees. Snow has blown in past strips of muslin partially covering several windows, collecting in the corners and on a metal folding chair. When I peer out, I notice nothing moving but tufts of yellow grass poking through the snow that wave each time the wind blows.

The blind gives me an easy advantage. But in all other ways whitetail deer here and throughout the eastern United States have the advantage, living free of predators such as wolves and cougars and increasing in number under the protection of laws that privilege game animals over other organisms. Deer have become overpopulated as a result and have ravaged not only wild-plant communities but also a good deal of agricultural land, not to mention threatening human lives through thousands of collisions with automobiles every year. As the number of hunters nationwide declines and the preferred habitat of deer (cleared land adjacent to patchy woods) increases, it's no mystery what this means for the future of biodiversity and forest health. Both will likely continue to suffer and decline.

To hunt, then, is to take part in a management plan set forth by one government agency or another; to not hunt is to take part in that same plan, albeit with different results. What I mean is that whether we are conscious of it or not, we are all members of an ecosystem, and taking no action means taking some kind of action after all. Deer have become overpopulated in the absence of predators every healthy landscape depends on, and doing nothing means letting the chips fall where they may and perhaps harvesting a deer with the hood of a car—as happened to me one night as a passenger riding in Joel's car.

I make my own attempts at becoming a conscious predatory member of the eastern deciduous forest once or twice a year, usually when I am visiting home over the holidays. Though my efforts end in failure more often than not, this is to be expected when my quarry are natural athletes skilled in evasion and survival.

A flock of birds crosses the sky in the distance. Geese, or perhaps tundra swans. I wonder if they ever feel their own potency while on the wing, necks torpedo-straight and beaks plowing the air like the bow of a ship. If they ever feel the same spark of pride and satisfaction an athlete feels when in top form. If they're aware even for an instant of how graceful they appear to the human eye. We ask what it means to us when we encounter wildlife—a hummingbird, say, flying through an open window to flap frantically around a room or a raccoon bounding across the road in front of us at night—but what does it mean to the hummingbird, or the raccoon?

Ben, like Steve, was a colleague who had a Neanderthal streak. He sometimes dressed in nothing but a loin cloth and would come running out of the woods into the company of shocked students and teachers. Communicating by way of grunts and hand gestures, he would get the students to help him build a fire and light it using a hand drill and then disappear back into the woods, leaving everybody to guess when Earth Man would next show up. Ben went exploring in the woods one day and happened upon a young deer browsing on forbs. The startled fawn looked up but didn't run, uncertain what to make of the human being, apparently the first it had ever seen, standing in such proximity. Kneeling on all fours, Ben began making the same motions as the fawn by pretending also to dine on the forest's greenery and then inched closer. The pair was only a few feet apart when after ten minutes the fawn's mother showed up and snorted in alarm: *What are you doing?* The fawn, according to Ben, registered a look of confusion. There was a threat somewhere—his mother had told him so. But where? She snorted again, and at last he understood it was his newfound human playmate and fled after his mother. Like all the times Earth Man descended out of the woods, it was a moment when the divide separating the human world from the wild temporarily disappeared.

Though rested and caffeinated, my mind has wandered. Recovering my attention, I peek once more through the cloth-covered window. The yellow grass. The snow and water tower. Still no movement.

When two deer bound out of the trees below the gas well and pause in the middle of the field, I'm all eyes and ears. My .30–06 rifle has a maximum range of three hundred yards, and the pair is standing only one-third that distance from me. Any second, I'm certain, something will alert them to my presence—my scent, the muslin cloth I push out of the way, or the muzzle of the gun I poke through the opening and point in their direction—and they will bolt.

But they don't. Instead, they trot a few feet more and stop again to look and listen and sniff the air. They're facing the wrong way, hind end toward me, which makes taking a shot unwise. But then the one in front, the larger of the two, turns so her flank is broadside and I locate her neck, a thing of strength and beauty, in the crosshairs of my scope and pull the trigger.

Ears ringing, I climb out of the stand. Though she lay still in the place where I watched her fall, I wait several minutes before approaching. It's a sobering moment and no time for rejoicing. I have shattered bone, shed blood. Ended a life.

It seems certain when I finally come over to her that my shot was clean and killed her instantaneously—or almost. Tracks show where she bounded ten feet away before dropping to the ground. Air escapes her lungs when I press into her rib cage with my hand. There's another set of prints in the snow belonging to her companion, who at the sound of my rifle made a beeline for the trees.

I put on rubber gloves and open the blade of my gutting knife and quickly get to work. Field-dressing an animal is a simple if messy procedure. The organs and viscera must be removed within about a half hour if I don't want the meat to become ruined. I have been successful only once before when I had Mike's help dressing and transporting the animal to my car so I could deliver it to the butcher. Today it's just me.

Within the hour Mike will return from running errands in town and lend me a hand moving the doe the final distance from field to house, where I will load her into the trunk of my car. I will drive to Cunningham Meats, located a few miles away, and ask for permission to observe them while they strip off the hide, which I will take home and tan. I will transport the meat to Tennessee in the used Toyota Prius my wife and I have just bought, which will inspire her to dub me an "NPR redneck." I will make room in the freezer for forty-five pounds of meat that will take me over a year to consume.

For now, though, it's just me and the doe. She is heavy. I have no rope and no other means of moving her. So I hook my arms under her forelegs and neck. Her fur rubs against my face as I hug her to my chest and begin dragging her through the snow in an intimate embrace, trying to hold up my end in one of the oldest, hardest dances on earth.

Snake Bit on the Ogeechee

I had just done an incredibly stupid thing. That's what I told myself as I rubbed my rapidly swelling right hand. It was clear now. Everything had been wrong about the behavior and appearance of that sixteen-inch water snake. It swam with its head lifted above the surface of the river, and it didn't dive when I approached it in my canoe. As I grabbed its tail after I pinned it against the bank with my paddle, I saw the white inside the snake's mouth and the long left front fang. In retaliation the snake latched on to me, wagging its head back and forth to work in its long teeth. The sharp, burning pain in the index finger of my right hand felt like a nail being driven deep into my flesh, unlike the numerous bites from nonvenomous snakes I had gotten over the years.

Pete, a middle-aged man sporting a pony tail and wearing a baseball cap, was in his kayak twenty yards away. I'd just met him. We were on the Ogeechee River above an old mill in central Georgia. He was there attending a camp-out meeting of the Georgia River Keepers, and I was there to promote a collection of nature essays with two of my writer friends. I had decided to take one last paddle early that morning before heading home to the South Carolina upstate. Pete had been paddling in front of me and had stopped when he came to a fallen tree that blocked the river, and I had caught up with him.

We had both considered pulling our boats over the tree's slim trunk and continuing up the river but had decided there wasn't time and had turned to go back. It was a bright, mild Sunday morning in mid-September. Because of the mill dam downstream, the river was almost motionless. Our boats cut the stillness of the dark water into sparkling waves. Black willows, box elders, and alders thickly bordered the river banks on either side. The day couldn't have been more perfect.

Pete and I had paddled only a few strokes from the fallen tree when he pointed out the snake crossing the river in front of us. I told him that, in addition to being a fair birder, I was something of a snake guy and announced confidently that what we had swimming before us was a nonvenomous banded water snake. While Pete made a point of keeping his distance, I paddled off to catch it. As I closed in on the snake, I was already going over in my mind what I would tell Pete about the serpent once I had it in hand, and I imagined how impressed he would be when I showed it to him.

My attraction to the snake and need to catch it and Pete's wish to be far away while I did reflect the two different reactions people typically have toward snakes, with Pete's response by far the more common. As the psychologist Hal Herzog points out in his interesting book *Some We Love, Some We Hate, Some We Eat,* our attitudes toward animals are often divided, complicated, and even contradictory. None, I would add, more so than our attitudes toward snakes. Most people are powerfully attracted to animals like baby seals, puppies, and kittens. The great ethologist Konrad Lorenz theorized that these animals' large eyes, high foreheads, prominent cheeks, and rounded skulls, resembling those of human infants, serve as "baby releasers" and prompt instinctive parental behaviors and caring emotions. Psychologists call this the "cute response." Snakes don't elicit the cute response. Herzog cites a 2001 Gallup poll that asked Americans to name things they most feared. Snakes ranked number one.[1]

Experts have long debated whether human antipathy toward snakes is innate, learned, or some combination of the two. Harry W. Greene, one of our leading contemporary herpetologists, argues it's innate. He notes that large boas and pythons very likely hunted, killed, and ate our primate ancestors. This evolutionary history would have selected for an instinctive fear of snakes.[2]

The old herpetologist, sea turtle expert, and writer Archie Carr also believed that the fear of snakes is inborn and suggested that stereotypic behaviors go along with it. In his book *The Windward Road* he describes the typical actions of people who have encountered a snake. They have a "fixed downward stare" and crouch in a "half aggressive and half recoiling posture," with "quick sidelong searching of the ground for a stick" or something else to throw. There is "the upraised arm, the clutching of young and beating away of dogs," and "the grave mien of the most responsible male." I call this peculiar behavior Archie's Dance. Carr claimed that he could identify these snake-killing behaviors from a quarter-mile away and had used them to collect "many a fine specimen."[3] My own experience bears him out. On two occasions Archie's Dance has helped me to find and rescue harmless snakes.

Others argue that fear of snakes is completely learned. The psychologist Susan Mineka found that captive-raised Rhesus monkeys had no fear of snakes and learned to fear them only when they saw the fright response of wild-caught monkeys. And while many people are afraid of snakes, some are attracted to them. More than fifty percent of Americans claim not to be afraid of snakes, and around four hundred thousand of them, like me, keep snakes as pets.[4]

Whether people's reactions to snakes are innate or learned, very few people are neutral toward them. This lesson was brought home to me years ago on a family trip to a zoo. As I wandered through the exhibits, I spotted a four-foot-long black rat snake slowly crossing the trail between cages. Intending to remove it to nearby shrubbery out of harm's way, I picked it up. The harmless snake glided placidly between my hands. Immediately a dozen people turned their backs on the antics of the gibbons and other exotic primates and crowded around me. Some were fearful; others were excited; all were curious. They eagerly asked me questions about the very common, glossy-black snake I held in my hands.

Some snake men, I suspect, develop an addiction to this kind of attention. When people get bored with their capturing and handling harmless snakes, like my rat snake, they show them venomous copperheads. When copperheads no longer get attention, they handle more dangerous cottonmouths, then much more venomous eastern diamondback rattlesnakes, up the continuum of peril. Pride goes before a fall. In this case it also goes before a life-threatening bite.

"Boy, that hurts," I said to Pete after the snake bit me. I knew then that it was a cottonmouth and not a harmless banded water snake, but I was too embarrassed by my mistake to tell him. Pete paddled over to get a better look, still keeping a good distance between us. Securing the snake behind its head, I transferred it from my bitten right hand to my unbitten left and held it at waist level while he took a picture of it with his cell phone.

In his guidebook, *Reptiles and Amphibians of Eastern/Central North America*, a holy volume for reptile enthusiasts like me, the late Roger Conant, expert on both water snakes and cottonmouths, cautions that these "very dangerous snakes [cottonmouths] closely resemble several of the nonpoisonous water snakes and are difficult to tell from them in the field" and warns his readers to "beware of any semiaquatic serpent within the range of the cottonmouths."[5] Conant's first commandment, and the practice of every good snake hunter, is never to handle a snake unless you're absolutely sure you know what it is.

I could use the excuse that cottonmouths live no farther west in Georgia and South Carolina than the fall line, that they don't live in the Carolina piedmont, where my home is located and where I usually encountered water snakes, and that I hadn't realized I had crossed over into cottonmouth territory in central Georgia on the Ogeechee. None of that, of course, mattered. I had violated the first commandment of snake hunting, and now I would have to suffer the consequences.

After Pete took a picture, I released the snake unharmed into the water. That was only fair. I had chased and harassed it, not the other way around. If anyone ever deserved to be bitten by a cottonmouth, it was me.

We slowly floated a little farther down the river. I still said nothing about the bite. Pete heard some birds calling and asked me what they were. "White-eyed Vireo and Acadian Flycatcher," I said. He briefly nodded. He felt no need to take pictures of them.

Between 20 and 25 percent of all bites by pit vipers, a class that includes cottonmouths, are "dry," meaning that the snake doesn't inject its venom.[6] I tried to justify what I was doing by convincing myself that I was having an allergic reaction to the snake's saliva, a response people sometimes have, and not to envenomation. But the sharp pain and rapid swelling of my hand told me otherwise.

Pete noticed none of this. A few minutes later he told me that his family was waiting for him and that he had to hurry. I resisted confessing to him what had happened and asking him to stay with me. Instead, I wished him a good paddle and watched as his kayak quickly disappeared around a bend in the river. Then I canoed slowly downstream, trying to remain calm. One thing was clear: my foolish pride had put me in this spot, and now I would have to get myself out.

Part of the reason snakes provoke strong feelings in us is that they are peculiar. They are legless, so they not only appear odd, but their wriggling movements seem bizarre and, for many people, disgusting. They are covered in scales and shed their skins all in one piece; some cultures have viewed this as a miraculous renewal. And they are exothermic rather than endothermic, meaning they maintain body temperature primarily by positioning themselves in warmer or cooler places rather than by generating body heat internally as mammals and birds do. Because they do not need to burn many calories for body heat, they can go for very long periods without eating. In spring in colder climates, snakes emerge in great numbers from underground dens after long months of winter, a mass resurrection of sorts. All this has made snakes a creature ripe for folklore. This seems particularly true in the South.

Southerners often mistakenly believe that all water snakes, which they call "moccasins," are venomous, that "pilot snakes" act as guides for groups of venomous snakes, that venomous snakes always go in pairs, the second seeking revenge if its mate is killed, that almost every snake is venomous, and that a bite from even a mildly venomous snake, like a copperhead, inevitably leads to death. I had to keep these notions in mind when I did snake shows in elementary schools or used my snakes in a nature appreciation class I did for my college's summer camp for kids.

But Southern myths about snakes have deeper roots than folk wisdom. One little boy's reaction in summer camp illustrates this. I had snakes in aquariums on two sides of my room. The first day the boy cautiously examined them, not daring to come any closer than five feet. Finally he turned to me and said in a thick Southern accent, "That just ain't right. You shouldn't oughta do that."

"Shouldn't do what?" I replied, puzzled.

"Them boxes," he said, an offended tone in his voice. "It ain't right to have snakes in them boxes."

There were small boxes in each of the cages with a hole in the side for the snakes to retreat, but I couldn't see a problem with them. "Why's that?" I said.

"It says Holy Bible on them boxes."

It did. My Methodist college has a long and somewhat odd tradition of handing out Bibles signed by the faculty and administrators to our seniors at graduation. As a result there is always an abundance of Bible boxes available, and these make perfect hide-places for my smaller snakes.

"So?" I said.

"You can't have snakes in no Bible box. It's like the Devil," the boy said, shaking his head and holding up his hands as if to ward off evil.

Then I understood. The boy's reaction to my snakes came from his fundamentalist Baptist upbringing and his Church's literal reading of the Garden of Eden story in the King James Bible. I knew because I came from the same religious background. His preacher's sermons from the book of Genesis would've described how the clever serpent, who is "more subtle than any beast of the field," lies to Eve and tells her she will not die, as God has warned her, if she eats the apple and promises her that her "eyes shall be opened and ye shall be as gods, knowing good and evil." From the book of Revelations the boy's preacher would have identified the snake in Genesis as "the great dragon," the Devil, Satan himself, who "deceiveth the whole world."

For eating the apple God punishes Eve, declaring that "in sorrow thou shalt bring forth children." Because Adam "hearkened unto the voice of [his] wife," the very ground he and Eve walk on will be cursed. God also punishes the snake, saying to him, "thou art cursed . . . above every beast of the field" and "upon thy belly thou shalt go, and dust shalt thou eat all the days of thy life; and I will put enmity between thee and the woman, and between thy seed and her seed; and it shall bruise thy head, and thou shall bruise his heel."

The preacher would have reminded the boy that the wages of sin are death. It's no wonder the little boy didn't want my snakes in a box that read "Holy." No wonder he and other children like him hate snakes. The serpent had brought tribulation and death to all of us.

Not all cultures have viewed snakes as evil. In one of the oldest Greek myths, Ophion, the snake, incubates the cosmic egg from which all creation emerges. Egyptian myth has Ra the Sun and all existence reborn each morning from a many-coiled snake called Amduat. In Hindu myth the god Vishnu rests on the back of the cosmic cobra Shesha, whose hood supports each of the planets. Hinduism presents the snake as a symbol of pure desire. In ancient Greece and India snakes were believed to bring good fortune, and people kept pet snakes or wore snake amulets to ward off the evil eye.

Some religions have also portrayed snakes as guardians, protectors, and healers. In Buddhist tradition an immense cobra named Muchilinda spread his hood to protect the Buddha from a fierce storm that raged for a week as the Buddha meditated under the bho tree. Then the serpent transformed into a young man and bowed before him, the first person to do so. Snake statuary appears around Buddhist temples as protecting spirits. In Greek mythology Asclepius, the God of medicine, carries a staff with a snake wrapped around it. The image of a snake or snakes entwined on a rod, the caduceus, goes back thousands of years and is a symbol of medical practice today.

A snake with its tail in its mouth, thus forming a circle, representing the totality of existence and the cyclical nature of life, is also widespread. Called the Ourobouros, the image appeared in ancient Egypt, in classical Greece, in Roman culture, and in medieval alchemy. Clearly our complicated ideas and feelings about snakes are derived, in part, from millennia of myths and symbols.

I paddled on, trying to keep my composure, slowing down by pulling the paddle through the stroke on a five count. It wouldn't do to get my heart rate up. I designated trees along the river and measured how quickly I got to them. If I arrived too soon, I increased my count to ten. And I took deep breaths to calm myself.

Whether myths portray snakes as evil or benevolent, there is an underlying biological reality to them and, in some species, real danger. Many snakes possess venoms, and some of these venoms have devastating effects on the body. Of the more than 2,500 species of the superfamily of advanced snakes, the Colubroidea, which makes up the great majority of snake species, half or more are venomous. But only between 250 and 500 of these snakes have venoms potent enough to cause serious harm to humans, and just 50 species do most of the damage.

All the elaphids, the family of snakes that includes cobras and coral snakes, and all the pit vipers, a viper subfamily that possesses heat-sensing organs between the eyes and nostrils and that includes rattlesnakes, copperheads, and my cottonmouth, are venomous. Worldwide snake bites kill around twenty thousand people each year.[7]

It's difficult to describe exactly what was happening to me once the cottonmouth's venom entered my body. Venoms are complicated chemical mixtures. Traditionally they are classified into two broad types: hemotoxic venoms, characteristic of the viperids, and neurotoxic venoms, which are more typically found in elapids. Greene prefers the term "tissue destructive" to "hemotoxic" because these venoms destroy far more than just the vascular system. Viper venoms contain lethal proteins that immobilize prey so that they can be located after they have been struck. In addition, the venoms have enzymes that destroy tissue, so the prey animal is being digested from the inside even before it dies and before the snake swallows it.

Another enzyme produced by pit vipers promotes absorption of venom through connective tissues. Venom spreads in human beings primarily by way of the lymphatic system, which recycles blood plasma from many parts of the body, plays a central role in the immune system, and flows to the heart. Other components are enzymes that act to destroy linings of blood vessels and kill red blood cells.

Multiple symptoms accompany a pit viper bite. Normally swelling occurs almost immediately, and sharp pain is felt within five minutes. If there is no sign of edema, the collection of fluids between the tissue cells, or redness around the bite within eight hours, envenomation probably has not occurred.

The swelling around the bitten area spreads, and redness or bruising appears around the bite. Lymphatic channels become inflamed and lymph nodes enlarged. Victims of timber and eastern diamondback rattlesnake bites may experience a metallic or rubbery taste in their mouths. Muscle contractions around the bitten area and in the face, neck, and back may occur and may be present in other parts of the body as well.

The destruction of the circulatory system leads to leaking of plasma and red blood cells into tissues, producing a great accumulation of fluid between the cells and thus massive swelling. Fluid accumulation can also occur around the heart and in the lungs. There may be a loss of a third or more of the volume of circulating blood in a limb, and this can deleteriously affect the functioning of the heart and kidneys.

Blisters full of blood or fluids may appear, indicating a severe bite. The worst effects of pit viper bites on humans are typically death of tissue around the bite, hemorrhage, kidney failure, and buildup of fluids in the air sacs around the heart. Those who survive a bad bite might suffer permanent crippling, the loss of an arm or the full use of a leg, and permanent lung and kidney damage. The typical cause of death in humans from pit viper bites is heart failure due to the internal loss of blood, with its accompanying collapse of blood pressure.

There are other common symptoms that are produced not by the effects of the venom but by panic and fear. These include loss of emotional control or its opposite, lethargy and withdrawal, diarrhea and vomiting, fainting, feelings of dizziness, cold and clammy skin, and an abnormally elevated heart rate.

In contrast, neurotoxic venoms block the transmission of impulses from nerve cells to muscles and rapidly spread through the blood system. The person may experience little pain or swelling from the bite, and in some cases symptoms may not occur for one to five hours. When they do appear, they can involve drooping eyelids, difficulty swallowing, loss of ability to move parts of the body, the inability to speak, effusive salivation, and, later, loss of deep tendon reflexes and difficulty in breathing. Death usually results from respiratory failure.

A good number of snake venoms, including that of the eastern diamondback rattlesnake, have both toxins. To make the issue of the effect of venoms even more complicated, different species of snake vary in the toxicity of their venoms. For example, the venom of cottonmouths is considered less potent than that of rattlesnakes but substantially more toxic than the venom of their close relative, copperheads. Populations of the same species of snake differ in their toxicity from one area to another; snakes of some species may vary in the potency and type of toxicity of their venoms according to their age, and even individuals from the same litter may greatly vary in venom potency. Also, people differ in their reaction to envenomation.

There were probably birds singing and no doubt the river was still lovely, but I heard and saw none of it. My mind was fixed on making it back to camp and my friends. One thing troubled me more than any other. My hand was swelling so rapidly I didn't know how much longer I would be able to hold the paddle.

I have had a long association with snakes. As a boy I lived outside San Antonio, Texas, on a dirt road lined with small houses. On one side of the road was a mile of thick, thorny brush land, on the other a small creek and pastures. Our neighborhood represented a tendril of invasive suburbia that would sweep over the area ten years later.

I spent my early childhood wandering through the brush and fields catching and keeping nonvenomous snakes, fence and horned lizards, ground squirrels, rats, and baby rabbits. At twelve my older brother gave me a .22 rifle and a 20-gauge shotgun to hunt rabbits and doves on our grandparents' farm, and in my early twenties I hunted quail on my father-in-law Buck's South Texas ranch/farm. He put me to work like his sons and daughters. As I walked his fence lines spraying herbicide on brush, I often encountered western diamondback rattlesnakes. Hunting quail was fun but didn't compare to the thrill of finding a big western diamondback reared in a dramatic defensive coil, sounding off and striking from the cover of thorny mesquite.

Because I was busy in undergraduate and graduate school, I missed the heyday of snake hunting in the United States. It was in the 1960s and 1970s, promoted in part by two books by the Staten Island Zoo's herpetologist, Carl Kauffeld: *Snakes and Snake Hunting* and *Snakes: The Keeper and the Kept.* Much

Gerald T. Thurmond

to Kauffeld's regret, his books inspired great numbers of people to begin hunting snakes, using his detailed essays as reptile treasure maps. Swarms of hunters and collectors invaded the low country of South Carolina, Florida, and the desert grasslands and mountains of southeastern Arizona. The Okeetee Hunt Club in South Carolina, one of the places Kauffeld's essays made famous, was closed to the public after snake hunters began showing up in chartered buses in the spring. Populations of some rare snakes were devastated and precious snake habitat destroyed. To protect threatened snake species from amateur and professional hunters, state and federal governments enacted laws greatly restricting snake hunting and collecting.

When I got my sociology teaching job at Wofford College in Spartanburg, South Carolina, I met my friend Ab, academic polymath and expert on reptiles. With Ab as leader and with his permits to study and collect snakes, I and other faculty and students camped and hunted venomous and nonvenomous snakes and amphibians in the low country of South Carolina and in North Florida, the desert Big Bend area of West Texas, the desert grassland and mountains of southern Arizona, and the Sierra Madre Occidental Mountains and Copper Canyon of western Mexico.

Catching a venomous snake was the biggest adrenalin high I'd ever known. We kept only a few of the snakes for class use, and most of these were later released where they had been caught. Ab eventually stopped doing his long snake hunting trips in the United States and Mexico and retired, and I did much less snake hunting. But the habit of find-a-snake, catch-a-snake, if only to immediately release it, had become deeply engrained in me.

A few more river bends and I saw my campsite. My writer friends John and Thomas were already packing up our gear. I called for Thomas to help me pull my canoe out of the water and, as he did, explained that I was snake bit. Pete's camp was next to ours, and I could see he was also getting ready to leave. I told him I had been mistaken about the snake and that he shouldn't handle one like it because it was a cottonmouth. Pete said not to worry, that he never came within twenty feet of any snake. Several people from neighboring camps, overhearing our conversation, came to examine my swelling hand.

I explained to John and Thomas that I didn't want to go to the emergency room, at least not until I could see how bad the bite was going to be. I didn't want to inconvenience them without good reason, and I didn't want to risk being hospitalized so far from home. For a while I sat on a log and watched my friends carry gear to the truck, but, not wanting to spend the time watching my hand swell and worrying, I soon joined them in packing up. I remained calm. "You have the right personality for snake bite," Thomas said.

Over the centuries people have applied a range of remedies for envenomation: various plants mixed with other substances like alcohol or, in the case of Native Americans, a warm stone rubbed on the bite, or, for Europeans in the southeastern United States, a split chicken carcass tied over it. Both the stone and the chicken were wrongly thought to draw out venom. Because a fair percentage of bites from venomous snakes are dry, because venoms vary widely in their toxicity so that the effects of some bites can be mild, and because people mistake nonvenomous for venomous snakes, any treatment will appear to work at times. For that reason the use of ineffective or even harmful ways of dealing with snakebite have persisted and have been used even by doctors.

When I was a boy, my parents gave me a snakebite kit. I often carried it with me when I went hunting. I remember opening up the dull-red rubber capsule it came in. There was a clear rubber tube to serve as a tourniquet, two razor blades, and a small suction device. The page with drawings that came folded inside the capsule showed me how to tighten the tourniquet above the bite, cut several x's up from the wound, and then use the suction cup to pull out the venom. I occasionally practiced the treatment, without actually cutting myself, before going into the woods.

This remedy goes back at least 2,600 years and probably originated in India. It was the standard procedure for the treatment of snakebite in the United States until recently. I was lucky I never had the occasion to use it. We know now that suction removes little if any venom and cutting can sever nerves, increases infection, and quickens necrosis of surrounding tissue. If the tourniquet is too tight or left in place too long, it can kill tissue and even result in the amputation of an arm or leg.

Physicians have applied a variety of other useless and sometimes harmful treatments. One was cryotherapy, the application of ice or very cold water; another was electric shock to the bite area. Cryotherapy has been found, because of the resulting restriction of blood flow, to possibly do more damage from frostbite than the venom does. In one small study three-quarters of those treated with cryotherapy had to have a limb amputated. The cooling also retards the effect of antivenom, and, once cryotherapy is stopped, leads to the sudden release of the venom and its toxic byproducts into a person's system, sometimes producing shock. Electric therapy is no better. It can lead to a severely abnormal heart rhythm and even heart attack.

Today the suggested treatment for snakebite is for the victim to be kept warm and calm. Rings and other restrictive wear should be removed, and the bite area should be immobilized and kept below the level of the heart. The victim shouldn't be given coffee, other stimulants, or alcohol, because these speed up the absorption of venom. Then the victim should be taken to a hospital as quickly as possible. If there is going to be a delay of several hours in getting treatment or if the bite involves neurotoxins, a restrictive band should be applied five centimeters above the bite or below the next joint. It should be loose enough that it doesn't greatly reduce blood circulation.

Once the person is at the hospital, medical personnel will record information about the bite and about the treatment the person has received, plus an extensive medical history. They will also measure the circumference of the limb every fifteen to twenty minutes to gauge the rate of swelling. Before antivenom is given, the patient will be tested for an allergic reaction. Antivenom does the most good when given within four hours of the bite. It's less effective after twelve hours, but even after twenty-four hours it's found to ameliorate problems with blood coagulation produced by venom. In most cases bites from copperheads and pygmy rattlesnakes are not severe enough to warrant the use of antivenom.

If a person shows sensitivity to the antivenom serum or if the bite is severe, the victim will be placed in an intensive-care unit for twenty-four hours or more. Those showing an allergic reaction to the serum will be given antianaphylaxis medicines. The most common threatening side effect of treatment is serum sickness from a hypersensitive response to the antivenom. These reactions can occur anywhere from one to two weeks after the person has received antivenom and can produce fever, joint pain, rashes, and swelling of the lymph nodes. In rare, more life-threatening cases, serum sickness produces inflammation of nerves, inflammation of the pericardial sack around the heart, and encephalitis.

This was one of the reasons I didn't want my friends to take me to an emergency room. I was afraid the doctors would insist on giving me antivenom. In the past, up to 50 percent of people treated with antivenom had allergic reactions. In the case of a mild bite, serum sickness can produce more serious medical problems than the venom and can lead to a long and very expensive hospitalization.

It is also true that in the United States, because of good, available medical care, including the use of antivenom, only five to six people die from snake bite each year. These are mostly children, the elderly and infirm, and those who refuse medical treatment.

Once we were loaded, I got in back in the pickup's jump seat. John drove and Thomas sat in front of me. Coming to the Ogeechee, John had driven back roads through economically depressed small towns full of ramshackle abandoned buildings and empty store fronts. This time he took a more direct route to the interstate.

I became concerned with the continued swelling of my hand and now my arm and had John stop at a couple of convenience stores in Warrenton, Georgia, looking for a small bag of ice. The second store had some. I put the bag on my hand. Still uneasy, I asked Thomas to call my herpetologist friend Chuck, who teaches at my college. Chuck has been bitten several times by the copperheads he studies. If anyone would know what to do about a snake bite, it would be Chuck. After what seemed like a very long time, Thomas got him on John's cell phone. Chuck told me that icing the bite was a bad idea because it would keep the venom concentrated in my hand and promote more tissue damage. I immediately took the ice off. He asked me if there was any discoloration or blistering around the bite. When I said there wasn't, he told me to keep an eye out for it but that I was "probably going to be O.K."

The three of us traveled in awkward silence. Before John and Thomas had been anxiously questioning me about how I was feeling and what I wanted to do. Now that I had decided not to get treatment, there seemed to be nothing more to say. I was relieved when they began talking about familiar topics for writers: grants, writers who had gotten them, those who hadn't, those having success and finding jobs, those who weren't, and the general politics, woes, and frustrations of getting stuff published.

Because they carry a heavy load of folklore, symbolism, and myth, snakes are natural subjects for writers and poets. Essayists and novelists have occasionally used them for dramatic effect. For example, in his memoir *North toward Home,* the fine Southern writer Willie Morris describes a water-skier falling into a "nest" of cottonmouths and quickly dying from multiple bites. In Larry McMurtry's great Western novel *Lonesome Dove,* a rider tumbles off his horse into a nest of cottonmouths while crossing a swollen river and suffers the same painful death.

Poets have also explored the diverse meanings we give to serpents. In her poem "Snake," Emily Dickinson tells of her encounter with a harmless little garter snake, whose movement she describes as a "whiplash." In the poem she expresses kinship with all of earth's creatures. All, that is, except the snake. "But never met this fellow," she writes, "Attended or alone, / Without a tighter breathing, / And zero at the bone."[8]

The Southern poet James Dickey wins the prize for the most menacing portrayal and the greatest hatred of snakes in literature. In "Reincarnation" Dickey imagines a man reborn as a rattlesnake, hatching from an egg buried in the sand. The reincarnated and vengeful human-now-snake waits "not for food, but for the first man to come by the gentle river" while "minute by minute [his] head becomes more poisonous and poised."[9] In "Blowgun and Rattlesnake" Dickey describes killing a rattlesnake by sending a sharpened section of a coat hanger into its head. The snake's death is justified, Dickey writes in an essay, because snakes "hate you and the human race instinctively hates them" and nothing can change that.[10]

Gerald T. Thurmond

Edward Abbey's essay "The Serpents of Paradise" in his environmentalist classic *Desert Solitaire* presents a very different view of snakes. One cool morning in April, Abbey is drinking coffee while sitting on his trailer's doorstep in the Arches National Monument in the Moab Desert of southeastern Utah, where he is working as a seasonal park ranger. He looks down and sees a coiled faded midget rattlesnake warming itself in the sun a few inches from his bare feet. Abbey considers reaching for his pistol and shooting it, but the bullet might ricochet, the gun is out of reach, and, besides, he writes, "where would I set my coffee?" Then there are his sacred principles. "I'm a humanist," declares Abbey. "I'd rather kill a *man* than a snake."[11]

He finishes his coffee, carefully lifts his feet, takes the other door to get out of the trailer, and uses a spade to persuade the snake to leave. As he does, he warns it that next time, should pragmatism win out over principle, he'll chop off its head.

A week later the same snake, or its twin, is back, waiting to ambush one of the numerous mice that live inside Abbey's trailer. If the mice are attracting the small faded midget, he fears that they might also attract the much larger and far more dangerous western diamondback rattlesnake. On his park rounds, Abbey finds his solution. He catches a large gopher snake. Gopher snakes are known, he says, to kill and eat both mice and rattlesnakes. He keeps the snake inside his trailer, an amiable and useful companion. The mice and rattlesnakes disappear. Eventually so does the gopher snake.

That's not the end of the story. One hot afternoon in May, Abbey is drinking a beer on his steps when he sees what he thinks might be his gopher snake, returned with a companion. The two snakes, a "living caduceus," wind and unwind around each other, crawl in tandem, and rise up and fall together. Abbey describes their dance as a passionate ballet and wants to think of them as lovers. He gets on his belly for a closer look. The snakes sense him and turn and crawl directly toward his face, forked tongues flickering. Responding to a "fear too ancient and too powerful to overcome," Abbey scrambles backward. In unison the snakes veer off and move rapidly into the brush. Abbey doesn't see the gopher snakes again but feels "their presence watching over [him] like totemic deities, keeping the rattlesnakes far back in the brush," controlling the mice population, and "maintaining useful connections with the primeval."[12]

Reflecting on the apparent passion motivating the snakes' actions, Abbey rejects the "foolish, simple-minded rationalism" that "denies emotions to all animals but humans and their dogs" and concludes that "we are obliged, therefore, to spread the news, painful and bitter though it may be for some to hear, that all living things on earth are kindred."[13]

In a series of poems Margaret Atwood examines the diverse symbolic and mythic significance of snakes. She portrays them as sublime and horrible, alien and beautifully mysterious, objects of simple, salacious humor and central mythic figures. Atwood begins her poem "Psalm to a Snake" with "O snake, you are an argument/for poetry." Some of the lines of this poem are reminiscent of Dickinson's. She describes the snake's movement as "a thin line moving through/that which is not time, creating time" and "a shift in dry leaves / when there is no wind." Atwood also uses the word "whiplash," but in her poem it has a darker meaning, referring to the snake's strike "across the eye" of its prey that produces "the kill." She calls the snake "a voice from the dead, oblique," the "Prophet under a stone," and a "long word, cold blooded and perfect."[14]

Snakes also evoke horror. In "Bad Mouth," Atwood lists atrocities by different types of snake, starting with the venomous puff adder, "for whom killing is easy and careless / as war." Atwood goes on to describe the boa constrictor, "looping like thick tar out of the trees / to squeeze the voice out of anything edible," and the pit viper with its heat sensing ability, "honing in on the deep red shadow / nothing else knows it casts." The poet asks, "shall I concede these deaths?"[15]

Snakes are also alien beings, their scale-covered bodies "pure / shiver, pure Saturn."[16] Serpents can't scream, she writes, nor can they sing, and, contrary to Abbey, it's inconceivable that in their mating they feel passion, since for them it's merely "a romance between two lengths / of cyanide colored string." And snakes are also a mystery: "Those who can explain them can explain anything" because "the reason for them is the same / as the reason for the stars, and not human."[17]

In "Eating Snake" Atwood describes lunching on fried rattlesnake. "Forget the phallic symbolism" she writes: "two differences / snake tastes like chicken, / and whoever credited the prick with wisdom?" Her poem "After Heraclitus" advises us to leave out a bowl of milk for a snake and "watch it drink." In "Quattrocento" she inverts the Garden of Eden myth, with the snake, the central figure in the story, creating meaning for human life with its gift of death.[18]

In using snakes for dramatic effect or investigating their symbolic significance, these writers often repeat snake folklore. Cottonmouths don't congregate in nests in the water as Morris and McMurtry say. Rattlesnakes don't emerge from eggs; they are live born, and snakes don't hate people as Dickey suggests. It's only human hubris that would make us think we're that important to them. Contrary to Abbey, gopher snakes don't eat rattlesnakes, and what he observed was not a passionate mating dance but male combat. Atwood gets some things wrong as well. Some snakes, such as pine snakes, make very loud sounds, much like a hoarse scream, and no snakes drink milk. But a reader couldn't find a better exploration of the diverse symbolic significance of snakes than those provided by these authors.

Gerald T. Thurmond

Now my palm was dimpled with the swelling, I could barely bend my fingers, and the swelling was marching quickly up my arm. We drove along, listening to the radio. I held my arm up and examined it closely, anxiously looking for blisters. When I lowered my hand, it throbbed with pain.

Outside Columbia, South Carolina, John pulled into a gas station to get ice cream. I had fallen into the role of the bravely bearing up victim and thought I was playing it well, but this struck me as a little too casual a response to my emergency. Plus, once he had brought my ice cream to me, I had trouble eating it because I couldn't hold the cup in my snake-bit hand.

When we reached my house in Spartanburg, I helped John and Thomas unload my boat and gear, waved goodbye, and then went upstairs to my bedroom, sat in a recliner, propped up my arm on a pillow, and began watching a football game. After a few minutes I told my wife, Teresa, who was lying on the bed reading, that I had been bitten by a cottonmouth but not to worry, that it wasn't a bad bite and that I was going to be O.K. Chuck had said so.

She came over, examined my arm, and quickly said I needed to go to the E.R. I told her I didn't, made excuses and stalled, and continued to watch the game. After another thirty minutes she calmly said I could tell my friends that she had made me go, if that's what I was worried about.

By then it had been more than four hours since I had gotten the bite. I had expected the swelling to begin going down or at least stop spreading, but it continued. Now my entire right arm, absent the green color, looked like it belonged to the cartoon character The Hulk. I told Teresa I wished that my other arm looked like that. For all my pretended bravado, what was happening to my body was unnerving. Yielding to my wife's repeated argument that I was being an idiot, I finally agreed to go to the E.R.

We left our teenage son in charge of our eight-year-old daughter, and Teresa drove me downtown to the E.R. We walked through the sliding glass doors and into a room crowded with glum and anxious people seated on rows of uncomfortable plastic chairs, most of them staring at the floor. I expected to join them for hours of waiting, but after my wife told the nurse at the reception desk that I had been bitten by a venomous snake, she immediately called over another nurse, who led us past the crowd and down a long hall to one of several curtained-off areas with a bed in it and a small TV mounted high on a wall. Clearly the way to get quick attention in an E.R., Teresa said, is to say that you're snakebit.

An attractive, heavyset nurse in her mid-twenties gave me a hospital gown and fed my medical information into a computer. She later took a blood sample and inserted an I.V. into my arm. Another even younger nurse, a pretty woman with big brown eyes named Cherish, watched.

Following procedure, the first nurse made several horizontal marks up my arm and measured the distance between them to gauge the progress of the swelling. Later a tall, young, blond doctor came in to see me. He wanted to give me antivenom. At first I refused. While it was true that the old horse-serum antivenoms caused a high percentage of victims to have a hypersensitive reaction, he answered, the newer ones had only a 13 percent rate. He said he couldn't let me go home until the swelling had gone down and added that he would have to put me in the hospital if I didn't improve soon. Putting aside the last bit of my pride, I agreed to receive antivenom. I wouldn't actually get the serum until 4:30 in the afternoon, more than eight hours after the bite.

Experts classify snake bite into three categories of severity. The least severe envenomation involves effects around the bite but does not result in any systemic symptoms. A moderate bite has symptoms beyond the bite but no life-threatening effects or signs, such as muscle spasms, the experience of unusual tastes and sensations around the mouth, and nausea and vomiting. Severe envenomation is indicated by swelling over an entire limb or region, shortness of breath, rapid breathing, drastic loss of blood pressure, loss of consciousness, and, in the case of rattlesnake bites, vomiting of blood and blood in the victim's urine. A bite that appears minimal may cause much more serious symptoms later. It typically takes several hours for the full and most damaging effects to appear from North American snake bites.

Above the bite my skin was as tight as a drum head. The nurse's repeated measures of the marks showed that the swelling was continuing up my forearm and upper arm. When I asked if I could have something to eat, she said no. They might have to do surgery to keep the skin on my arm from splitting.

Eventually the blond doctor, who seemed determined to put me in the hospital, went off duty and was replaced by a short, thickly made young doctor with a northern accent. I liked him immediately. He seemed much more concerned with his football team, the Philadelphia Eagles, losing the game on the tiny TV above my bed, than with my snake bite. When it didn't appear that my skin was going to burst from swelling, my wife left to check on our children and returned bringing me a McDonald's Happy Meal with a plastic toy inside.

At eight at night, the football-loving doctor released me. The swelling hadn't gone down much, and it wouldn't for a long time, but it wasn't increasing. Once home, I propped my hand up on a pillow to keep it from hurting. The next morning I discovered that my right breast and my entire right side down to my waist were swollen as well. But I was lucky. I had received only a moderate bite.

I took Monday off from teaching but came into work the next day to a great deal of kidding from my biologist friends. Chuck made up a printed, laminated card for me that reads:

Lifetime Member
[crest]

Loyal Brotherhood
Of Dumbass
Order of the Snake

Gerald Thurmond
Member since September 11, 2010
Heyual Watchdis
President

Pete, the River Keeper, sent a picture of me holding the cottonmouth. I have it framed, with Chuck's card inserted in the corner, sitting on my office desk.

Most of the swelling in my arm was gone in six days. And I wasn't one of the unlucky 13 percent who have reactions to antivenom. But I carried a reminder of my stupid act. The bitten finger remained swollen much longer than a week (and, after more than four years, I still can't bend it completely). When the bill came from the hospital, it was for $44,000. My insurance reduced it by 90 percent, but it would take me years to pay off the remainder. Although I had become far more cautious, these things didn't stop me from keeping, caring for, occasionally catching, and loving venomous snakes.

The question remains, Why, after my experience, did my fundamental feelings about venomous snakes not change? At the end of his extraordinary book *Snakes: The Evolution of Mystery in Nature*, Harry W. Greene offers an explanation. The happy pursuit of snakes in the field with good friends, Greene writes, "blurs the distinction between science and art, between what we know and what we feel." For him, "venomous serpents have been icons of danger, of life and death—as if in that crystalline moment when the fangs pierce another creature, I might finally understand my own fears and losses."[19]

To walk in the habitat of dangerous pit vipers is both exciting and humbling, Greene says. It teaches us wonder and respect for nature because in "venomous snakes we contemplate violence and mortality without implications of real evil, devoid of anthropocentric traps laid by fur, feathers and facial expressions" and that "with pit-vipers and their unusual infrared vision, we arrive at the very cusp of mystery, the illusive but tantalizing limits on empathy."[20]

Greene is right. I have never been happier than when I was with good friends like Ab, wandering through some desert grassland, clambering down a rocky mountainside in Arizona, or driving slowly along a Southern country road in the low country after a heavy rain, looking for snakes. The pursuit of them, as Greene argues, destroys the artificial divide between the heart and the mind. Ask my herpetologist friends Ab and Chuck about a particular snake, and they will reply with a densely factual, informative, important, but nevertheless dry list of particulars. Ask them to talk about their fieldwork with snakes, and they will be transformed into storytellers and poets, revealing the personal significance these animals have for them.

Snakes remain entangled in myth and folklore. Hunting and handling snakes teaches us that we are only a very small part of a vast, interrelated universe and that our world and its beautiful creatures do not exist for our pleasure, safety, use, or convenience. Or, as Margaret Atwood put it, "the reason for [snakes] is the same / as the reason for the stars, and not human."[21]

Gerald T. Thurmond

Contemporary Medieval Boar Hunting

"And there is neither lion nor leopard that slayeth a man at one stroke as a boar doth, for they mostly kill with the raising of their claws and through biting, but the wild boar slayeth a man with one stroke as with a knife, and therefore he can slay any other beast sooner than they can slay him. It is a proud beast and fierce and perilous, for many times have men seen much harm that he hath done. For some men have seen him slit a man from knee up to the breast and slay him all stark dead at one stroke, so that he never spake thereafter."

Edward of Norwich, *The Master of Game*

| The Charge |

Archers, spearmen, and a bay dog were the order of the day. Unlike catch dogs, which are trained to chase, catch, and hold quarry, bay dogs are trained to bring a boar to bay—to force him to turn and fight. When archers are boar hunting, bay dogs are preferable as they slow the progress of the boar without getting too close to the target or blocking the line of fire as much, making possible devastating bowshots from close range.

Two boars had emerged from the swampy ground ahead of us, flushed by our single bay dog. Our two archers took the center, advancing cautiously, flanked by two spearmen. The spearmen were armed not with throwing spears but with stout thrusting spears with large blades and heavy iron crossbars. Should either boar charge, the spearmen were to hold firm, letting the archers dodge behind them for safety—a tactic as old as bows and spears. But the two hogs were bent on escape. Sprinting to our left, the pair couldn't quite outrun our hound. The nearer of the two turned to face its pursuer, the other boar continuing to race through the long grass to freedom.

When bayed by a single dog, a boar will often turn to face his pursuer only until he has caught his breath, then bolt again to try to escape. The chase resumes. While wild boar have been estimated to reach 30 miles per hour over short distances, they tire quickly at top speed. When the dog catches up, the boar again turns to fight or (more likely) face off and catch his breath again. If the hunters aren't fast enough to catch up and engage the boar, the cycle repeats itself until the boar reaches the safety of thick cover.

Despite the harrying of our bay dog, the remaining boar was outpacing our archers. I realized that we might well lose that boar too unless something blocked its choppy progress. While the bay dog intermittently slowed the boar's flight, I left my position as right flank spearman to sprint a wide arc to the left fore. Well out in front of the archers, I placed myself between the boar and the shelter it sought, hoping to keep it at bay until the archers caught up and engaged it from the flank.

Quartering away from the bay dog, the boar now saw me blocking its path of escape to the palmetto scrub and hammock of trees toward which it had been angling. Though it could easily have dashed around me on either side, the boar chose to charge. I lowered my barred spear, the inch-and-a-half ash shaft tucked under my right arm as tightly as ever I had held a jousting lance, my left hand well forward of my right to keep the aim true. Feet in line to prevent the boar from running between my legs and striking upward with its tusks (as they are wont to do), I crouched to lower my center of gravity and braced for impact. Unswerving in its charge, the boar struck the blade of the spear almost head on. A tremendous jolt was followed instantly by a brilliant white light, flashes of blue sky, green grass, then silence . . .

| Enlightenment |

Enlightenment is seldom cited as a reason for hunting. In fact, the conversion of the late seventh-century Merovingian nobleman and avid hunter Hubertus to a life of piety, religious service, and, ultimately, sainthood argues that "the stream runs in the other direction." As legend has it, Hubertus was pursuing a magnificent stag with his hounds on Good Friday when the stag turned to face him. Between the stag's antlers, Hubertus beheld a crucifix; then he heard a voice that advised him to repent and lead a holy life or he would soon go down to Hell. Although he forsook his passionate pursuit of hunting for a life of pious contemplation, in the end St. Hubert became the patron of hunters, not philosophers.

It was, however, in search of a rather mundane sort of enlightenment that I began my investigation of medieval *par force* hunting: the pursuit of game with horses, dogs, and primitive weapons quite literally known as "the Chase." For several years, I had been gleaning insights into various aspects of other forms of medieval hunting, first as a licensed falconer, then as an archer hunting with replica medieval longbows and crossbows. *Par force* hunting would prove far more intense in many ways.

My early interest had been further piqued by the discovery of kindred spirits. In 2006, an international brotherhood of the medieval hunt had been established in the United States, taking the name "St. Hubert's Rangers." Within the constraints of modern regulations, its members recreated various aspects of medieval hunting, including *par force* hunting. I was drawn to study "the Chase" not simply because it was regarded as the form of hunting most appropriate for noblemen but because numerous medieval sources unequivocally endorsed this method of hunting over the tournament as the best training for war. I found these assertions thoroughly intriguing. Having served in the U.S. Army for eleven years, I could appreciate the great physical and logistical demands of the field environment. But having practiced and taught swordplay for decades, I realized that there must be something profoundly important beyond mere skill with weapons to be learned from "the Chase."

| The Chase |

"chase v. run after. Before 1338 chasen to hunt . . . borrowed from Old French chace, chas, from chacier v. The meaning of pursuit, as of an enemy developed in Middle English about 1330."

Barnhart Concise Dictionary of Etymology:
The Origins of American English Words

In antiquity, hunting was regarded primarily as the armed pursuit of wild game with the assistance of dogs. Xenophon's fourth-century B.C. *Cynegeticus* deals more with dogs than with any other aspect of hunting: game, nets, weapons, tactics, and so on. Hunting dogs appear prominently in the art, literature, and mythology of the ancient world and were quite literally elevated to the heavens as the constellations Canis Major and Canis Minor, the hunting dogs of the giant huntsman Orion. Hunting boar with dogs, bows, and spears was regarded as a pastime worthy of demigods and heroes—Heracles, Theseus, Jason, Odysseus, Adonis—and dogs and hunters in these accounts were frequently injured and sometimes killed.

Likewise, during the Middle Ages, dogs for locating, flushing, and tracking game were seen as integral to hunting—not only *par force* hunting but also falconry and bow hunting. In the fourteenth century, Gaston Phoebus, Count of Foix, penned *Le Livre de la Chasse* (The Book of the Hunt), now widely regarded as the definitive medieval hunting text. The very word from the title that is translated as "Hunt" (Chasse) means "pursuit." Of its 120 chapters, a full tenth are devoted to the care and maintenance of dogs. The bulk of the text deals with hunting red deer (*Cervus elaphus*) and wild boar (*Sus scrofa*) with dogs. Methods of taking game without dogs are mentioned but usually only in passing and often with unveiled disdain.

Recreating Western European medieval-style "le Chasse" hunting in modern North America is problematic. The two most readily available analogous quarry are whitetail deer (*Odocoileus virginianus*) and feral swine (*Sus scrofa*). Hunting whitetail deer with dogs in the United States has effectively been legislated to death: outlawed in all but a few Southern states and increasingly de facto prohibited by requirements for special permits and limitations on vast land holdings (250-plus contiguous acre private property requirement) beyond the means of 99 percent of the population. Feral swine, on the other hand, provide fertile ground for research.

Wild Boar/Feral Swine

Since the arrival of Spanish explorers and settlers in the early 1500s, domestic swine have been both accidentally and intentionally released in the southern continental United States. Over the course of the past five hundred years, feral swine have become highly successful, expanding their range and numbers to current estimates of at least thirty-six of the fifty states and a total nationwide population in excess of 6 million. Within the past fifty years, these bloodlines have been augmented in some regions by the release (both accidental and deliberate) of physically larger genetic strains of captive bred Eurasian "aka Russian" wild boar stock.

Because they are nonnative, invasive, and highly destructive of indigenous flora and fauna, feral hogs are exempt from many hunting regulations. In some states, they may be hunted throughout the year, often with a much broader range of weapons and methods than are authorized for native game species, making them a preferred quarry for medieval hunting enthusiasts.

Medieval Boar Hunting

The medieval view of the wild boar was one of profound respect, if not awe, as is apparent from the quotation from the fifteenth-century hunting manual at the beginning of this essay. This admiration was not misplaced. Wild boar are formidable prey, disregarded at one's peril.

In *Le Livre de la Chasse*, Phoebus described a wide array of methods for hunting wild boar. Like writers today, the author wasn't above a bit of hunting snobbery, dismissing ignoble methods of boar hunting that employed pitfalls, enclosures, snares, nets, and the like.

Phoebus went into greater (and more approving) detail when he described how to hunt boar with crossbows from raised mounds or platforms, how to ambush boar with a combination of dogs and crossbows, and how to confront boar with dogs, spears, and swords. Wisely, he advised against the fashionably daring practice of taking boar with one's sword while on foot—the method employed by the lord Bertilak de Hautdesert in the medieval classic *Sir Gawain and the Green Knight*. Rather, Phoebus recommended: "If one dares attack a boar in his den one should do so with a 'barred' spear, i.e. one that is equipped with a crossbar below the head, or 'winged,' to prevent the weapon from entering too deep, thus enabling the hunter to keep out of range of the boar's deadly tusks. For the same reason one should grip the shaft in the middle and not near the head. If the boar is attacking one must not couch the spear but wield it with both fists. But if the hunter has struck, one should couch the spear and with all one's might press against the boar. If the beast is stronger than the hunter, the latter should change from one side to the other but not for a moment relax his hold, and keep pushing until God or men come to his aid." It is primarily according to Phoebus's work that my colleagues and I equip ourselves, train for and conduct our hunts, having taken more than thirty feral swine to date using medieval methods. With the exception of the use of horses mentioned later (we always hunt on foot), the passage from the fourteenth-century Arthurian romance *Sir Gawain and the Green Knight* therefore closely describes our hunting experiences:

> While the lord was racing over the fields,
> After the ferocious boar that rushed up
> Hillsides and broke the backs of his best
> Hounds, holed in till arrows drove him
> On, out of shelter, to run
> In the open—arrows falling like flies
> On his hide. He held them off, leaping
> Wild, until at last running
> Was over and, weary, he worked his way
> To a rocky hole over a river,
> The hill was behind him; his hooves pawed
> At the ground, foam grimaced on his snout;
> And he sharpened his tusks, waiting. Tired
> And still afraid, the hunters stood safely
> To the side; they wanted to annoy him, but no one
> Came near:
> So many had been gored
> By those tusks that fear

Of being torn
Held them: he seemed wild, he seemed weird.

And then the lord rode up, urging
His horse, and saw him holed in and his hunters
Watching. He jumped lightly down, drew
His bright-polished sword and began to approach him,
Hurrying across the ford to his hole.
And the boar saw him, saw his bright sword,
And his hackles rose, and he snorted so loud
That the hunters were afraid for their lord's life.
Then the beast rushed out at him, straight and quick,
And man and boar blended in the steaming
White water; but the boar had the worst, for the lord
Had measured his charge, and aimed his sword
Into his throat, and planted it deep,
Down to the hilt, so the heart was cut,
And snarling as he fell the boar surrendered
And dropped.

As presented in the passage, once scented by the hounds, the feral boars we hunt have usually begun by running in search of shelter. When hard pressed, they head for water or turn to fight. When fighting, they seek trees, embankments, or other obstacles to place behind themselves to avoid being flanked. Other behaviors described in the passage (pawing, foaming, clashing tusks, snorting) are all quite common. The sudden, forceful charge is classic. The full force of such a charge received on a sturdy boar spear even while employing textbook technique can easily throw a two-hundred-pound man six feet backward through the air—which is precisely what happened to me.

| The Charge—Continued |

A tremendous jolt was followed instantly by a brilliant white light, flashes of blue sky, green grass, then silence.

In a moment, I heard my fellow hunters rushing to my side. It was clear that my loss of consciousness had been only fleeting. My whole body was a-tingle, almost palpably vibrating. My hearing was muffled, the sunlight oppressive. Time passed almost comically slowly.

The shaft of the spear was still tightly clasped in my hands. Beside me lay the mortally wounded boar, transfixed by the spear's blade. The large crossbar had done its job admirably, preventing the boar from riding up the shaft of the spear after it impaled itself on the blade. When the boar hit the crossbar, the kinetic energy of the impact from the charge had been transferred up the shaft of the spear. My grip had held, and I had been sent flying backward like a rag doll, landing a little more than six feet away, unharmed. A fellow spearman arrived in moments and deftly administered the coup de grace with his dagger. . . .

| Historical Context |

More than a decade before my first boar hunt, I had begun a wide-ranging review of primary and secondary sources, including medieval hunting texts, literature, forest law, artwork, and commentaries. While an exhaustive knowledge of historical context was no guarantee of understanding, ignorance of it was an almost certain guarantee of misunderstanding.

Hunting was an integral part of medieval culture. Unlike in our modern era, hunting references in medieval culture were ubiquitous and, more often than not, positive. Artwork was disproportionately made for and paid for by members of the upper class, for many of whom hunting was nothing short of an obsession. Hunting images (both positive and negative) abound in tapestries, paintings, frescoes, stained glass, and the marginalia of religious texts such as Bibles, psalters and books of hours. Literature, poems, sermons, and legal documents frequently contain hunting references, though many of these escape the casual reader. Forest law and weapon and hunting rights were recurrent points of social conflict. Words as simple as "forest," "park," and "chase" are woefully misunderstood if not taken in their medieval hunting context.

To see how historical context is essential to understanding word meaning, one need look no further than the modern use of the term "fair chase." Medieval usage of the term was unequivocally associated with the pursuit of game with dogs. The French *chasse,* the German *jagen,* the Spanish *caza,* and the Portuguese *caçar* all meant both "to hunt" and "to pursue or chase." In the fifteenth-century tract *The Debate between the Heralds of France and England,* a French herald challenges the English practice of bow hunting in deer parks and provides a clear and concise late-medieval definition of "fair chase": "To what you say, that you have fair chases, and such a wonderful number of parks, all of them full of venison, I answer that to catch an animal in a park is no chase. I say that it is a chase when a wild animal, in a state of nature, is at full liberty to run through woods and forests, and a man by his diligence, with the help of dogs and hounds, forcibly overcomes him. Then are to be seen the excellence of the dogs, the courage of the hounds, and the perseverance of the man. This, I say, is a real chase, and I call Count Phoebus to witness."

To eliminate any possible ambiguity, the French herald goes on to declare bow hunting deer in parks "a certain sort of pastime, but it is no chase."

Modern English definitions of "fair chase" make no mention of the use of dogs. As defined by the Boone and Crockett Club, "FAIR CHASE is the ethical, sportsmanlike, and lawful pursuit and taking of any free-ranging wild, native North American big game animal in a manner that does not give the hunter an improper advantage over such animals."

Some modern hunters have gone so far as to argue that, because pursuit of game with dogs provides what they deem to be an improper advantage, somehow hunting with dogs violates the principles of "fair chase." This is a fundamental misunderstanding of the origin, history, and nature of the term "fair chase" with a subsequent complete reversal of the original meaning.

While my studies brought a degree of understanding, it was at best imperfect. A bookish grasp of the lexicon, theory, and physical mechanics of medieval hunting may facilitate comprehension of the actions described in medieval literature, but to a mere reader the intense visceral reality of medieval boar hunting remains as elusive as a description of skydiving to a person who has never leapt from a plane. Actually physically hunting in the fashion described is essential to gaining a deeper, more practical understanding and thus a common frame of reference. It was my urge to experience this common frame of reference that ultimately prompted me to begin hunting wild boar using medieval weapons and tactics.

Because they shared a common frame of reference, medieval authors could directly communicate the visceral, psychological components (valor, prowess) of medieval hunting to their upper-class medieval audiences. Many readers had witnessed or participated in *par force* hunting. In the excerpt from *Sir Gawain and the Green Knight*, the contrast in demeanor between the reluctant huntsmen staying at a safe distance and the lord boldly dismounting to engage the boar on foot with a sword affirms the chivalric ideal: that valor and prowess were the purview of the nobility, while simultaneously reinforcing the notion that these qualities were present to a lesser extent, if at all, in the lower social classes.

In medieval culture, seeking out dangerous situations in order to demonstrate one's skill and self-control was regarded as a virtue. While this perspective persists in some sectors of today's society (the military, police, firefighters), it is largely absent from the contemporary Western worldview. Modern readers, hunters and nonhunters alike, who do not regard the concepts of valor and prowess as virtues tend to see the actions of the lord as simply reckless and foolhardy. The original psychological element of the narrative is lost on them. Conversely, for readers who embrace the importance of valor and prowess, the lord's actions are not only commendable but expected from someone of his station. For those willing to risk serious injury to emulate the lord's actions by engaging in medieval-style boar hunting, unique insights emerge.

The efforts of our small group of medieval-hunting enthusiasts are well rewarded. Physical insights garnered during our medieval-style boar hunts include things as mundane as how to walk up a steep slope on wet grass in medieval shoes, how to run in a group over broken terrain while carrying unsheathed swords, how to cross a stream while holding naked spears at the ready, and other similar insights.

Cognitive insights obtained while participating in such hunts are more complex: the nature and behavior of quarry, communication and cooperation in the field, how to maneuver together as a group over complex terrain, how to work as a unit in a rapidly developing situation with multiple threats emerging independently, tracking, engaging, and defeating the "enemy." It quickly becomes evident why this form of hunting was so highly regarded as training for war during the Middle Ages, as it exercises so many of the same skills.

Whether psychological insights obtained while pursuing medieval-style boar hunting go beyond the level of small-'e' enlightenment is a matter for debate. What is indisputable is that profound psychological insights do occur. Many of these psychological insights are inseparable from the transformation that takes place during and after the intense physical encounter of medieval-style boar hunting. Employing a sharp weapon to lethal effect at close range with human-size quarry that is actively trying to harm you irreversibly changes you as a human being. Among other things, it alters how you are perceived, most obviously by others. Since I returned from my first successful medieval-style boar hunt, spear-hunting wild boar has become the defining characteristic by which my coworkers know me.

This is not an isolated or even uncommon experience. Regardless of the level of his education, personal accomplishments, and so on, the medieval-style boar hunter is often subsequently defined by colleagues primarily or even solely by the uniqueness and intensity of that hunting experience. As an emergency-medicine physician, I constantly meet new people: patients, family members, staff from other departments, and others. When new acquaintances in the workplace begin making conversation, more frequently than any other subject I am asked about hunting boar with dogs, spears, and swords. How do all these people know? Second only to my name, it is how my coworkers describe me to others.

Hunting in medieval fashion also alters how you perceive others. Once you have participated in a medieval-style boar hunt, it is common to begin viewing others as falling into one of two groups: those who will hunt boar in medieval fashion and those who will not. Over the years, I have invited more than twenty coworkers (including military veterans and peace officers) who regard themselves as hunters to join me on a number of medieval-style boar hunts. Between declined offers and last-minute cancellations, it became clear that the vast majority of modern gun hunters I knew and worked with did not possess the wherewithal to hunt boar in medieval fashion. None of them lacked the physical ability. All of them lacked the will.

Similarly, on three occasions I have been approached by journalists eager to write about spear-hunting wild boar. Because of the intensely visceral nature of this style of hunting, I explained that I would grant an interview only after the journalist had participated in a hunt with me. Two immediately declined, and the third canceled shortly before the planned hunt when I asked about his medical insurance coverage.

For those who make it as far as the field, the intensity of medieval-style boar hunting quickly reveals a great deal about each individual's character. I have seen the simple act of witnessing a medieval-style boar hunt turn a would-be boar hunter into a cringing mass incapable of action. Conversely, a cameraman who had never hunted before in his life was so inspired by witnessing the charge described earlier that later that morning he took up a spear and joined the hunt.

Medieval-style boar hunting also alters how you perceive yourself by providing an opportunity to display those qualities so valued by medieval authors: valor (personal bravery) and prowess (technical skill in the use of arms). By engaging in a physically dangerous activity in the company of one's peers, the medieval-style boar hunter is able to demonstrate to himself that he has the both the psychological fortitude and the physical ability to acquit himself favorably in a lethal encounter with primitive weapons at extremely close quarters.

Often perceived by others as self-confidence, it is this self-knowledge that results in an increased ability to function effectively in comparably stressful situations. Countless times, nurses with whom I work have told me that they feel safer in the emergency room with me than with my fellow physicians because of my willingness to confront, grapple with, and restrain violent, intoxicated patients who threaten their safety. My ability to remain calm in the presence of constant verbal abuse and imminent threat of bodily harm while directing coworkers in the application of measured force is due in no small part to similarly intense confrontations while boar hunting. For those with less stressful occupations, the benefits may be less immediately evident, but they are no less real. The self-knowledge that permits one hunter to calmly face workplace violence enables others to pursue excellence in their respective disciplines: academia, athletics, business, and other pursuits.

Certainly, I've gained a much deeper understanding of medieval *par force* hunting and a more profound respect for my quarry by participating in actual hunts. I've witnessed the transformative effect of the experience on every hunter who accompanied me to the field. And in the end, I glimpse a source of wisdom more than half a millennium old in a new light.

While the twenty-first-century combat psychology term "stress inoculation," described by Grossman and Christensen in *On Combat: The Psychology and Physiology of Deadly Conflict in War and Peace,* was unknown then, the concept was clear in the fourteenth century. Engaging in *par force* hunting, an activity that closely simulated the physical, cognitive, and psychological conditions of the medieval battlefield, was the best preparation for medieval warfare. Centuries later it possibly remains the best tool for understanding that preparation, as King John I of Portugal makes clear in his *Livro da Montaria:* "For hunting is a training for all types of fighting met with in war; against a foe crossing in front, in a head-on encounter or in a pursuit; in an awkward situation or a sounder one. For every kind of military encounter, hunting is a better training than jousting. If the tourney teaches a man how to strike with a sword on a helmet, how much better he will learn by striking down a boar when his only chance of saving himself is by a good thrust with the spear."

| Works Consulted |

Almond, Richard. *Medieval Hunting.* Gloucestershire: Sutton Publishing Ltd., 2003.

Anonymous. *Sir Gawain and the Green Knight,* trans. Burton Raffel. New York: Signet Classics, 2009.

Baillie-Grohman, William A. *Sport in Art: An Iconography of Sport Illustrating the Field Sports of Europe and America from the 15th to the End of the 18th Century.* Honolulu: University Press of the Pacific, 2004.

Edward of Norwich. *The Master of Game by Edward of Norwich, Second Duke of York: The Oldest English Book on Hunting,* first paperback ed., ed. William A. Baillie-Grohman and F. N. Baillie-Grohman. Philadelphia: University of Pennsylvania Press, 2005.

Robert K. Barnhart. *The Barnhart Concise Dictionary of Etymology: The Origins of American English Words.* New York: HarperCollins, 1988.

Boone and Crockett Club. "Fair Chase Statement," 2015, http://www.boone-crockett.org/huntingEthics/ethics_fairchase.asp?area=huntingEthics (accessed January 15, 2016).

Cummins, John. *The Hound and the Hawk: The Art of Medieval Hunting.* London: Phoenix Press, 2001.

d'Orleans, Charles, and Henry Pyne. *England and France in the Fifteenth Century,* trans. Henry Pyne. London: Longmans, Green, 1870.

Dalby, David. *Lexicon of the Mediaeval German Hunt.* Berlin: Walter de Gruyter, 1965.

Duarte, Dom, king of Portugal. *The Art of Riding on Every Saddle: A Translation into English of King Dom Duarte's 1434 Treatise,* trans. António Franco Preto and Luis Franco Preto. Lexington, Ky.: Chivalry Bookshelf, 2006.

Dryden, Alice Slivr, ed., *The Art of Hunting or Three Hunting MSS.* Northampton: Old Swan Works, 1908.

Florida Fish and Wildlife Conservation Commission. "Wild Hog: *Sus Scrofa*," http://myfwc.com/wildlifehabitats/profiles/mammals/land/wild-hog/. (accessed January 15, 2016).

"Getting Medieval: Serious Hunting with Gear from the Middle Ages," *Field and Stream Online,* http://www.fieldandstream.com/photos/gallery/gear/hunting-gear/2011/08/getting-medieval-serious-hunting-gear-middle-ages. accessed January 15, 2016.

Gaston III/X, count of Foix-Béarn. *Manuscripts in Miniature No. 3: The Hunting Book of Gaston Phébus.* London: Harvey Miller, 1998.

Grossman, Dave. *On Combat: The Psychology and Physiology of Deadly Conflict in War and in Peace.* Second ed.. Millstadt, Ill.: PPCT Research Publications, 2007.

Haslewood, Joseph, ed. *The Book of St. Albans by Dame Juliana Berners.* New York: Arno Press, 1966.

"St. Hubert." *Catholic Online,* Catholic Encyclopedia, http://www.catholic.org/encyclopedia/view.php?id=5931 (accessed January 15, 2016).

Lebaud, Philippe, ed. *Le Livre de la Chasse: Texte intégral traduit en français modern par Robert et André Bossuat.* Paris: Philippe Lebaud, 1986.

Marvin, William Perry. *Hunting Law and Ritual in Medieval English Literature.* Cambridge: D. S. Brewer, 2006.

Mississippi State University. "Mississippi State University Wild Pig Info," http://wildpig info.msstate.edu (accessed January 15, 2016).

Niederwolfgruber, Franz. *Kaiser Maximilians I: Jagd- und Fischereibüch*er. Innsbruck: Pinguin-Verlag, 1979.

Phillips, A. A., and M. M. Willcock. *Xenophon and Arrian on Hunting.* Warminster, England: Aris and Phillips, 1999.

Smith, Kathryn A.*The Taymouth Hours.* London: British Library, 2012.

Treitzsaurwein, Marx. *Der Weiß Kunig: Eine Erzehlung von den Thaten.* Leipzig: Seemann Henschel GmbH, 2006.

Wilson, David M. *The Bayeux Tapestry: The Complete Tapestry in Colo*r. London: Thames and Hudson, 1985.

Wood, Casey A., and F. Marjorie Fyfe. *The Art of Falconry by Frederick II of Hohenstaufen.* Stanford: Stanford University Press, 1943.

Woolley, Linda. *Medieval Life and Leisure in the Devonshire Hunting Tapestries.* London: Victoria and Albert Museum, 2002.

Richard Swinney

An Ode to Machines

On Coming Late to Hunting

The small liberal arts college where I teach abounds with hardwoods, towering oaks especially. The campus teems with dopey, trashcan-diving squirrels. It is also home to smart hawks that, despite the constant mobbing by crows, can't resist the easy pickings. If you look up as you make your way across campus, you'll see from time to time a red-tailed hawk picking apart a recent catch. The squirrels' ease with people is so different from their woodland cousins', whom I've spent the break hunting. It's discouraging to return to campus the first January morning of the spring semester and see so many scurrying across the quad, chasing one another.

To hunt and to work in the academy makes for sometimes uncomfortable exchanges with students and colleagues. "What did you do over break?" "I went hunting for a few days." "You *hunt?*" Indicating that, specifically, I hunt squirrels is somehow worse: folks expect hunters to go after deer, and to them that's bad enough. But a squirrel? The responses seem to indicate: "What's the point? Do you *eat* them?" As though the answer to the latter must be *No,* and if that's the case, then one must shoot squirrels because one must love to kill. And *fuck* that.

The college where I teach reaches to its Quaker roots to add legitimacy to its platitudes of independent thinking, social justice, and stewardship of the earth in promotional materials. The principles hang on banners around the quad. While many students live and breathe the spirit of those principles— spending breaks in the Chihuahuan Desert leaving caches of water and providing medical care for those making the crossing from Mexico to the United States—when it gets down to it there is little evidence of the principles' influence on the institution. Just ask the housekeeping staff about social justice on campus.

The hunting aside, my owning and using firearms are alien to most of my colleagues. Down the hall from my office, a sign that sums up the sentiment hangs at the Office of Public Safety. It reads: "In accordance with Quaker tradition, firearms are not permitted on campus." The prohibition of firearms on campus doesn't concern me in the least: it makes all kinds of sense. In this regard, I am, perhaps, an aberration among gun owners in this state: I don't think it's an inherent right that I be able to own a firearm, much less to carry one wherever I go. But to pin the prohibition on Quaker tradition speaks to a deeper prejudice and misunderstanding of history. The campus library houses the Friends Historical Collection, and hanging on the wall in the reading room is a Jamestown rifle. A gorgeous piece of craftsmanship, it is a slender muzzle-loader lightly ornamented with simple brass diamonds. The Jamestown rifle was a utilitarian tool used by those in this area, an artifact from a time when leftward thinking and firearms were not at odds with each other.

The night is unending and cold. And windy. I wake up shivering many times. Bad shoulders make it difficult to close my bivy sack, though I doubt I'd sleep any better with it zipped all the way. The campsite, on a small promontory a mile walk from the car, is littered with limbs, and the periodic crack and thump of more falling nearby is worrisome. In this moment, I can't say why I do this. I'd like to walk out of the woods and go home, where it is warm and my children are asleep.

One of the times I wake up, I determine that I can't bear to chase sleep anymore. The clouds have gone, and the moon, just beginning to wane—big and crisp—throws light across the forest floor. The oaks haven't let go of their leaves, which shake dryly in the breeze. Other rustlings are probably leaves twisting over the ground in little vortices, though it could be something else: deer move frequently up the draw below the campsite, as it is far from the trail that so many hunters stick close to. With the moon, they shift to nighttime feeding. Could be raccoons. Or mice.

Or it's just the breeze.

Regardless, I'm thinking of game, and two hours before shooting light I struggle out of my sleeping bag, get my shoes on, and light a small alcohol stove my hunting buddy showed me how to make from cat food cans, J. B. Weld, and a bit of fiberglass insulation. I boil water and make instant coffee to sip in the dark in an attempt to get warm. It is hopelessly cold. The coffee does not take the edge off, and I shiver.

I stow my cooking gear by my hiking pack, and then, with a smaller hunting pack over my shoulder, I pick my way through the dark toward an oak I've hunted from before. I know this small corner of the Uwharrie Mountain Range well; I know dozens of trees in these woods that must be good for hunting.

Trees from which I have shot squirrels and other trees that are situated perfectly—good shooting lanes, excellent mast with squirrel cuttings, among trees that surely hold active nests—from which I *ought* to be able to shoot a squirrel.

The Uwharries are an old range. Hardly mountains now—the highest peak is barely more than a thousand feet—they were once majestic. This oak sits near the top of a rounded-over ridge and offers 270 degrees of clear shooting lanes out to a hundred yards—farther than I'm willing to shoot, but perfect for spotting movement and setting up for a shot as the squirrels move closer. Several ghostly hardwoods with their tops missing and hollows drilled into them stand before me, promising (almost certainly falsely, I know) the emergence of sleepy, hungry squirrels after sunrise. Moreover, there are acorns all over the place, and on some logs, I observed yesterday, reasonably fresh cuttings. The logs on the ground and those leaning against other trees are squirrel highways. It is a good place to hunt.

With the side of my foot I clear the leaves slowly in a circle around the base of the tree, wide enough to stretch my legs. I can move around the tree silently. I sit with my back against the trunk and open my backpack to retrieve hand warmers, activate and slip them into my gloves, then deposit them on the ground beside me. I pull ten Remington Yellow Jackets from a box, one by one, and with numb fingers nudge each little .22 cartridge into the rotary magazine. Dropping one, I find it on top of the compost without much trouble in the moonlight, load it, and gently push the magazine into the receiver with a click. Shooting light is at 7:00, and it is 6:00. I settle in.

My father didn't hunt. Around the time he was discharged from the Navy in 1965, he bought a Winchester Model 94 in .30–30—the classic, ubiquitous lever-action rifle from Western pictures—from the Navy Exchange in Pearl Harbor. He left it with my mother's brother, Warren, on the farm long before I was born. I don't imagine he used it much. I don't believe he ever hunted.

On the farm, where my brother and I spent long summers, Uncle Warren taught us how to use a Marlin Model 60 in his back yard, shooting at a cardboard target across the pond. He showed us how to load it and how to handle it safely, how to aim and to breathe. Shooting that little rifle was exciting and special, but it wasn't unique. Those were summers full of dangerous things Uncle Warren and Grandfather taught us how to do—things that made us feel mature and trusted. A rattling sickle-bar mower, for instance, is a menacing thing: aggressive teeth and clacking knives. Working with anxious livestock in the head gate. Riding high on the hay wagon behind the bailer, stacking bales thirteen tiers high. So much of the work was inherently risky, and we felt brave and capable for doing it. Shooting that Marlin was part and parcel of the experience.

Beyond teaching us to be respectful of dangerous things, my uncle and grandfather taught us about machines. When I hold a rifle and slowly cycle the action, I'm admiring a machine. It's little different from admiring the way an old bailer works. Spinning the flywheel slowly, the teeth of the pickup turn, the augur rolls, the feeder forks lift-reach-drop-pull, the plunger drives back and forth. More interesting, even, is the knotter, the way it, in a fluid moment, twists and bends the twine and then drives the tails through the eyes with what they call a needle, though so much larger and forceful than the needle we think of. *Chunk-chunk,* and two knots are tied, the twine is cut, the counter advances by one, and the next bale commences. In the field it is an elegant and delicate operation on an otherwise clamorous and menacing contraption.

There are no electronics and no plastic parts that make the bailer operate: it's all about the precise interplay of durable metal components. The same is true of a firearm, and in this day and age that's a rarity. For better or worse, the machines we use every day—from toasters to cars—are full of plastic and electronics, rendering them delicate and incomprehensible. Companies that make mobile computing devices also make vacuum cleaners and dishwashers. I grew up in a household of early adopters—my father taught computer science in the 1980s, so we had computers from the time I was six or seven years old. I revel in new technology. But this is exactly what makes the rifle and the old baler so appealing. They can be disassembled, understood, and their mechanics admired. They last forever.

In the stone garage we built things and fixed things. We disassembled motors, replaced engine blocks and clutches. We built a raccoon trap from discarded gravel-sifting screens. By disassembling and reassembling machines, my brother and I understood how things worked. There was joy in it: seeing how the knotter, full of potential energy, stands by for the moment the bale is long enough and then engaging. Taking apart the trigger group for my squirrel gun and for the first time understanding the sear—a part that stands by for the moment when a finger applies just enough pressure and then releases the potential energy of the hammer, the firing pin, and all that energy sitting in the wee brass case—felt familiar to me.

I hunt two ways: When I'm hunting with other people, we move around. Set up at a tree for half an hour, move on after a while. Hardwoods and good mast. When I'm by myself, I'm inclined to set up and stay put, and that means sitting against that oak for hours on end. The virtue of this kind of hunting is that it allows the woods to wake up and makes you invisible—by not moving, you start to blend in after a while. But, probably the real reason I hunt this way is that I'm more lazy than I am impatient.

Between the advice I've gotten and the few squirrel hunting books I've read (which have got to be about all the squirrel hunting books that have ever been written), I'm supposed to look for the squirrel silhouette, a flicking tail, or some bump on a tree that just doesn't look right. I don't think I've ever located a squirrel this way. It's always a rustling of leaves first, and I think, "Is that the breeze?" Once I pinpoint that the rustling is more regular or less random than the breeze, I wonder if it's a bird—a chickadee or a finch scratching in the forest floor. At the same time I ask that, I try to figure out where it is. It's amazing in the woods that something within seventy-five yards could be coming from any direction. There must be a good explanation for it, but my working theory is that such a light sound with so many surfaces to bounce off makes it difficult to pinpoint the location. It's not an echo, just location-less. The sound comes from everywhere. If it's a squirrel, slowly the sound resolves into a pattern, something that sounds like three good hops and then silence, as the squirrel digs around under the leaves for five to ten seconds, three more hops, searching again. After moving around the tree quietly and slowly, which is possible only because I cleared the leaves from the base of the tree, I either am able to pinpoint the squirrel by sound or actually see it.

The farm is in Lincoln, Massachusetts, roughly fifteen miles west of Boston. My mother's family settled there in the mid-seventeenth century and have been farming there since. Families that live in one place for so long tend to accumulate things. The houses on the property are full of my ancestors' stuff: a pre-revolutionary grandfather clock; locks of a Victorian ancestor's hair woven into a bracelet; the old flintlock converted to percussion lock, a vestigial link to my family's firearms past.

While the farm is old, the land itself is geologically young. It is a range of features, owing to the last ice age: within a stone's throw the soil goes from peat, to sand, to gravel, to beautiful, rich loam. An esker, a ridge of gravel sediment deposited by a stream within the glacier, wide enough to drive a truck down and flanked by peat bogs, runs through the woods behind the back pasture. The land is in its infancy compared to the Uwharries in North Carolina.

Along the esker we harvested white pine and white oak for firewood and lumber, hauling it up on top of the ridge with a backhoe and logging chains and bucking it into logs to load on the old farm truck. Some of those logs we milled into lumber at Quincy Adams's place. Some of that lumber we used to build a hut the summer I turned twelve. It was a loose approximation of the hut built by Thoreau, a figure who persists in family lore, as he once petitioned Major Ephraim Flint, my grandfather's great-grandfather, to build a cabin on Flint's Pond, as his friend and Harvard classmate Charles Stearns Wheeler had done.

Thoreau had a poor reputation, though, among many in the area, having in 1844 started a fire in Concord Woods that singed nearly three hundred acres. The old Major denied the request, an offense that Thoreau never forgave, writing in the Ponds section of *Walden:* "What right had the unclean and stupid farmer, whose farm abutted on this sky water, whose shores he has ruthlessly laid bare, to give his name to it? Some skin-flint, who loved better the reflecting surface of a dollar, or a bright cent, in which he could see his own brazen face; who regarded even the wild ducks which settled in it as trespassers; his fingers grown into crooked and bony talons from the long habit of grasping harpy-like."

We constructed our hut in the barn—my grandfather, my brother, and I—the frame in oak and the floors and sheathing in pine. We took three days to build it, then got an old axle under it so we could tow it out to the back pasture. My brother and I spent our nights there, listening to bullfrogs, whippoor-wills, and bachelor mockingbirds. Those days we didn't have work to do, we made it our base. It was in this hut that I first thought about hunting. Books we were reading—this must have been around the time I read *Where the Red Fern Grows* and *The American Boy's Handy Book,* which had instructions for building shelters, making primitive hunting tools, and training crows—along with the fact that we ate food we raised on the farm, stirred in us a desire to gather our own food. Added to this was our grandfather's deep and outspoken frustration with a gaggle of nonmigratory Canada geese that spent their days pulling seedlings from corn fields. From our hut we made plans to hunt those geese.

We made bolas from bailing twine and small field stones. We practiced stalking across the pasture, walking quietly along the abrupt edge of the backwoods, bellying up to the crest of the knoll, and waiting for the geese to land in the swimming pond. We killed two geese that summer. The first Grandfather hung from a gnarled pine and helped us pluck, then dressed it in an empty stall in the barn. He was proud of us.

We learned with the second goose, when my little brother called a taxidermist, that there are seasons for hunting, and midsummer was decidedly not a time for killing geese. My grandmother called back and apologized, explained that we were kids, didn't know better.

The farm was a place outside hunting seasons, perhaps because of long family history, perhaps because it is a place where we naturally took food from the land without considering legal statutes and perhaps because of childhood naiveté. It was a place where we came to terms with birth and death, risk, and machines. The farm was for us about heritage, about the transference of practical truths. My uncle and grandfather passed down the knowledge—the reality—that the meat we eat bleeds and dies. . . .

However, I am aware that my participation in this heritage is also about the

J. B. Weir

apparent conflict of my brother and me hunting geese from our approximation of Thoreau's hut. Apparent, but really Thoreau was a poseur. He didn't live in the wilderness; he lived on a few acres in Concord, which was a sizable, sprawling town with fewer woods than now. Being aware of the heritage *and* the conflict also leads me to the realization that I'm the same kind of poseur. That is, like Thoreau—even generations removed—I long for some harder, truer, more visceral way of living than what the contemporary world, for the most part, has to offer. Except, even saying that I long for some truer way of living in the world isn't entirely honest. I want to dip into it, go squirrel hunting in the freezing cold, and then return to my gas-heated home, streaming video, and packaged, free-range chicken breasts.

I came to guns and hunting in my mid-thirties. That's late by most standards, but seems especially so in North Carolina, where so many rural youngsters cut their teeth on squirrels and sit in stands with their fathers, uncles, grandfathers—nearly always men—throughout deer season. I know so little about hunting. I am the embodiment of someone who has come to hunt not through heritage but through the academy.

Hunting for me often feels like fumbling, but more often it feels like tinkering, and from tinkering I feel like I problem-solve on a much more primal level than I do when I'm solely living in a world of ideas. I suppose I view hunting through an academic lens, but I don't actively think about it at all. There's something about getting out of the stifling ivory tower—especially for an adjunct, which I have been for more than fifteen years—in favor of the basement, the root cellar, the garage. There's nothing noble about it, but it's nourishing in a way that academia is not. Academia is like trying to draw nourishment from sand—whereas working on the farm, working with machines, and hunting draw nourishment from loam. I like the world of ideas. I like the challenge of thinking through problems, but, as a counterbalance to that, hunting is also a kind of thinking through problems—haying, fixing a tractor is thinking by feel, fumbling, tinkering.

At my grandparents' house, a grandfather clock stood in the piano room. This beautiful, old, noble, stately machine. It is itself a kind of symbol, an academic symbol, in a way. What I mean is that, of all the furniture in my grandparents' house, the clock is the piece that feels like it went to college. It's a pre-Revolutionary grandfather clock, and a clock like that, in its era, didn't just tell time. It's a piece of furniture that conveys information. In this day and age, we take time for granted; clocks are everywhere. But in its day it was a rarity. And it has continued to tell time, several hundred years later, a wise, old machine. At the same time, when you open the door of the clock, you can smell the oil. If you go inside the case, you get dirty, like from tinkering with the rifle and the baler. But the clock is both stately and gritty, from a time when being these weren't at odds with each other, in different camps.

Every year I hunt the winter solstice. While the timing may be romantic in some ancient and primal way, the date is set not directly by an astronomical calendar but by the academic calendar: there is a small window between submitting final grades and holiday travel during which I can take a few days to hunt.

Around 6:30, a grey fox lopes lazily up the draw and over the ridge. The clouds are gone, and the stars are just beginning to fade. By 7:00 the woods are waking up. A downy woodpecker lights on a tree nearby and makes its way around and up the tree, calling *pik, pik, pik* as it feeds. A chickadee settles on the ground nearby and commences to kick leaves, a vexing sound that, as I become more eager to locate a squirrel, will become increasingly difficult to distinguish from a squirrel foraging.

The hunting is nearly always hard this time of year. The cold and the short days keep the squirrels holed up in their hollows. One balmy year they were active in the morning, and I bagged three in under an hour. Most years, though, they bark shortly before dusk, and the hunt is on. An hour or two of looking for grey silhouettes among grey limbs against a grey sky. With luck, it means cleaning squirrels in failing light, a treacherous uphill hike to the campsite, and building a cooking fire by touch.

DAVID BRUZINA

Squirrel Hunting and the View from Here

| The Practice |

Despite my four-plus decades, my devotion to bookish pursuits, and my faculty responsibilities in the English department at the University of South Carolina Aiken, every fall I rearrange my course syllabi and neglect my research and personal relationships to indulge my obsession with squirrel hunting. I hunt deer, turkey, and sometimes other game, too, but the puzzle squirrel hunting presents so fascinates and attracts me that I often sacrifice other pursuits to wrestle with its complexities.

Where I hunt in northwestern South Carolina, the public-land squirrel season opens on October 1, when the trees are still full of leaves and their branches constitute a jagged hemisphere of seething colors. I'm in the woods before sunrise. Dazzling light breaks through the dome and distorts tree trunks and branches and leaves, and every surface is draped in writhing shadows. In this environment, the sensory task of finding something as small, skittish, athletic, and camouflage-colored as a squirrel requires from me a seemingly meditative concentration and a degree of physical coordination that forever outstrips my means. Making even basic sense of the landscape—grasping more than visual and auditory gibberish—demands close, conscious attention. I stare for long minutes at a time. I bend and peer and crane and freeze, peering, trying to stay quiet and unobtrusive, attempting a stealthy self-effacement. Or sometimes I sprint, wheezing and creaking, up the steep slopes from the creek bottom, chasing a receding scuffling, a flutter of tail, a potential, promising sign of squirrel.

When I hunt, I feel as if I'm groping with my eyes and ears, reaching past tree trunks and leaves, reaching and groping and withdrawing and reaching out again. A dark patch that seems at first like a distant shadow turns out to be a beetle crawling on the other side of a nearby leaf. A scuffle turns out to be one of the innumerable species of little invisible birds that kick up leaves and sound like squirrels. A tree branch dips and springs, which could be a turkey scratching, or an out-of-season white-tailed yearling ambling through the brush, or one of those strangely pale woods armadillos I've been seeing lately, or a squirrel, heart-stoppingly digging for a beech nut not that far away. The need to sort and react, to match sound, image, action, and circumstance, is constant and absorbing. Hours slide by. Colors change. Sounds swing ninety degrees as the wind veers. Somewhere out there, a tasty squirrel is imitating a branch knob or a woodpecker or a breath of wind or a colorless area of nothing. And if at the right moment from the right location I face the right way with my head tilted at just the right angle, I can maybe catch a glimpse of my quarry—can maybe sneak within forty yards and peer through my .22's scope and calm my breathing and muscle tremors and hold a sight-picture 99 percent still while I move my trigger finger and *only* my trigger finger, and the rifle fires. Otherwise, all I'm doing is walking around the woods, and the guests I've invited for squirrel tacos will have to make do with beans.

Cleanly headshot, a squirrel transforms abruptly from a weightless, lithe, scampering, sometimes purring and squalling emotive entity into a shapeless inert weight crashing discourteously, almost blasphemously, through the branches and hitting the forest floor with a startling thwap. Sometimes on impact, for reasons I don't know, a headshot squirrel will flop feet off the ground, thrashing and leaping like a fish for five or more seconds—though afterward I find the squirrel's brains are missing, the .22 hollow point having struck perfectly between the ear and eye and blasted a hole the thickness of a pencil through the skull. I'm thrilled and relieved. I breathe deeply, sometimes wishing for a witness. A good shot feels like an accomplishment, and I'm guilty of afterward reviewing and bragging about what I did right.

Occasionally on days when I've bagged no squirrels—when I've walked for hours and miles without seeing a single squirrel—or if I've missed shots and wounded a squirrel and witnessed it kicking, gasping, gnashing, and writhing and trying to escape—or if I've been talking to people with deep moral doubts about hunting—I wonder what the hell I'm doing out here with my gun and my backpack and my weird obsession with killing squirrels. This is what I do, seriously? I wander around shooting tree-dwelling rodents when I could be more carefully reading my students' papers and contributing in small, indirect ways to their success—when I could be studying law or economics or legal procedure or history and trying to better oppose in some tiny fashion the deadly contemporary squeeze on American public institutions, not least my own university? At least, I could be cleaning the house or sitting inoffensively in my back yard doing nothing deadly. There's something sobering about the experience of killing—of having caused even a small, forgettable, but unnecessary death.

But mostly when I'm hunting, I don't pause to reflect on the killing. I retrieve my squirrel. I skin it by making an incision beneath the tail and unsleeving its body. I cut off its head and gut it, and if the weather's warm, I sprinkle it with salt, inside and out, before putting it in my pack and preparing to move off in search of more meat. I'm grinning and pleased and happy to be hunting in the woods.

One of my colleagues—an Orange County, California, transplant to the South, who a few years back expressed a desire to learn to hunt and who has since spent a few seasons accompanying me as we've developed and honed strategies for taking local whitetail deer, turkey, squirrel, frogs, and bass—this colleague and friend keeps prodding me to consider more deeply why I hunt.

I wonder why he wonders. The question seems academic: it seems to originate in a deliberate critical reflection and not in an immediate practical problem. (I understand my distinction here is wobbly.) The question also seems somehow hostile: *Why (do you) hunt?* feels vaguely like an accusation. An adequate answer, it feels, would have to be more than a casual causal biography. A personal history of my coming to hunt would only beg the further question of why I continue to hunt. As I hear the question—now that I'm donning my academic mortarboard—*Why (do you) hunt?* seems to ask for a justification, an objectively sound moral justification; it contrasts hunting with an array of other less violent recreations and asks for an account of the deliberations that lead me to choose hunting from among my infinite preferable options.

As an academic with an interest in philosophical ethics, I can't resist wrestling with the problem.

| The Problem |

When I first consider the question *Why (do you) hunt?*, two responses spring immediately to mind:

(1) I hunt because I'm morally weak. Stripped of its illusory romance, my squirrel hunting is gratifying but deeply purposeless and ultimately unconscionable. Humans evolved in ways that leave intact neurological and cultural susceptibilities to the sensory stimuli hunting provides. As a result, hunters experience pleasure when hunting—even though it's been established that killing (even animals, without compelling mitigating reasons) is wrong. In short, hunters hunt because hunting is pleasurable and gratifying the way masturbation or drug use is pleasurable and gratifying. Though it has the chemical feel of profundity, in the end these feelings signify nothing.

(2) There's something authentic, beneficial, and even sublime about hunting. It is transhistorically important. Plato praised hunting as a means to attaining a practical understanding of courage. In his 1942 bible of modern hunting, *Meditations on Hunting*, the philosopher José Ortega y Gassett claimed man (*sic*) hunts because of a reflex that is "the residual fossil of an instinct that man retains from the time he was a pure beast."[1] Archibald Rutledge, the first poet laureate of South Carolina, wrote in *An American Hunter:* "It has always seemed to me that any man is a better man for being a hunter. This sport confers a certain constant alertness, and develops a certain ruggedness of character. . . . Moreover, it allies us to the pioneer past. In a deep sense, this great land of ours was won for us by hunters."[2]

Responses like this second one are popular among hunters. When contemporary American hunters are moved to philosophize about hunting, one is apt to hear murmured invocations of a purer, more primordial self hunting in arcadia. From reading Cooper and Hemingway, watching fish and game TV shows, and listening to other, older hunters, young American nimrods learn that stepping into the woods equals stepping back into a more instinctual and therefore truer state of being. Our encounters with game become visitations and gifts from Nature. We feel grateful for and a little religious about them. It is still standard practice to paint the forehead of a new hunter with the blood of his or her first deer.

Personally, however, I find this second kind of answer unhelpfully sentimental. By temperament and experience, I'm too skeptical and cynical to accept the notion that through hunting one encounters intimations of atemporal significance. While understanding that other hunters might object to my quick dismissal of Ortega y Gassett, Rutledge, Hemingway, et al., I find that their venerable defenses/explanations require too much metaphysics, too much faith to explain my own twenty-first-century attachment to squirrel hunting.

The first explanation of hunting—that it satisfies a spurious animal hunger, a spandrel appetite—seems to me true but also dangerously and misleadingly inadequate. It has the feeling of explaining love in terms of neural patterns or music in terms of equations or (to paraphrase the poet Richard Hugo) good whisky in terms of chemistry. It's true *but*. . . . A more satisfying response would identify *some* legitimizing quality of hunting as a contemporary practice, *my* contemporary practice—something analogous to the nutritional value of fruit that justifies my indulgence in its sugar, something objectively good in a way that counterbalances the badness of the deaths that I, as a hunter, continually cause.

For example, as an academic, I could justify my pursuit of squirrels if hunting them uniquely pushed me toward important insights and better explications of crucial strands of humanistic thought. It is natural for academics to enrich their research with language and discoveries prompted by their hobbies.

David Bruzina

And hunting appears both literally and figuratively in writings by any number of thinkers important to the development of Western culture.

One of my favorite philosophers, David Hume, in his *A Treatise of Human Nature,* compares philosophy itself to hunting:

> There cannot be two passions more nearly resembling each other, than those of hunting and philosophy, whatever disproportion may at first sight appear betwixt them. It is evident, that the pleasure of hunting conflicts in the action of the mind and body; the motion, the attention, the difficulty, and the uncertainty. It is evident likewise, that these actions must be attended with an idea of utility, in order to their having any effect upon us . . . To make the parallel betwixt hunting and philosophy more compleat, we may observe, that though in both cases the end of our action may in itself be despised, yet in the heat of the action we acquire such an attention to this end, that we are very uneasy under any disappointments, and are sorry when we either miss our game, or fall into any error in our reasoning.[3]

Sir Thomas Wyatt, the sixteenth-century ambassador, courtier, and poet who helped found English poetry by introducing Petrarch's Italian forms to the Tudor court, sees the pursuit of the beloved as a kind of hunting in his best-known and most beautiful sonnet:

> Whoso list to hunt, I know where is an hind,
> But as for me, hélas, I may no more.
> The vain travail hath wearied me so sore,
> I am of them that farthest cometh behind.
> Yet may I by no means my wearied mind
> Draw from the deer, but as she fleeth afore
> Fainting I follow. I leave off therefore,
> Sithens in a net I seek to hold the wind.
> Who list her hunt, I put him out of doubt,
> As well as I may spend his time in vain.
> And graven with diamonds in letters plain
> There is written, her fair neck round about:
> *Noli me tangere,* for Caesar's I am,
> And wild for to hold, though I seem tame.[4]

And Classical Greek and Roman literature is rife with treatments of hunting, including this lyric glimpse at an ancient foodie's lucky accident, attributed to the first-century Roman Bianor:

The Octopus

Having found it enisled in a rock pool after
the tide withdrew, the fisherman snatched
an octopus up and, afraid that it might latch
itself around his wrist, pitched it over

onto a grassy clearing in the underbrush.
With a woozily unhinged liquid swirl,
it oozed over sideways and as if by will
slumped against a rabbit asleep in the grass.

Like melted wax, the tentacles spilled,
hardened, then contracted around
the bone cage of the rabbit's head.
By grace of the gods (he imagines still),

the fisherman's haul from the sea trove
was redoubled by a second haul on shore.
(Translation by Sharon Santos)[5]

As an academic interested in defending his hunting, I find such frequent allusions to hunting tantalizing. If first-person singular hunting experience is required to understand, for example, Hume's analogy, I might justify my hunting as necessary for gaining insight into the meta-philosophy of an important figure in the development of Western philosophy. If only a hunter can appreciate the intensity of Wyatt's speaker's weariness and obsession—the bulging of the poem's poignancy against the sonnet's formal squeeze—I can perhaps legitimize my hunting as a means to better understanding the Anglo-American lyric tradition. If only a contemporary hunter can recognize how a Roman poet astonished by his good fortune could feel a little religious, I'd have some evidence to use in justifying my indulgence in shooting squirrels.

Unfortunately, though I've struggled to obtain from my hunting some genuinely useful academic insight, I am unable to see how hunting provides the kind of scholarly benefit I'm searching for. I think anyone acquainted with both philosophizing and, say, poker or soccer or bird watching can understand the experience of philosophizing that Hume is intent on explicating in the passage presented. The parallel he draws seems more conventional than dependent on the particular nature of hunting as opposed to, say, serious bowling. And in Wyatt's poem, first-person hunting experience seems unimportant to appreciating the tension between the speaker's desire and exhaustion; most undergraduates grasp immediately the speaker's desperate passions regardless of their exposure to hunting. And as for Bianor's lyric, I imagine any

David Bruzina

contemporary cook who has discovered, for example, an accidentally free frozen chicken (or a bag of soybeans?) when unpacking groceries at home can empathize with and chuckle at Bianor's lucky hunter/gatherer.

Despite my enjoyment of and attention to the appearance of hunting in literature and philosophy—and although hunting feels important and worthwhile to me, especially when I'm hunting—when I think as carefully and objectively as I can in the quiet of my study, I suspect my hunting fails to contribute significantly (even if indirectly) to my own scholarly work, my teaching, or the world's overall good. My initial knee-jerk response to the question *Why do (I) hunt?*—that I'm addicted to a pointless and violent practice—seems uncomfortably hard to avoid. No matter hunting's limited but real objective benefits—food, my own pleasure, social opportunities that might not otherwise arise—those benefits seem either trivial or obtainable by less violent means. My personal joy in hunting seems petty when weighed impartially against living creatures' demises, and I don't want to be petty.

But neither do I want to stop hunting. Against my reluctant acceptance of hunting as an apparently unjustifiable indulgence, another uneasy intuition presses, one that suggests my squirrel hunting has legitimate value despite my inability to identify the objectively justifying good it produces. If hunting constitutes self-indulgence, is self-indulgence always petty? Does the demand that moral human beings act only out of impartially justified motives distort something important about the nature of human values? (I hear the great skeptics—Sextus Empiricus and Nietzche and Lyotard and Bernard Williams et al.—whispering from their graves.)

| The Problem Reconsidered |

In her influential article "Moral Saints," the American philosopher Susan Wolf suggests there's something fishy about moral philosophy's fixation on objective/impartial justification. She writes: "I don't know whether there are any moral saints. But if there are, I am glad that neither I nor those about whom I care most are among them. . . . Moral perfection . . . does not constitute a model of personal well-being toward which it would be particularly rational or good or desirable for a human being to strive."[6] For Wolf, a moral saint is someone who impartially weighs all options and acts unrelentingly on the judgments obtained. Such a person, Wolf worries, would be "dull witted, humorless or bland"[7] since a more cynical or sarcastic sense of humor "would require one to take an attitude of resignation . . . towards the flaws and vices to be found in the world."[8] Similarly, she argues that "an interest in something like gourmet cooking" would be proscribed since "there seems no plausible argument" that could impartially justify "producing a *pate de canard en croute*" when human resources could be devoted to more compelling moral needs.[9]

While Wolf acknowledges the value of the demand that people impartially consider their actions' impacts on the larger world, she insists that moral philosophy also take seriously the value of real-world personal attachments and the roles they play in motivating our actions: "One cares about [a friend]'s good not just insofar as it constitutes a bit of human good in general; one loves opera not just in proportion to its providing one with pleasurable experience. One's attachment to this person, this activity, this cause is what moves one to act even if it is not optimally beneficial to oneself or to what is worthwhile from some detached impersonal perspective."[10] For Wolf, reducing personal attachments to petty self-indulgences obscures the very values that our real-world decisions aim to preserve. Personal attachments play a crucial role in the decisions that define human lives, but, as Wolf urges, their value can't always be reconciled with a demand for objective moral reasoning nor can they be reduced to frivolous self-interest.

For Wolf, this means there's something wrong with the moral demand that human decisions be reached through impartial deliberation, and her concluding suggestion is that "we" (philosophers) should "free ourselves more thoroughly from the grip of the metaphor that takes morality as a whole to be a matter of acting in accordance with the judgments of a single unified and coherent point of view." Instead, Wolf hopes, we should "look further and more imaginatively at the possible structures moral thinking can take."[11]

If, following Wolf, we abandon the notion that justifying a practice means producing an objectively sound moral argument, a hunter might answer the question *Why (do you) hunt?* by describing a complex and inconsistent web of considerations, including personal, historically located, and sometimes powerfully irrational attachments. These are the kinds of attachments that allowed the eminent (and notorious) philosopher Peter Singer—a seminal figure in antihunting ethics—to famously veer from his strict utilitarianism when his Alzheimer's-stricken mother needed expensive care. (As Singer later admitted, "Perhaps it is more difficult [to act impartially] than I thought before, because it's different when it's your mother.")[12] And these are the kinds of attachments that move people to protect commercially unimportant endangered species; to block the development of beautiful beaches; to admire a friend's perseverance even when we know his or her individual talents offer no chance of significant success. This is not to say that hunters needn't examine their hunting practices as rigorously and objectively as possible. But it's not clear that the verdicts that emerge from such examinations should preclude or trump more nuanced stances. Instead, they can offer a perspective that must be reconciled with other aspects of our lives. As Wolf describes the process, "When I deliberate . . . about what to do, I simply deliberate, as it were, from here. I consider a variety of values that have no common measure, taking into account, at least sometimes,

David Bruzina

when the occasion warrants, both how attached I am to the values and goals in question and how important or worthwhile these goals and values seem to be independently of my attachments to them. I juggle, I balance, I choose—and I assume that with respect to this general characterization of decision-making, I am not unusual."[13]

| Three Points of Attachment |

So why do *I* hunt?

(A) In part, my attraction to hunting derives in convoluted fashion from my family's history and my desire to remain close to my parents, both of whom are nonhunters but serious cooks and eaters. In my family, the planning, execution, and consumption of meals have been and remain a central activity, one that occasions a great deal of discussion, argument, work, cooperation, and skill. Participating in the preparation of meals, demonstrating and appreciating culinary ability, and sharing, praising and criticizing food has always been the single most important and stable requirement of membership in my family. We regard vegetarians and those content with prepackaged food with resignation at best and biting contempt most of the time.

I suspect this attitude toward food and cooking has its origins in the multicultural, multigenerational, and linguistically complex composition of my family. My father grew up in Ohio and Wisconsin but spent much of his adult life in Germany and France, where he was first exposed to serious culinary traditions. My mother grew up in Canada, the daughter of recently arrived Japanese immigrants, whose diets were fusions of Japanese tradition and local ingredients sometimes made scarce by the impositions of World War II. As children, my sisters and I were exposed to an ever-changing mishmash of languages—including Kentucky-Canadian and Japanese-Canadian-inflected English. It wasn't until I was eight or nine years old that I discovered that a phrase my parents frequently used, "touchez pas," was French and not, as I'd always assumed, Japanese.

Because family members were frequently away from home for months at a time—and extended family members and international guests were frequently present—food offered an alternative to the sometimes headache-inducing demands of conversation. We didn't always talk; we cooked and ate.

And now—having lived away from home for decades, having learned to dislike both the gastronomic qualities and the ecological and cultural implications of commercial farming—and as my parents age and my relationship with them grows ever more important and overshadowed—I've discovered in hunting an activity that permits me to remain a family member. While both my parents share a liberal suspicion of firearms and hunting—my father in particular avoids confronting the live animals he eats—they appreciate hunting as a useful means of obtaining the freshest ingredients, and they have been gratified and excited by the meals my hunting has yielded.

(B) I also hunt because hunting seems to balance the time I spend reading, writing, and thinking. Through the physical, sensory overload of its demands, squirrel hunting reminds me of my own senses and my material body in a way that contrasts starkly and refreshingly with my academic life. As an academic, I spend much of my time in the state of disembodied consciousness that serious reading requires. As I work through Hume's or Susan Wolf's arguments or Frank Bidart's poetry or Halliday's criticisms of Vendler—or as I try to understand and fairly evaluate my students' sometimes challenging papers—the meanings of words, phrases, and paragraphs displace my study, my desk, my body, my book, the words. Outside my office door, a student can shuffle his or her feet. My colleague Gwen can shout at that fascist Cajun fiction writer Ned by the copy machine. Far away in Aiken, South Carolina, we might be experiencing a once-in-a-decade earthquake. But if I'm working on a problem or a lesson plan or an essay or a poem, I don't care. Without conscious effort, I deflect noise or movements that threaten the borders of my attention. I am somewhere else, an intangible homunculus rummaging through a symbolic landscape of relationships and implications that aren't physically anywhere. I'm engaged in a metaphorical kind of hunting, and if I'm lucky and careful, my reward will be the sustaining fat and protein of understanding. . . .

But this is *only* metaphorical hunting because, in part, it doesn't involve my body. For an academic, the displacement and disembodiment—the vanishing of the here and now and the physical me—is a sign of deep concentration, a hallmark of the focused reader and the dedicated working geek. But for a literal hunter—especially a squirrel hunter—the same retreat from the immediate is disastrous. Hunting squirrels involves interacting with a material landscape, an auditory universe and a visual field many magnitudes more complex and subtle than any page or computer screen. It is the opposite of reading, and I enjoy thoroughly the offsetting exercises of both reading and hunting.

(C) And, finally, I hunt because, in my moral deliberations, the lives of individual squirrels weigh relatively little. When driving, I try to miss one that darts into the road—and when hunting, I try to make clean headshots and kill as quickly as possible—but I value a squirrel's life in a way differently from how I value the lives of people or dogs or members of endangered species or people's pets. When I consider my hunting, I factor in my other pursuits and do a kind of calculus. I weigh my virtues—I am a devoted teacher and an easy-to-get-along-with department member. I subtract my faults—stubbornness, impatience, a tendency to avoid confrontation. I offset my weaknesses, moral and other. I read and brood about books and articles about the value of animals' lives and the morality of hunting.

And I find myself unpersuaded that I ought to stop hunting.

I can imagine my commitments changing. My squirrel hunting could be displaced by other activities. The world moves mysteriously: if my job or social life changed substantially in ways that made squirrel hunting less appealing, I don't imagine the change would necessarily entail a diminishment of my life's quality. But there'd have to be a long lever exerting considerable force on my decisions from outside and a rich something to replace my hunting.

In the meantime, I'm stockpiling .22lr CCI mini-mags (in lieu of Winchester Power-Points) and tearing paper towels into easy-to-dispense squares. I'm checking my scope's zero and sharpening my hunting knife and arranging my course sequences so major assignments and exams don't conflict with ample time afield.

Much as I love teaching, reading, writing, arguing, books, literature, philosophy, and seminar tables, libraries and the rituals, practices, and tools of academia, I've learned to schedule my hunting for days when I don't have to participate in academic work. Or if I must, I plan to hunt later in the day *after* I'm done with the day's academic responsibilities. Though I sometimes drive from class to the woods to hunt in the evening, I don't like returning from hunting in the morning to teach or write or read. When I do, I feel as if someone has dropped a lid on me. I have a hard time switching my senses off. The intellectual curiosity, the hunger that at other times blinds me to anything but the literary or pedagogical question at hand, seems bloodless and dispassionate. I walk through the halls of USCA's Humanities and Social Sciences building, and the halls seem beige and constrictive, and though I'm looking at faces and faces are one of the most interesting things to look at, it's discourteous and discomfiting to look too closely, too actively at them.

And so I stop looking and withdraw into my thoughts. I change my ontological status. I become temporarily a faculty member and not a squirrel hunter, not a cook, not the host of tonight's squirrel feast. . . .

Because We Hunt

Intellectualizing Hunting

DAVID GRAHAM HENDERSON

Hunting Ethics

Reflections from a (Mostly) Vegetarian Hunter

I did not grow up in a hunting family. There was no opposition to it; we just didn't do it. We fished a little and even shot skeet on occasion. But hunting had not been part of my dad's childhood, which was spent on various Air Force bases around the world, and so it did not make it into mine. We kept busy with other things. But woods and wildlife were vitally present. The many hours spent alone in the Texas pinewoods encountering copperheads and red-tailed hawks nurtured my growing enchantment with nature and continue to animate my work as an environmental philosopher.

I first started hunting while in graduate school. The idea had long been attractive to me, but it had mostly been a pipe dream, a vague romantic longing to recover traditional and primitive ways of participating in the land. But it was my growing academic identity as an ethicist focused on responsible human relationships to the land and animals that motivated me to buy a license and a weapon. As I became more educated about the actual conditions of contemporary agriculture, it became clear that I could no longer in good conscience eat the tortured flesh of animals produced in the factory farm system. It was not the meat but the cruelty that I could not stomach. Hunting promised a chance to take moral ownership and control over my relation to the animals I ate.

Hunting is contrary to the confined feeding operation in every way. The distance and hiddenness of the animal's life and death from the consumer are gone. The life of the animal is free of all mechanization and mutilation, unfettered in its natural habitat. The killing is as compassionate and respectful as I can (or can learn to) make it. I would, in the words of Aldo Leopold, prefer to seek my "meat from God."[1]

Although few other hunters share my convictions exactly—I have not met any who are otherwise vegetarian—I came to appreciate the importance hunters generally place on their moral codes. They take pride in clean shots or express remorse and shame at having wounded animals. Most have strong convictions about the impropriety of waste or wanton destruction. Like Augustinian just-war theorists, they are concerned that killing be done only for a right reason and in a right manner.

But during the required hunter education courses, I began to worry about the coherence of these codes. The instructor and a wildlife official were talking about the importance of mentoring for young hunters, and it became apparent that the delinquent behavior that worried them was the shooting of doves that are perched instead of in flight. It was unsporting. The importance of only taking a clean shot, which had been firmly emphasized with respect to deer, was completely overridden in their minds by a principle of sportingness when it comes to doves. I struggled to see how putting the bird at greater risk of wounding in order to give the hunter a greater challenge was about being fair to the bird. Whatever moral substance there is to this idea of sportingness, it is not to be found in the concern for animal welfare that had motivated me.

The question simmered: Should I write sportingness off as an incoherent tradition, or is there something real there to be learned and respected? Some help and understanding came from the works of Theodore Roosevelt and Aldo Leopold, which I was reading for my dissertation on wilderness. I had come to hunting with a contemporary moral problem in mind; I wanted to subvert and resist the inhumanity of factory farming. So I had consequently framed my sense of right hunting almost entirely in terms of humane hunting. Roosevelt, Leopold, and other late nineteenth- and early twentieth-century conservationists had also looked to hunting for help in resolving a moral problem, but it was a very different problem. They transformed hunting into a practice for building and maintaining strength of character in the face of a rapidly changing world. Sportingness and fair chase are best understood as the central pieces of this project.

| Sport and Character Building |

The history of this project, using sportsmanship in hunting to build character, is multifaceted, and Charles List's essay in this volume tells it more fully from another angle. But a key factor in its origin is nostalgia over the loss of the frontier. The frontier experience shaped the character of American culture in a number of ways. The constant availability of land to those willing to work made America the land of opportunity. Frederick Jackson Turner, in his 1893 essay "The Significance of the Frontier in American History," attributed our individualist, egalitarian, and democratic tendencies to the frontier experience. How right he was has been hotly contested, but the thesis was widely accepted and discussed at the time. Just as the 1890 U.S. Census had declared that the frontier was officially no more, Turner declared that it had been the cause of all that was best about America. Attempts to preserve a semblance of the frontier experience in the lives of postfrontier Americans proliferated, including the Boy Scouts and the national park movement.[2]

Probably nobody worried about this loss of American character more than Theodore Roosevelt, who feared that flabbiness and sloth would replace the manly and masterful virtues cultivated on the frontier.[3] While advocating for the adoption of many strenuous endeavors to combat this modern dullness, he put special emphasis on the promise of hunting: "Hunting in the wilderness is of all pastimes the most attractive. . . . The wilderness hunter must not only show skill in the use of the rifle and address in finding and approaching game, but he must also show the qualities of hardihood, self-reliance, and resolution needed for effectively grappling with his wild surroundings."[4] And in 1887, together with like-minded hunters, he organized the Boone and Crockett Club to promote and preserve the wilderness, along with big-game hunting, and to thereby foster qualities of manliness, hardiness, and self-reliance in the American people.

The Boone and Crockett Club promoted the ideal of fair chase as an ethic for hunting that would both cultivate the desired character traits in the hunter and preserve wildlife populations from wanton destruction and decline. Fair chase, which appears to be the source of the sense of sportingness that troubled me in the hunter education course, requires hunting "in a manner that does not give the hunter an improper advantage" over the animal.[5] Too great an advantage would be improper not because it would be unfair to the animal but because it would demean the sport and challenge of the hunt. Easy hunting would not serve to cultivate the virtues by challenging the hunter's abilities. A hunting ethic that embraces difficulty and emphasizes restraint also helps balance the promotion of hunting with the conservation of wildlife. Nostalgia for the frontier, especially in people like Roosevelt, included nostalgia for the great herds of bison and other wildlife whose numbers and habitat had been decimated by the conquest of the frontier.

Aldo Leopold represents a bridge from the romanticizing of the frontier to a modern ecological understanding of the land (or perhaps a synthesis of the two). He was a seminal figure in the development of scientific wildlife management and an early proponent of the designation of roadless wilderness areas. His essay on the land ethic, which emphasizes human membership in a broader biotic community, became extremely important for my field of environmental philosophy. Leopold identifies the cultural value of wildlife sport, including but not limited to hunting, as threefold: historical (or "split-rail") value, a reminder of ecological dependency, and the ethical restraints of sportsmanship.[6] The first idea is closely tied to frontier nostalgia; by reenacting our national history, we are better prepared to face the political realities of the present. This is the same sentiment in which Leopold urges the preservation of canoeing and pack trains as primitive recreation. The second idea holds that hunting is valuable because it "reminds us of our dependency on the soil-plant-animal-man food chain and of the fundamental organization of the biota"[7] These connections are everywhere obscured by modern industry, but such ecological literacy is desperately needed if we are to avert environmental catastrophe. Neither of these cultural values is inevitably realized by hunting, but both may be achieved by appropriate forms of hunting.

Sportsmanship, in Leopold's framing, is a set of ethical constraints "aimed to augment the role of skill and shrink the role of gadgets in the pursuit of wild things."[8] Some of these constraints are ideals derived from frontier necessities: going light, not wasting, one-bullet-one-buck, and so on.[9] But the really important, distinctive feature of these principles for Leopold is that they are rules that one usually keeps in solitude, with "no gallery to applaud or disapprove."[10] To show restraint when no one is watching is powerful training for moral integrity in all things. But to break the rules when no one is watching is just as powerful training for depravity. Thus, keeping a code of sportsmanship that requires restraint appears to be essential for hunting to fulfill its greatest character-building potential. However, this restraint need not and ought not take a cruel form (such as encouraging chancy shots) in order to serve this function.

The relationship of skill and challenge to virtue may not be immediately obvious, but it is not spurious. This may be seen by looking at hunting in terms of Alasdair MacIntyre's account of how virtues are cultivated through and depend upon practices. A practice for MacIntyre is a very particular kind of activity: "any coherent and complex form of socially established cooperative human activity through which goods internal to that form of activity are realized . . . with the result that human powers to achieve excellence, and human conceptions of the ends and goods involved, are systematically extended."[11] There are many practices, from baseball to particle physics, and what sets them apart from other activities is a kind of richness. To begin with, practices have goods and satisfactions internal to them, sought for their own sake and known only to those who participate. Becoming a great pitcher or batter is a good internal to baseball. Working out a theory that unifies diverse phenomena is a good internal to physics. There are usually no shortcuts to these kinds of goods. They are had only by learning and building on the work of those who came before and by a disciplined personal pursuit of excellence. In contrast to these goods that are internal to practices are external goods like wealth and reputation. Unlike the internal goods, external goods may very well be had by cheating, and

David Graham Henderson

the unconstrained pursuit of them can corrupt or undermine the practice as a whole.

In addition to having internal goods, practices are complex enough to provide an inexhaustible space for the development of excellence in the pursuit of those goods. Tic-tac-toe is not a practice, because anyone can learn to become the best possible player in an afternoon. The game has been solved. Chess, on the other hand, with a bit more complexity, is a practice that many people spend large portions of their lives trying to master, without ever exhausting the challenge or satisfactions of the game. It is also important that there are many other people devoted to chess. The social richness of a practice contributes to its character-building potential; a person who plays only against the computer will be short the lessons in winning and losing graciously and on how to take instruction.

Practices cultivate virtues, according to MacIntyre, because people can achieve those internal goods only if they also exercise characteristics such as patience, self-control, fairness, honesty, courage, and the humility to accept the evaluation of others. Without patience and perseverance, no great achievements could be made in baseball or physics. And dishonesty among the practitioners would quickly sink either endeavor. These virtues are developed in the context of a practice, but then they carry over into other relationships and other practices.

Hunting is clearly a practice in MacIntyre's sense. It offers many satisfactions known only to the hunter, goods internal to the practice. These include not only making a clean kill but also things like making a good approach or the ability to call in elusive quarry. Hunting also has the requisite complexity. One can never exhaust the possibilities of becoming better at it, whether those skills be in marksmanship, tracking, camouflage, or game management. Continuous improvement is as doggedly pursued in sport hunting as in chess. And the practice of hunting is socially cooperative in that it has been developed and invested with meaning over generations, such that its practitioners may care about the current state and future of hunting itself.

The benefit of applying MacIntyre's account to hunting is that it clearly shows how hunting can cultivate certain virtues. And it does so without having to accept uncritically the conceptions of virtue handed down to us from previous generations of hunters, which, as in Roosevelt's case, may be deeply tainted with sexism and racism. Hunting will always require patience, despite the gadgeteer's best efforts to circumvent the need for it. Lessons in courage and humility are also regularly meted out by nature. But MacIntyre's account also suggests that almost any practice could develop these virtues, from guitar playing to gardening. Simply that something is a practice that develops virtues is not enough of a justification for participating, especially if there are prima facie moral objections to the practice. Roosevelt also advocated war for its internal goods and character-building tendencies, writing in a letter to Francis V. Greene, on September 23, 1897, "I should welcome almost any war, for I think this country needs one."[12]

The particular value of the practice of hunting must be found in its relations to our other values and the present context. For Roosevelt and Leopold, the particular value of hunting was found in its potential to ameliorate the felt loss of the frontier and what that meant for the relationship of people to wild nature. But what about today?

| Moving Forward |

Nostalgia for the frontier has grown dim. Concerns persist about Americans' tendency toward crass materialism and our modern sedentary lives. But our worries about our relationship to wild nature have been transformed by a broader and more pervasive sense of environmental crisis, going far beyond the loss of the frontier. If the practice of hunting is going to continue to play a distinctive role in teaching us to be good citizens and stewards of the land, then the hunter's moral code will have evolve to address these new problems. I am hopeful that it can do so and believe that it is already.

Lessons might be learned from how the ethics of another outdoor practice have transcended its roots in frontier nostalgia to address contemporary problems: the transition in hiking and camping from a woodcraft ethic to the Leave No Trace program. Leave No Trace has been remarkably successful in its goals, but I am as interested in the lessons of its failures as in those of its strengths. The problem that Leave No Trace handles so well is the conflict between nature preservation and the enormous increase in the numbers of campers and hikers. The alliance between outdoor recreation and the preservation and appreciation of wilderness was threatened by the impact of too much visitation. In particular, if recreational use of wilderness had to be strictly controlled to limit its damages, far less political support would be available for official wilderness designation. The solution was found not in limiting the numbers of hikers and campers but in transforming their impacts though a new ethic.

The old ideals of woodcraft included being able to make food and shelter from what the forest provided. Knowledge of the wild plants and animals, along with a good axe, gave one a healthy independence from civilization and a chance to relive the frontier experience. In the Leave No Trace ethic, the axe, the snare, and even the campfire have been largely replaced by modern equipment. Knowledge of the land is no longer as necessary as knowledge of gadgets. The result is a radically reduced impact on the landscape—the camp stove and the aluminum-frame tent save a lot of wood from being chopped for warmth and shelter—but it is achieved by putting an insulating layer of consumer goods between the backpacker and nature.

David Graham Henderson

This strategy of further insulating people from nature is clearly not compatible with hunting, which unabashedly seeks greater participation in nature. The question must be how to participate well—how to leave responsible, even beneficial, traces. In the backpacking ethics discussions, some are pushing back against the alienation and purely negative aspects of Leave No Trace. There are possibilities for having positive impacts even in hiking, from removing invasive plants to adopting and maintaining trails. There are also moves to counter the consumerist tendencies of Leave No Trace by promoting more sustainable manufacturing, buying secondhand, sharing, repairing, and drawing on the DIY and Maker movements. These trends creatively recover some of the go-light and heritage aspects of woodcraft, but in ways that address contemporary environmental concerns with the consumer economy.

What would strategies like this mean for hunting? Hunting may have some things to learn from Leave No Trace, especially where overcrowding is having some of the same negative impacts on hunting that motivated the change for backpackers. But hunting must also concern itself with the ecological consequences of its primary impact—the killing of animals. Removing invasive species like feral hogs and limiting species that tend toward overabundance, such as deer, can clearly have positive impacts, beneficial to the ecological health of the land. The removal of other animals, such as rare, threatened, or keystone species, can be very detrimental. The ecological benefits of predators are now well understood, and with that understanding comes a greater obligation to let them be. Through thoughtful prey selection, hunting has the potential to ameliorate other problems ecosystems may face, such as mesopredator (for example, raccoon, skunk, snake) release. The more ecology the hunter knows, both in terms of theory and in terms of what is happening locally, the more environmental responsibility the hunter can exercise.

Like those seeking to extend the environmental responsibility of Leave No Trace beyond the immediate impacts of the camp, today's hunters can also extend their sense of conservation beyond the immediate results of the hunt to its peripheral effects, taking responsibility for the ecological footprint of their gear, weapons, and transportation. Many hunters already strive for independence from excess gadgetry, for which this just adds another reason. Maintaining and handing down weapons across generations is also already valued in terms of heritage. Avoiding buying additional, unneeded new weapons or choosing less toxic ammunition may require a larger change of mindset. Expanding the traditional conservation-mindedness of hunting into a broader ecological consciousness is vital for the ongoing moral relevance of the practice of hunting. But a robust moral code for hunting will include more than that. There are a number of principles to be held in balance, including but not limited to ecological stewardship, regard for the creature, preservation of heritage, and the intentional cultivation of virtue.

Getting back to the principle that first motivated me to hunt, I must admit there are real obstacles to reconciling the practice of hunting with a robust moral regard for individual animals. The animal liberation movement has been overwhelmingly hostile to the practice, and hunters have often dismissed any moral regard for animals as a pathological Bambi syndrome. However, I would argue that hunting is the most humane way of acquiring meat. The life of creatures in the wild, especially in a suitable and healthy habitat, is usually the life to which the animal's capacities are best suited. The life of the wild animal may include hardship and suffering, but these are unlikely to rival those imposed by the factory farm. And, unlike the consumer of farmed meat, the hunter of wild game does not bear much responsibility for any sufferings the animal may have experienced prior to being hunted. Gary Varner has argued compellingly that, at least for deer and other "obligatory management species," hunting is a permissible means for preventing a significant amount of animal pain, even under the moral philosophies of the animal liberationists Peter Singer and Tom Regan.[13]

Bambi rhetoric notwithstanding, consideration and respect for the individual animal are a regular and established part of hunting ethics. The ideal of the clean kill is taken seriously by nearly all and is part of the challenge that the hunter develops skills and capacities to meet. The problem is to work this out with greater consistency and mindfulness, so that it not only constitutes a goal of marksmanship but also informs the selection of methods and game. Regard for the animal is also more than minimizing its suffering. Many hunters experience respect, gratitude, and even feelings of kinship toward their prey, as well as compassion. This richer sense of respect toward the animal holds promise for further transforming the reasons for and the ways in which we hunt.

I suggest that one such transformation should be an appreciation of the capacities and interests particular to each species. We already discriminate among species in our regard for animals but mostly in unreasonable ways. Rattlesnakes hunted for roundups are treated to cruelties and indignities that would cause an outrage if done to any other species of game, but the explanation for this singular treatment has nothing to do with respect for the rattlesnake's capacities or interests and everything to do with animosity on the humans' part. Recent years have seen an explosion in our understanding of animal cognition; no longer can we dismiss whole classes of animals as having three-second memories or any such foolishness. These revelations have the biggest impact on our treatment of those species of animals whose capacities for caring relationships, complex reasoning, sustained planning, and anticipation of the future approach our own: elephants, great apes, cetaceans, and possibly crows. If these animals are to be hunted at all, it can only be with very strong justification and with due regard for how the hunting impacts their social structures.

David Graham Henderson

Besides what we owe to the biotic community and to our prey, there is what we owe to ourselves and to one another. I have argued so far that hunting can be a virtuous pursuit, when done well. But done wrongly it has the potential to be, as Leopold said, "training for ethical depravity."[14] So it is important to hunt in a way that requires the exercise of patience, self-control, mindfulness, compassion, and the like. Avoid the shortcuts, and perpetually work to improve. These virtues have both personal and social value. Hunting can also develop other capacities, such as ecological literacy and a personal knowledge of public lands, which while not strictly virtues are sorely needed in civic engagement. But acquiring these is not automatic either. It is only the hunter who studies natural history in order to excel at hunting who gains ecological literacy.

Heritage is another way of thinking about what we owe one another, a way that looks across generations in both directions. Previous generations have invested the practice of hunting with aesthetic, social, and moral value, developing tools and traditions and passing down hard-won knowledge. There is a debt of gratitude for what is received and an obligation not to snuff it out. Not everything old is of value, but much of it has endured precisely because it is. If I find that traditional woodcraft skills, such as tracking or foraging, have enriched my life, then I must be a good steward of that knowledge, passing it on and contributing to it if I can. To fail to do so would be to thwart the legacy of my elders and rob the heritage of my children.

| Application |

These principles—ecological responsibility, regard for the creature, preservation of heritage, and cultivation of virtue—are not meant to be an exhaustive list of the moral principles relevant to hunting. I have not mentioned anything about public safety. But together, with their complex interactions, these principles capture the heart of the ethical knot (or paradox or conundrum) that hunting poses. I offer now some reflections from my own experiences in trying to work through these, not because I am a moral exemplar but because of the difficulties of writing from anyone else's experience.

After deciding to hunt, a decision based on my judgment of hunting's superiority to industrial agriculture in terms of both ecological responsibility and regard for the creature, I made the further decision to bow hunt and have mostly kept to that. The bow not only draws on a deeper heritage of traditional ways but further reduces the distance (physical and psychological) between hunter and prey. And, based on an analogy to the accidental experiences of having cut my finger with a sharp knife and having hit my finger with a hammer, it seems plain to me that the broadhead is more humane than the bullet. And should I err and give a nonlethal wound, a cut from an arrow seems likely to be both more bearable and easier to recover from than damage from a bullet, although I admit to mere speculation here. The bow is also environmentally friendlier than the rifle: I can reuse and repair my arrows, and I leave no lead around to bioaccumulate. Archery is also a skill that I already enjoyed developing, and it is easier to train regularly and at home. And bow hunting is generally thought to require the development of greater skill to be successful. In bow hunting, these principles all converge and reinforce one another fortuitously.

At other times these principles pull in conflicting directions. I recently had a chance to join a friend on a hunt for hogs in a forest managed by a community college. Removing feral hogs is as ecologically beneficial as hunting gets, and I had been on the lookout for such an opportunity. This particular opportunity had the added benefit of supporting an educational institution, so I went. The catch was that the stands were set up for rifles in a way that would make using a bow awkward, and I had to borrow my friend's spare rifle. It was a fine gun, but there was no chance to practice with it beforehand. In this case, I let the environmental good of hog removal outweigh my concerns about animal welfare and my lack of due diligence in preparing for a clean kill. In the end, I killed two hogs with reasonably well-placed shots, but I was not comfortable with how they died. I regretted not insisting upon using my bow.

My choice to hunt is also connected to a broader, daring hope that I have for the possibilities of the restoration of nature and the human place in it. The decimation of wild things has been tied up in part with the replacement of wild food systems with domestic ones. For pre-Columbian Americans, all meat was wild, and vast herds of bison supported many nations. Until but yesteryear seafood was entirely wild. People have tolerated the destruction of the creatures formerly relied upon and of their habitats because they have been offered a substitute. The transition from wild to farmed seafood seems barely to have been noticed. But the domestic food systems substituted are fraught with problems of cruelty, exploitation, pollution, and unsustainability.

The restoration of large portions of many of these destroyed ecosystems is still possible. It will not be perfect and will require a significant investment of work and political resolve. The idea of the Buffalo Commons and the work of the Rewilding Institute are promising signs in this direction. Wild game is unlikely to ever displace animal agriculture, and not all animal agriculture is cruel and unsustainable. Most of the meat I eat today is from a local bison farm. But if wild bison are to roam the vast prairies again, it will help for us to invest them with as much social value as possible, including as food and sport. It would mean healthier land and healthier people. Large-scale prairie and bison restoration would even be a step toward admitting and righting at least one of the terrible wrongs of the frontier expansion. The dream may be a long shot, but a generation of civically engaged hunters with a clear vision of ecological responsibility and the possibilities of recovery could go a long way toward making it happen.

David Graham Henderson

The Catch and Release Conundrum

"Fascinating as the art of fly fishing is, with all its wonderful tools and the graceful flow of the cast, it is still a way to catch fish, sometimes to eat. There is something—something stronger than mere sentiment—that connects us to the animals we hunt or fish for. Casual hikers and weekend boaters do not know this deep attachment, but hunters and fishermen do, and it is the basis for their willingness to contribute money and countless hours of effort to protect them and their habitat. To deny this is not only to overlook a fundamental dimension of human nature; it opens the way to those who argue that catch and release fishing is merely another way of tormenting other creatures to gratify ourselves, like cock-fighting or bull baiting."

Donald Larmouth, *Riffles and Back Eddies*

One of the things philosophers regularly do is question received truths in order to discover whether these stand on a basis in logic and evidence or wobble on weak argument and unsubstantiated claims. I intend here to engage philosophically and critically with the ethical correctness of catch and release fishing, surely one of the received truths of our time among those of us who practice the angling arts.

The idea of catch and release fishing was once considered an effete affectation practiced only by the wealthy who disdained anything that smacked of the kind of "meat hunting" best left to servants and lower classes. But it has now caught on big time in the fly fishing world—although I suspect not so much among the worm runners and treble hook hardware tossers (some of my best friends, by the way). The enormous rise in the practice of catch and release fishing has multiple origins—certainly in Lee Wulff's now famous and often misquoted dictum that a trout was too valuable a thing to be caught only once and in the CPR (Consider Proper Release) campaign promoted nationally by

Trout Unlimited and other sportsmen's organizations. It is based, too, in the outdoors community's growing awareness of the need to protect and maintain increasingly scarce and/or threatened populations, and finally it has thrived in the growth of fly fishing as practiced increasingly by many sport fishermen for whom the catching matters more than the keeping.

First, as a broad and general definition, let's call an ethical issue one that arises out of a choice, decision, or action that positively or negatively affects the welfare or well-being of some entity. That entity might be the agent him- or herself—I should lose weight, quit smoking; or it might be some other person or persons—I should be truthful, deal fairly, give to charity; or it might be some generalized community such as "wildlife," "nature," "humanity," or even "trout"—I should live sustainably, not pollute, and so on. Thus, actions that have no consequences for anyone's or anything's well-being are not ethical issues. But as should be evident, very many of the choices we make and actions we take, most of which require no deliberation, do have some such consequences and so might be seen as generating ethical issues. Thus, not all ethical issues are the "big" issues, and lots of small decisions, choices, and actions count as ethical issues because they do or can affect someone or something's welfare. Clearly, fishing raises ethical issues because it does or can affect the welfare of individual fish, fishermen, fish populations, and ecosystems.

Second, let me distinguish between ethical issues that support an action or a practice and those that are generated by it. As an example, we note that human societies have long practiced various forms of capital punishment, supported by the notion that persons who engage in particularly heinous crimes against society must be punished with particularly strong measures. The need for society to address such crimes and criminals *supports* the taking of action by society against them. But, as we know, the practice of capital punishment itself *generates* ethical issues: is hanging, guillotining, or beheading ethically permitted? What about the electric chair, firing squad, or lethal injection? Or does the practice itself produce negative ethical consequences such that it can no longer be considered a morally acceptable response even to the most heinous crimes? So we see that there are ethical issues like dealing with serious crimes that lead to or support practices like capital punishment, and there are practices such as capital punishment that themselves produce or generate ethical issues. I want to look at both what ethical concerns support catch and release fishing and what ethical issues are generated by catch and release fishing and to weigh them in the balance.

So first, why catch and release in the first place? The principal argument, A1, put forth in favor of catch and release fishing is that it benefits the resource. Thus the principle, P1: *practice catch and release for the sake of sustaining the resource.* Not that it benefits the individual fish—we'll come back to that later—but that it benefits the fish population or that it benefits the ecosystem by ensuring that trout especially but other game fish as well survive and thrive. The idea here is that the ecosystem and its fish are *intrinsically* valuable, that preservation of nature, or at least some form or part of nature, is a thing worth doing *for its own sake*, regardless of its possible benefits for humans. As Aldo Leopold famously argued, it is the integrity of the system that counts in itself, not for any further aim or purpose. My sense of this is that most of us have come to accept some form of this principle as well as its implication that we are all collectively and individually responsible for supporting and sustaining the integrity of the ecosystem. Of course, some of us do so more actively than others, but certainly those of us who actively engage with nature by fishing, hunting, bird watching, hiking, and other such activities have the greatest responsibility here. I won't take issue with this line of thought; I generally agree with it, though as a professional philosopher I believe that it deserves a far better and more systematic justification than it has hitherto received.

However, it seems clear to me that although most of us accept this idea as true, *it is not the primary motivation* for most of us who practice catch and release some or all of the time. Rather, the motivation is nicely captured in Lee Wulff's handy phrase. It is clear, or should be clear, that in Wulff's view the primary beneficiary of catch and release is the *fisherman,* not the ecosystem. For Wulff and for many of us, we put fish back because we want to be able—or want others to be able—to catch them again. The motivation is self-interested, though not necessarily selfish. The argument, A2, is simple: if we keep all the fish we catch, pretty soon there won't be any fish left for us to catch. And we want to keep catching fish. Thus the principle, P2: *practice catch and release so that we will continue to be able to fish.* Commercial fishermen learned this lesson, though the problem was economic rather than recreational, and the solution was to set limits on the catch. So, however much we are careful about how we play, handle, and release fish, we do so essentially for our own benefit and address the welfare of the fish only as a means to our own ultimate aims and agendas. I am not arguing that there is anything wrong with that; it's just important to be clear about our real purposes here.

But let's return for a moment to the broader environmental justification for catch and release, namely the welfare of the species or the ecosystem. Even if it isn't our primary motivation for catch and release, it surely sits somewhere in our consciousness when we're on the lake or stream. We are told that we should limit our catch, not catch our limit, or that we should practice CPR to ensure that the target species and its web of interrelationships with other species is sustained in a healthy fashion and not threatened by overharvesting. Yet this line of thinking appears to lead us into a problematic realm, thus P3: *if the "resource" or the system is threatened or at risk, then for the sake of its well-being we should avoid all activities that contribute or might contribute to its decline or demise.* Why should we accept halfway measures that allow us to do only a little bit of harm? After all, catch and release still results in some fish mortality. If the sole or primary purpose of catch and release is the protection of the resource, shouldn't we prohibit all actions that might be harmful to the resource? And, of course, we sometimes do; we close seasons by ending the wolf hunt or the sturgeon-spearing seasons in Wisconsin when the "harvest" quota is reached; we establish "no kill" zones on some rivers to protect native species; we close fisheries by ending commercial harvest of striped bass along the Atlantic coast when the population crashes just for that reason. But we do this only rarely because we have to contend with competing interests—the desire of fishermen to exercise their "God-given right" to fish, the economic welfare of the communities that depend on the income from fishing and fishing-related businesses, and so on. And since fishing regulations, like other matters of public policy, are determined only in part by ethics (and often, unfortunately, even less by science) but also and significantly by the adjustments made to many competing interests, we make do with catch and size limits, defined seasons, bait and hook restrictions, and catch and release requirements. This has very little to do with ethics and much to do with politics. P3, then, seems to be ruled out on practical grounds despite the fact that it appears to follow from the preceding considerations.

In summary, then, the ethical matters that *support* the practice of catch and release are: A1, the general concern and respect for the environment and the fish species that are integral to it, and A2, the self-interested motivation of ensuring that there are fish for fishermen to catch, *not necessarily in that order.*

All of the preceding, while necessary to our understanding of the practice, seems relatively, if not completely, uncontroversial. What follows, however, must give us pause. Let's turn now to the question of the ethical issues *generated by* the practice of catch and release fishing. If I am right about what I've said so far, it follows that the well-being of the individual fish is no part of the supporting reasons for catch and release. That being the case, it appears that catch and release fishing, from the standpoint of the fish, cannot be morally justified. This has little to do with the question of whether fish feel pain, though that is a persistent and I think unresolvable question that hinges not so much on data as on definitions. *Morality, ethics, regardless of what theoretical or theological source we take it from, makes a general demand upon us not to deliberately inflict avoidable harm.* Many systems amplify this stricture by especially condemning the harming of the helpless and defenseless. Moreover, most codes of ethics and systems of morality condemn especially strongly the doing of harm for the sake of one's own pleasure, behavior often called "sadistic." Clearly, catching, playing, and handling a fish is necessarily doing it some harm, no matter how minimal. Even if fish don't feel pain in some technical sense, clearly they do not benefit from being punctured by a hook, restrained by a line, "played" to exhaustion, removed from their natural element, handled—however gently and lovingly—by an alien being in an alien environment, "revived," and then released, regardless of what the disputed mortality data show. Dying is not the only possible harm that these fish might suffer. And, not to put too fine a point on it, all this is done for one and only one reason—the pleasure or enjoyment of the fisherman. Rather than catch and release fishing occupying the "moral high ground," as some contemporary apologists would argue, it appears to constitute the moral basement—a morally impermissible practice. An agent, the fisherman, causes harm to another sentient being, a fish, solely for the sake of the agent's pleasure. Paradoxically, then, a practice presumably created for the moral good of preserving and protecting the integrity of the natural environment and the well-being of a species has the consequence of causing the moral evil of wanton harm to individual members of that species.

It is worth noting that these kinds of arguments hold only with regard to a voluntary practice like sport fishing, one that we could choose not to engage in without causing any significant harm to ourselves or our loved ones. The central ethical dilemmas of hunting and fishing in the twenty-first century spring precisely from the fact that we sportsmen and sportswomen do not need to hunt or fish in order to feed ourselves. Even those of us who also—and/or solely—practice catch and release, that is, fish for "sport," are in for a hard ride here. We engage in a practice supported by the desire to do moral good, yet the practice apparently produces moral harm.

Those of us who occasionally catch and kill fish for the table have little to worry about from the moral point of view (other than to defend our actions from the assaults of PETA or the ethical vegetarians). So long as we eat carnivorously, it matters little who kills our food for us, and in fact there may be good moral arguments—I would support them—in favor of our killing our own food. Further, certain harms to individual members of some species may directly serve the good of the species as a whole, for example culling (read "killing") individual animals where overpopulation, invasives, or disease may threaten the entire group.

So what are we to say? Is there some flaw in this argument against the moral acceptability of catch and release? Is there some overriding argument on the other side that outweighs the moral harm done to individual fish by the practice of catch and release by appealing to some greater good that the practice creates? The environmental argument—the good done to the ecosystem and species by not killing fish—so far appears insufficient by itself to override the moral evil of wantonly causing harm to individual sentient beings solely for our own pleasure. Following that argument to its logical conclusion would demand the immediate end to all sport fishing, as P3 requires.

Let me give you some fanciful examples to show this clearly. It is well known that in parts of Europe and elsewhere, migrating songbirds have been regularly trapped in gill nets and killed for the table. Years ago, when I was younger and dumber, I even ate some at a small village café in Italy—delicious! Now suppose that the European Union proclaimed the practice of catch and kill for songbirds to be illegal. However, because of the lobbying of "sportsmen," it was decided to permit songbird catch and release. This would lead many people to set out baits of various kinds, attached to, of course, barbless hooks, by means of which they would be able to catch songbirds, play them until they were exhausted, and then gently and lovingly release them back into the wild. Or suppose instead that over the years, a similar practice had grown up among some indigenous tribes somewhere in the world who, recognizing the interdependence of all nature as such tribes are famously supposed to do, ended their ancient practice of killing all of the local small animals for food (perhaps they saw that larger predators made bigger and better meals and that the predators needed the small animals for their own food) and began instead to practice catch and release of these small animals, with baited, barbless hooks, which they did for their amusement and for the entertainment of their children or for the sake of maintaining their cultural heritage.

We might go further to imagine a race of superior space aliens who decide that catch and release of humans, on the lightest possible tackle and using barbless hooks, would make great sport. Setting aside the question of whether the birds, small mammals, or humans feel pain, what would we say of such behaviors? Wouldn't we condemn them in the strongest terms—this deliberate torture, we would say, of sentient beings solely for amusement and pleasure, for "sport"? So why is it any different for fish?

I am a fisherman. I am a fly fisherman. And I am primarily a catch and release fisherman. There are, for me, only three possibilities: (1) that I am a conscious, deliberate, and regular committer of moral wrong; (2) that, like so many human beings, I am in a state of radical denial, somehow living a life filled with unresolved moral contradictions and/or the hope of some miraculous resolution or revelation; or (3) that there is a moral solution to this paradox, one that has not yet made itself evident.

I said earlier that the good to the species and the ecosystem doesn't appear to outweigh the harm done to the individual fish. This seems intuitively correct and squares with the arguments of philosophers who fault utilitarian arguments that appear to permit or even require that individuals be sacrificed for the sake of the common good. Ursula K. Le Guin's well-known story "The Ones Who Walk Away from Omelas" illustrates this notion clearly. We have no doubt that enslaving a few for the benefit of the many, or torturing one to save others, or killing one's companion to prevent the enemy from killing one's platoon are all prima facie morally impermissible. Not that these examples aren't problematic or that some arguments to the contrary can't at least be proposed. We can give examples—eradicating the Chronic Wasting Disease–infected deer herd to save the uninfected, the mandatory kill regime for nonnative trout species in some parts of Yellowstone, or rotenone poisoning invasive fish species from a stream or lake in order to reintroduce natives—where the case can be made. However, none of these cases appears to provide sufficient analogy to the problem of catch and release, since I take it that, with the exception of the removal of invasive species, no one would argue that we have in the first place any obligation to catch—release or not—for the sake of the well-being of the species or the ecosystem. I'd like to take another look at the case of catch and release from a very different angle, to see whether I can make good on the third option.

Let me first propose a very rough principle of moral respect or moral concern, MR_1. Initially, this principle is intended to reflect actual practice rather than moral preference; that is, it is, for now, descriptive only and not prescriptive. The principle is this: *those entities that are most like me receive the greatest degree of moral respect and concern; that respect declines or diminishes as the entities become less and less like me.* As a matter of empirical fact about how humans tend to make ethical judgments, I think this is indisputable. Thus, we tend generally to give greater weight to the well-being of humans, including especially human fishermen, than to the well-being of fish. But now suppose that, for the sake of argument, we treat this principle as prescriptive. Thus, other white adult male humans like myself deserve the highest degree of moral consideration from me, chimps and bonobos quite a lot, dogs and cats somewhat less, lizards and fish still less, and insects just a tiny bit. (It is not clear where to put porpoises and parrots!) Thus, *we ought to give greater weight to the well-being of humans than to the well-being of fish.* As I said, this is intended to be a very rough sketch and will require a lot of refinement. First of all, there is the problem of what is meant by "like." We should, at the very minimum, mean "like in the morally relevant respects," for it is immediately obvious that, as an empirical fact about how people do make moral judgments, MR_1 has produced horrendous consequences such as the treatment of women as chattel or the enslavement or genocide of other humans whose race or creed is judged to be insufficiently "like" those making the judgments. But the concept "in the morally relevant respects" is going to be a hugely difficult notion to parse. Here the question of just what are the morally relevant differences between fishermen and fish might be the subject of some particularly pithy Gary Larson cartoons.

Alternatively, we might propose the operating practical moral principle MR_2, namely that *those entities that are the most complex neurologically deserve the highest degree of moral respect and concern and that respect declines or diminishes as the entities are seen as less complex.* On the one hand, trout are among those beings that, while sentient, are not much like us; they are cold-blooded, small-brained, relatively neurologically simple, gill-breathing, water-living creatures and therefore pretty low on the scale of entities deserving of our moral consideration under MR_1 or MR_2, maybe just a tad higher than the mayflies, stoneflies, caddisflies, and grasshoppers whose imitations we use to catch them. A difficulty with MR_1 and MR_2 is that in the absence of any clear "objective" criteria, we might in practice come to see those entities for which we have the greatest degree of sympathy—charismatic megafauna, for example—as being the most like us or the most neurologically complex. MR_1 and MR_2 thus simply rationalize our moral prejudices. Moreover, both MR_1 and MR_2 seem prima facie to rule out moral respect for rocks and trees and rivers and ecosystems, the very things that Aldo Leopold enjoined us to respect morally. These are beyond any reasonable limit of "likeness" or neurological complexity.

There is yet another moral ideal, MR_3, that seems to be left out of this way of thinking about what is or is not due moral respect and ethical concern, namely that *we moral agents owe a particularly strong obligation of moral concern to those (or at least some of those) least able to look out for their own welfare.* Infants, the handicapped, the helpless, that is, those most vulnerable should, it seems, receive a very high degree of moral consideration from us. This notion, of course, is one of the ways that we come to see ourselves as morally responsible for, that is, "stewards" of, the well-being of ecosystems and species. Both the individual trout and the species, not to mention the ecosystems in which they live, fall under the principle that the vulnerable are deserving of a high degree of moral respect and consideration. Both are capable of being harmed by human actions, and both therefore require some degree of protection from harm as a part of our moral duty. Moreover, the ethical duty to look after the well-being of the vulnerable seems clearly to be enhanced and strengthened when the possible harms to which they are vulnerable are ones produced by human action (or inaction). Indeed, it may well be the case that our duty to look after the well-being of the vulnerable especially comes into play when the harms that they might suffer are of anthropogenic origin (including, perhaps, the harms they might suffer from human-caused climate change). Thus principle MR_4: *we moral agents owe a particularly strong obligation of moral concern to those least able to look out for their own welfare, particularly when and if the harms to which they are susceptible are of human origin.* After all, it is absurd to suggest (though not so ridiculous as to have never been espoused by some recent philosophers) that we have a duty to protect prey animals from their natural predators. On the other hand, the argument may be reduced to absurdity (*pace* the Jains) that we have a moral duty to protect the ants and beetles that we might inadvertently tread upon or the mosquitoes or midges we might inadvertently inhale while fishing.

Argument MR_4 compels us to avoid harm to those entities especially vulnerable to harm from human agency. It demands this with respect to both "communities" or "systems" or "classes" and also to individual members of those classes. Clearly this duty generates moral conflicts. Our inclinations to see our moral obligations to avoid harm to individual fish under MR_1 or MR_2, however problematic, may well be outweighed by our less vexed sense of duty to avoid or minimize harm to the classes and systems of which they are members under MR_3 and MR_4. Whatever the definitional problems are that challenge MR_1 and MR_2, we have little ethical problem with killing mosquitoes or mice in our homes. (Even the Dalai Lama swats mosquitoes!) At the same time, we do not countenance pulling the wings off flies, so in some way immediate killing seems less wrong than cruelly torturing. In any event, we seem to be drawn to the conclusion that in the "big picture" our moral duty to the class overrides our moral duty to the individual. This is a striking and somewhat disturbing outcome especially with respect to the well-known objections to similar utilitarian arguments.

However, the usual objections appear to bear weight principally with respect to choices between the welfare of individual persons and that of groups of persons. That is, when confronted with the problem of harming one in order to benefit many, most if not all arguments against this utilitarian choice assume that both the one and the many are themselves autonomous rational agents. At the same time, most if not all arguments that support culling or other actions that harm individual members of communities or classes of nonhuman entities assume that the deer or rough fish or invasive plants are not autonomous rational agents. PETA and others might argue that it is mere sentience, rather than moral autonomy, that forbids such practices. While their arguments bear respectful consideration, there is not room here to show why they fail. A far stronger and more defensible argument based upon our principle MR_4 demands that we minimize, avoid, or prevent harm to individual members even of classes whose well-being trumps their individual welfare, without the need for questionable assumptions about their inner states, and it allows us to recognize duties to protect even inanimate entities that clearly lack such inner states.

Is there any way, then, in the light of MR_4, to continue to satisfy our desire (need? passion?) to continue to fly fish in a way that does no harm to our quarry? We have already seen that, however careful the catch and release fisherman may be, there is undeniable harm to the fish, harm whose sole cause is the process that gives pleasure to the fisherman. There is, in fact, a way in which we can preserve most of the aspects of our sport without causing harm to the fish. The elements of the sport—immersion in aesthetically pleasing natural environments, choosing and caring for the tackle, reading the water, matching the hatch, making the cast, presenting a fly in such a way as to overcome the natural wariness of the trout, and achieving a "take" by the fish—can all be accomplished without actually hooking the fish, by simply cutting off the hook at the bend so that although the fish strikes at the fly and may even momentarily hold it, the fish quickly releases the fly and swims away unharmed. There is some movement in this direction among some fly fishers, though, to be sure, it has caught on only among a rather small minority. Note that this practice is clearly suited primarily to dry fly fishing, where the take is visible and obvious, though less satisfactorily to nymphing or swinging streamers. Often, even with normal hooks, the take on a nymph goes undetected by the fisherman until the fish has already released itself. While using cut-off hooks might satisfy principle MR_4, it will not satisfy the fisherman. Moreover, such a proposal would surely be considered risible by the party of "big game" fishermen! Unlike the much-derided proposals that hunters should substitute the camera for the gun, an idea that quite clearly undermines the idea of the hunt whose objective, whether realized or not, must be the kill, fishing with the hook point removed remains fishing.

What is removed under this regime is "catching." Among some fishing communities, the l.r.r., or "long-range release," in which the hooked fish releases itself before it can be brought to net or hand is still considered successful fishing. This proposal simply allows for the auto-release of the fish that takes the fly but is not impaled by the hook. Under this proposal, which appears to satisfy MR_4, catch and release fishing releases the fish prior to the catch; call it "strike and release" perhaps.

To reiterate, if we accept principle MR_4, that we have a moral duty to avoid harming those sentient beings that are vulnerable to being harmed especially by human actions, short of quitting fishing altogether we should abandon catch and release fishing in favor of "strike and release" fishing with the hooks cut off at the bend, so that while much of the practice of dry fly fishing is preserved, the end of the process is the "take," rather than the bringing to hand or to net of the fish. This is clearly a radical proposal, and one unlikely to gain widespread acceptance. As a consequence of having accidentally injured a beautiful cut-throat trout that I caught in a required release area (when elsewhere I would have kept that fish for the table), I experimented with the proposed practice myself during the remainder of the past trout fishing season, and I regret to say that I have found it largely unsatisfying. The practice makes it impossible for the fisherman to distinguish between the successful attempt and the mere "miss," "short strike," or "refusal," though perhaps one must finally accept this as a necessary consequence of a morally correct practice. Moreover, as I pointed out earlier, this tactic is mostly inapplicable to steamer and nymph fishing, which occupy a substantial portion of the fly fisherman's practice. Thus we seem driven back onto the horns of the dilemma.

I suggest then that we have come full circle and are left with a "solution" that appears to work in practice but that remains unsupported by theory, namely P_1, that the utility served by catch and release fishing, a utility that we initially rejected as being insufficient to justify that practice under principle MR_4, finally may be the best that we can do. Not only does this seem to be a clear example of a morally permissible practice in that benefiting the class or community trumps the harm to the individual, but also it is worth noting that, in at least the majority of cases, the individual lives to fight and *to breed* another day. Catch and release is not a morally *required* practice, since it is embedded in the larger practice of fishing, and practicing fishing is clearly not a moral duty for anyone who is not dying of hunger. But if my argument here is correct, catch and release is a morally permissible practice.

As a philosopher, I find this less than adequate. As a fisherman, I believe it is correct and sufficient and that it mirrors the often noted paradox that hunters and fishermen generally feel and display a greater and more genuine knowledge of and love for their quarry than the casual nature lover or animal rights activist. As a philosopher, I desire to find moral clarity and strive for moral certainty. As a person, I recognize that I must accept a world that is filled with moral ambiguity. Other writers have wisely stressed the benefits of the environmental concern and activism generated and sustained by hunters and fishers. Still others have celebrated the spiritual aspects of communion with nature that comes from intense engagement with the natural world and interaction with its life and death cycles. I leave it to them better to express these virtues. While I share the views of many of these authors, I believe that these considerations are and must be secondary to the immediacy of the ethical dilemma raised by catch and release fishing.

Let me end with this admission from Paul Schullery's *The Fishing Life:*

> We fishermen know we're on the defensive here. We do everything we can to reduce the potential for permanently harming the fish. We debarb our hooks to ease the release of the fish. We approach a limited sort of mysticism when we experiment with flies whose hooks are bent closed, or that have no bend at all; unable to hook the fish, we want to see if just the strike alone is enough of a contact (sometimes, almost . . .). We spend more and more time watching and less and less time casting. We suspect, somewhat darkly, that we know where this is headed: to a day when society reverts for a time back to catch-only-if-you-mean-to-kill— a time that will ironically echo the earlier excesses of anglers who killed all too much—and then on to a time when sport fishing goes the way of hunting as an archaic thing people are embarrassed to admit their grandparent did. But we persist because we know, we know damned well, that we are onto something important and that in some troublesome, aching way this catching of fish matters beyond all doubt and all reason.

GREGORY A. CLARK

Vacating the Human Condition

Academics, Hunters, and Animals According to Ortega y Gasset

"The white man has been only a short time in this country and knows very little about the animals; we have lived here thousands of years and were taught long ago by the animals themselves."

David Abram, *Becoming Animal: An Earthly Cosmology*

José Ortega y Gasset famously claimed that hunting is a vacation from the human condition.[1] "The human condition" names humanity's mythic journey out of nature and into freedom. Hunting, then, according to Ortega, involves a temporary return to nature. In this essay, I first contextualize Ortega's claim that hunting is a vacation from history by describing in general terms the received story of the human condition and demonstrating that, according to that story, academics and hunters stand in an oppositional relation to one another. I then explain how Ortega, in contrast, argues that academics and hunters share a way of thinking about and intending the world such that they do not stand opposed to one another. Finally, I extend Ortega's argument to show that his own understanding of hunting as a vacation from the human condition is insufficient to his own analysis. Throughout, I will use the following as equivalent terms: "the story of the human condition," "the story of history," "the story of civilization," and "the story of the progress of freedom." Reflecting on the legitimacy of hunting leads Ortega to rework the story so completely that hunting can't be coherently understood as a means by which hunters temporarily leave history and return with their normative frameworks intact. Instead, Ortega's thinking entails that hunting vacates the basic structure of the story of the human condition.

Academic Dismissal of Hunting

Academics rarely notice the practice of hunting. There are important things on which we humans can be making progress, and "hunting" is not among them. If hunting does catch the attention of an academic, it will be dismissed or condemned in two ways. Hunting looks like a frivolous and retrograde diversion and so is not worth taking seriously. And hunting appears ethically problematic because it intends the death of an innocent animal. Academics can take hunting seriously just long enough to ignore it again or to condemn it.

The Human Condition: A Story of Freedom

Both forms of dismissal are grounded in the self-understanding of academics and, more generally, in humanity's separation from and elevation over nature. Our civilization was built on a story of what it means to be human. This is not a description or a statement of fact. It is a normative account of our human essence and destiny. In abbreviated form, the story goes like this:

> Once everything was part of nature. In nature, all physical events are caused mechanistically and all animal behavior is determined by instinct. Humans became distinct from and higher than nature by developing freedom. Freedom is the capacity to have one's actions guided by reasons we give ourselves rather than by natural causes that are external to our true selves. With the appearance of human freedom, history, properly speaking, first began, for history is the story of the progress of freedom. History progresses as humans extend the breadth and the depth of actual freedom. The instrumental use of reason enables humans to conquer nature, that is, to develop technology so that the natural world reflects our will. The moral use of our reason enables humans to develop political structures that recognize and extend further freedom for all. The name for the technological and political forces of freedom is "civilization." The human condition is to be on this journey from nature to freedom and to be the agent, the material, and the product of our own actions.

According to this story, to be biologically human—to be an animal we now classify as *homo sapiens sapiens*—is not sufficient to be fully human. Conceptually and historically, biological humanity has not been enough for admittance into "humanity" as a shared moral community. Our civilization's treatment and justification of the treatment of "savages" and "barbarians," that is, uncivilized peoples, make this clear. Our shared moral community is constituted by understanding oneself through the story of civilization as presented here.

Academics fit into the story by playing a crucial role: they articulate the knowledge that enables us to extend the story as far as possible. When we find limitations built into the story, academics suggest revisions for the sake of greater extension. Thus this story identifies academics as the story-tellers whose narratives determine the boundaries of our shared community. According to the story, the way we tell the story determines the place of animals and of hunters in the progress of freedom.

| Animals |

The story of the human condition not only explains what it means to be human; it defines, in negative terms, what it means to be animal. Animals are *that from which* humans distinguish themselves. They belong to nature; they act on instinct; they are not and cannot be free. In developing their reason, humans are leaving their own animal nature behind.

Recently some academics have argued that animals should have a positive role to play in our narrative. Animals are intelligent. They communicate with one another. Some have something like language. Some can be taught systems to communicate with humans. We reward and punish them as though we hold them responsible for their actions. They feel pleasure and pain, and they have an interest in the things that happen to them. Accordingly, the argument goes, animals need to be included in our story of freedom in some way. Our moral community should expand to include animals.

| Hunters |

The story of civilization, with its account of what it means to be human and what it means to be an animal, makes modern hunting an enigma for academics. When academics turn to think about hunting directly, they encounter it in two forms. First, anthropologists and historians may study hunting as it is and was practiced by hunter-gatherers. Hunter-gatherers seem to offer a glimpse of the human life-ways at the beginning of history. They are primitive humans still enslaved to nature, living a life that is "solitary, poor, nasty, brutish, and short." The hunting of hunter-gatherers, on our story, is the least developed form of reason. It marks a time when we had only just begun a journey toward freedom.

In addition, academics think of hunting as they imagine it practiced by rural populations, modern hunters who continue to hunt even though they are not driven to hunt by either hunger or instinct. Through the modern technological use of reason, food is available to anyone who can pay, but modern hunters instead use their reason to hunt. It is as if modern hunters use their freedom to return to the site of their own enslavement. They are a textbook

Gregory A. Clark

example of "bad faith." Worse, modern hunters, as depicted by media devoted to hunting, seem to take joy in killing animals. In this, they unreasonably refuse to expand our moral community, with its rights and freedoms, to include animals, and they show themselves as unworthy members of the moral community.

Academics and hunters, according to these accounts, are mirror opposites of each other. Academics are highly trained, dispassionate researchers seeking to discover truth and defend freedom. Academics' thinking and knowing are founded on reason, and their actions have made and continue to make the world more rational and free. Academics see themselves as the vanguard of the progress of civilization, the heroes of their own story. This, in truncated form, accounts for why many academics view hunters with suspicion and hunting as either irrelevant or atrocious. . . .

| Ortega's Argument That Hunting Is a Vacation from the Human Condition |

We can now specify what Ortega meant when he said that hunting is a vacation from the human condition. For Ortega, to hunt is to return to just before the beginning of history, before any social contracts with their rights, privileges, and responsibilities. It is to take a break from the arrangements to which we give our tacit consent because they promise (civil) freedoms. So far, Ortega's views are compatible with the story of the human condition presented earlier.

Next, however, Ortega argued that hunting should be afforded a limited measure of legitimacy because of its timeless quality. Ortega accepted that life is given to humans "empty" and that humans must choose how they will occupy their own lives. And he accepted that the possible forms of occupation are limited by our place in history, so most occupations in the past are no longer legitimate possibilities today. After all, one cannot decide to be one of the Knights of the Round Table. Those historical conditions no longer exist. Every Renaissance Faire in the country demonstrates that the attempt to return to Camelot is a farce. However, Ortega argued that any occupation that does not depend on specific historical conditions, which precedes all history, will always be a permanent possibility for humans. He actually named four such occupations: conversing, dancing, racing, and hunting.[2] Ortega's point was that life is not given to humans *totally* empty. And his interest, of course, lay in hunting, which he said names a "deep and permanent yearning in the human condition."[3] For Ortega, when hunters hunt, they are really hunting. They are not dressing up like hunters and pretending to hunt. He noted, "It has always been at man's disposal to escape from the present to that pristine form of being a man, which, because it is the first form, has no historical suppositions. History begins with that form. Before it there is only that which never changes: that which is permanent, Nature. 'Natural' man is always there, under the changeable historical man."[4] For Ortega, then, hunting is always a legitimate option, one that cannot be made obsolete by the progress of history because it is legitimated by nature and not by the story of the human condition. Put another way, hunting, on Ortega's account, is a vacation from the human condition.

If Ortega was right, when we take this vacation, we find that the world is put together somewhat differently outside history. First, the hunters do not find themselves alone. The academics too are there, not in an oppositional role but thinking and looking very much like the hunters. Second, hunters recognize that our stories cannot be stories only of human agency. Our own identity and actions as humans must be understood through our relation to the agency of other animals.

| The Academic |

For Ortega an academic is not first of all a soldier in the vanguard of the progress of freedom who on that basis opposes the hunter. (Ortega raised the question of what it means to be a "philosopher" rather than an "academic." Here, I conflate the two terms. Many features of the philosopher and philosophical practice can be generalized to academics and academic practice, but perhaps not all.) More fundamentally, for Ortega, the academic is someone who can truly think. She has the ability to understand that our story of the human condition is a way of thinking about what makes us human, and she has developed the ability to think critically about that story. For Ortega, an academic does not primarily pursue "inertial thinking," lines of thought laid down by and assumed by others. Rather, she sees how a line of thought loses touch with the reality it tries to describe and makes corrective adjustments. To understand Ortega's reconceptualizing of the academic, we need to grasp these two distinct forms of thought.

| Inertial Thinking |

For Ortega, inertial thinking begins with "an idea true in itself," but then, imperceptibly, it is itself captured by that idea, and it "continues thinking vaguely and mechanistically in the same direction."[5] For example, Ortega noted that the deer population had been declining for the previous thirty years. (He was writing in 1942.) Thus, if we take the past thirty years as marking a law of nature and we extrapolate backward to the Stone Age, we conclude that the deer must have been so thick that you couldn't turn around without tripping over one. Here is an obvious case where the initial idea is true and the extrapolation is false. Yet, Ortega pointed out, it is easy to think this way without realizing it.

Ortega's example may be overly simple, but it helps to get at two dimensions of inertial thinking that often characterize more sophisticated lines of reasoning. First, inertial thinking is thinking in the shadow cast by "habit, tradition, [and] the commonplace."[6] These sources make possible, and this is no small thing, the shared intelligibility of the world. But, stated differently, they also offer us the world with the hard work of understanding it already completed. Inertial thinking is guided by the assumptions built into our initial ideas.

Second, inertial thinking moves in one direction. With the work of understanding completed, all that remains is to follow out the implications and applications of an idea. Implications and applications are fascinating in themselves, and they can be carried out with surprisingly novel and refined methods, but they simply follow the direction set by the initial idea.

Inertial thinking offers many attractions. Parts of academia have always harbored a dream that thinking could be reduced to method and that method could be reduced to technique. If we had an ideal language, or a sophisticated calculating machine, or some perfect embodiment of technological reason, our hard problems would at last be solved. If we only paid attention to our technique, we could let the technique pay attention to the subject matter. We could say, with Leibniz, "Come, let us calculate together."

Ortega, however, claimed that inertial thinking is an incomplete vision of academic thought. Though application and implication are challenging in some ways, they can also be mechanistic, rule-bound procedures that are indifferent to questions of content, relevance, appropriateness, and importance. Application and implication can make the ruts of thought straighter and deeper, but they can't show us how or when to get out of the rut.

| Alert Thinking |

In contrast, Ortega saw alert thinking as "always ready to rectify its trajectory, to break its direction, attentive to the reality outside it."[7] It is tempting to think of alert thinking as the opposite of inertial thinking—but this would itself be a form of inertial thinking. Alert thinking *presupposes* inertial thinking as a *first moment*. All thinking charts a course with an orientation or a direction set for us by habit, tradition, or the commonplace. Inertial thinking stays the course and may not even notice whether it actually achieves what it set out to do. Alert thinking starts in a certain direction, but it is always on the lookout for signs that the journey is not progressing rightly. It constantly checks its course with other reference points and makes midcourse corrections. These checkpoints and new trails will challenge what everyone (including the academic) assumes is known to be true. Alert thinking requires that we "live in a perpetual state of detachment before one's own convictions."[8] Even then, alert thought makes no promises. It may dislodge our old assumptions, but it may not provide an alternative. For Ortega, academics who think this way "always runs the risk of returning empty-handed,"[9] and their critics will notice. But Ortega was also aware that alert thinking also opens the academic's attention to "the great rotundity of the horizon" and to the "thrill of delight" when thinking succeeds.[10]

On Ortega's account, alert thinking is hard work. Some lines of thought may be so powerful and so widely shared that we cannot imagine what it would mean to call them into question. Some seem so comprehensive that we cannot conceive that anything could stand outside them to serve as a reality check or point to an alternative. To think beyond these lines of thought is to already have one foot outside them.

Our story of civilization as the progress of freedom, as the human condition, constitutes one such line of thought. It is so comprehensive and fundamental that we can't imagine how ideas can stand outside our story of increasing freedom. Academics who fail to question that story dismiss the hunter as a prehistoric relic or a modern idiot. However, if, like Ortega, an academic alertly questions the story, she can reconceptualize what it means to be an academic (or a hunter or even a human). Then she may discover in hunters and academics a kindred spirit.

| The Hunter |

As we've seen, there are two kinds of hunters in our received story of the human condition. The hunter-gatherer—who stands on the border of the division between nature and freedom, and instinct and reason—was the first version of what it means to be human. But that vision of humanity is completely exhausted and has been surpassed by the rise of agriculture, industry, and now the digital age. The second kind of hunter, the modern hunter, is dismissed as a hick who doesn't know that in the twenty-first century the first version of humanity is passé. Hunters are those who have no role to play in the advance of civilizational freedom, and where they continue to exist, they are an embarrassment.

This story is so natural and obvious that our heads begin to nod, and our sleep is taken as assent. Ortega's goal was to remain alert in thinking about real hunters and real hunting, "to hunt down the hunt."[11] In order to do this, he started with the most traditional opening move of academic philosophy: he made hunting puzzling. He showed how traditional views of hunting are inattentive, don't square with actual experience, lead us into contradictory thoughts, and so lead us into a number of dead ends. That is, he tried to wrest the wonderful puzzlement of hunting from inertial thinking. He asked, "what the devil kind of occupation is this business of hunting?"[12]

He then made the second standard move in the philosophical tradition: he searched for a definition. A definition does not first of all direct our attention to marginal cases or poor exemplars. Rather, it identifies the best and clearest

Gregory A. Clark

account so that we can determine cases that do or do not fit within the definition. Ortega pointed out that, "As everyone knows, every well-informed rule only transforms the definition of an exemplary reality into an imperative. If someone says: to hunt well you should first of all and above all, do such-and-such, we must understand that what is being said is: really and truly to hunt is to do that."[13]

| Universal Attention |

So, for Ortega, what is it to hunt? He quoted from his friend Edward, Count Yebes, a hunter and the author of the book *Veinte Años de Caza Mayor* (*Twenty Years as a Big Game Hunter*) for which Ortega wrote *Meditations on Hunting* as an introduction: "Look, look, and look again; at all times, in all directions, and in all circumstances. Look as you go along; look while you are resting; look while you are eating or lighting a cigar; up, down, back over the ground you have just covered, at the hill crests, at the ledges and dells, with binoculars and the naked eye."[14] To hunt is to look.

Ortega, the philosopher academic, revised his friend's vocabulary and introduced a distinction. For Ortega, "to hunt" means "to be attentive." But there are different ways to be attentive, so Ortega distinguished "mere looking" from "being alert." Mere looking focuses on one point to the exclusion of everything else because you assume that what interests you lies precisely in that direction. Being alert is "completely opposite." The alert person still uses his eyes to see; he does not presume to know where the object of interest will present itself. Being alert employs a "'universal' attention," which keeps itself open to all directions. The attention of the hunter is not mere looking; it is being alert.

For Ortega, it is not by accident that "mere looking" and "inertial thinking" share a tendency to tunnel vision and that "being alert" and "alert thinking" are both versions of universal attention. Philosophers have long recognized that they share the attitude of being alert or of universal attention with hunters. Ortega noted that historically, "when a philosopher wanted to name the attitude in which he operated when musing, he compared himself to the hunter."[15] That is, Ortega argued, academics have developed their understanding of themselves and of their tasks by finding in the hunter and in hunting a reflection of themselves.

The emphasis on universal attention gets at the scope and direction of the hunter's and the academic's intentional attitudes, and this is the point of comparison Ortega emphasized. But alert thinking also names the ability to leave behind the habitual, the traditional, and the obvious. Ortega's work enables us to see clear parallels here between the academic and the modern traditional hunter.

Ortega acceded to the traditional story that humans have lost their animal instincts and replaced them with reason so that "reason" names what is uniquely human.[16] Ortega used the word "reason" in three distinct ways.

Mimetic Reason: First, "reason," as our supplement to make up for our deficient instincts, is just our good memory and a capacity for fantasy and imagination.[17] This form of reason makes humans masters of observation and imitation.

Mimetic reason is the capacity for human hunters to be alert in the ways noted earlier. It enables hunters to imitate the look, the smell, and the movement of the animals they hunt. They do this not only to fool the animals. They do it to imagine their way into the instincts of other animals. They try to experience the world as the animal does. In imitating the exterior of the animal, the hunter makes her way into the interior of the animal. The human hunter "cannot pursue if he does not integrate his vision with that of the pursued."[18] That is, the hunter is "imitating the perpetual alertness of the wild animal."[19] Mimetic reason makes possible the hunter's alertness by establishing a mimetic relation with the animals hunted.

Instrumental Reason: The second form of reason I will refer to is "instrumental reason." It envisions and creates technologies. From the standpoint of the traditional story of the progress of freedom, this is the kind of reason that enables us to conquer nature and bend it to our will. From Ortega's perspective, instrumental reason releases humans from the work of being alert and makes it likely we can succeed by merely looking. This form of reason can provide the basis for some forms of inertial thinking that we noted in academics.

According to Ortega, instrumental reason can also affect hunting. The technologies produced by instrumental reason augment the powers of the hunter or they trick, change, or cancel out the instincts of the animal. We see the attraction of instrumental reason at work in advertisers' promises (mostly unfulfilled) of success if one uses their new hunting gear. But technical superiority is not always an empty promise. On the contrary, it can turn hunting into *destruction* (Ortega's term); high fences and spotlighting, to name two examples, make success so easy that most states have made them illegal. Ortega referred to this second consequence of instrumental reason when he wrote, "reason can be described more appropriately as the greatest danger to the existence of hunting."[20]

Self-reflexive Reason: To these two functions of reason, Ortega added a third that I will call "self-reflexive reason." Self-reflexive reason is the capacity to recognize that the first and second functions of reason can come into conflict. Instrumental reason can make alert reason unnecessary or impossible,

Gregory A. Clark

and when it does humans no longer hunt; they destroy. Self-reflexive reason also enables the human to step out of the story of technological progress that guides instrumental reason and put on the brakes. In Ortega's words, "reason's most important intervention consists precisely in restraining itself, in its limiting its own intervention."[21]

Ortega saw self-reflexive reason as essential to hunting in two ways. First, it recognizes that in order to hunt, the hunter must leave the animal "free to practice its wily defenses."[22] Second, self-reflexive reason requires "a conscious and almost religious humbling of man [sic] which limits his superiority and lowers him toward the animal."[23] If hunting is possible, on Ortega's view, the hunter must "avoid making the prey and the hunter excessively unequal";[24] hunting requires that humans rely on being alert.

This "conscious and almost religious humbling" that occurs in self-reflexive reason shows that, for Ortega, hunting involves a *return* to mimetic reason. The modern hunter does what the hunter-gatherer does not; she *imitates* the hunter-gatherer. To do this, she steps outside the current technology that is on offer. She refuses to follow the path that says more technology will make hunting even better. Most radically, she no longer understands her own character or action as a part of history, the habitual and so obvious story of the past ten thousand years of civilization. Hunting involves not just the development of universal attention. It is also requires leaving the path implied by the habitual, the traditional, and the commonplace.

Thus, in *Meditations on Hunting*, Ortega could claim that the academic and the hunter are not opposed to each other as the story of the human condition claims. They are actually much like each other, and this points to a different line of thought. That is, the hunter is not by nature the failure of reason and freedom but rather their embodiment. For Ortega, the hunter does not play the role of the rear guard, the counterpart of the academic vanguard, in the quest for freedom. Rather, he saw the hunter-gatherer's universal attention standing as the original model of both the academic and the modern hunter, a model to which they each return for their own self-understanding and that suggests its own orientation for thinking beyond the story of the human condition. The second way Ortega's account diverges from the traditional story of the human condition emerges from this understanding of the role of animals in hunting.

| Animals and Hunting |

The traditional story of the human condition is a story about human freedom, human history, and human civilization. All agency is human agency. History begins when humans start to take charge of their environment and their food sources. According to this story, hunting is something humans have done and sometimes continue to do to animals. Animals are passive; hunting is done to them. Some modern (for example, animal liberationist) versions of this story claim that hunting should cease and that we should find ways to expand our definition of our moral community to include the interests or even rights of animals so that animals too may participate in the advantages humans enjoy because of the progress of freedom. Still, history remains a human-all-too-human story. Ortega thought this view of animals and hunting wrongly assumes that hunting is a uniquely human activity. But, as Ortega was aware, hunting was not invented by Cabela's. It was not invented even by hunter-gatherers. And it never was a way for humans to conquer nature. Agriculture and industry did that.

For Ortega, hunting is an activity of animals such that to hunt is to be an animal: "The most obvious thing in the world [is] that hunting is not an exclusively human occupation, but occurs throughout almost the entire zoological scale."[25] Specifically, hunting occurs when two sets of instincts have developed in response to the hunting relationship: "This is what hunting really is: *a contest or confrontation between two systems of instincts.*"[26] A unique instinctual system makes each animal what it is, and for many species, to be the animal they are entails hunting. Conversely, for other species, to be the animal they are requires being hunted. So, the wolf and the deer each know the other "in their instinctive depths."[27] According to Ortega, without hunting, there would be neither deer nor wolf. This is the metaphysics of ecology, the metaphysics of hunting.

Animals, then, on Ortega's account, are not the passive victims of hunters. Animals too are hunters, and both as hunter and as hunted they remain agents. This means that when humans hunt, they do so *as* animals and, more specifically, as human animals playing a role in an ecological system.

Here Ortega confronts us with a puzzle. If hunting is a confrontation between two systems of instincts, how do humans hunt, since humans do not hunt by instinct? Ortega solved this problem in two ways. First, he claimed that instinct, even in the animal, is really its form of being alert: "for him [the animal] living is being perpetually alert for the hunter."[28] At the end of the *Meditations* Ortega returned to this point: "But this itself—life as complete alertness—is the attitude in which the animal exists in the jungle. Because of it he lives from within his environment."[29] So, we can say that hunting is a contest between animals with two different ways of being on the alert for each other.

Second, while the hunter does lack the instincts of the animal, she has mimetic reason, which enables her to imitate the animal's alertness. The hunted animal is the original form of the embodied alertness of the hunter. To say humans' natural occupation is to hunt is to say that humans are naturally animals that hunt by imitating other animals.

For someone who can think only within the story of the human condition, this may seem problematic, and Ortega recognized that his account might not

Gregory A. Clark

sound attractive. We have already noted his claim that hunting will require the "conscious and almost religious humbling of man [*sic*] which . . . lowers him toward the animal."[30] Later in the *Meditations* Ortega mused, "It is possible that I may have offended some hunter who presumes that my definition of hunting implies that I have treated him as an animal." And indeed, this is exactly what he had done. However, he continued, "But I doubt that any real hunter will be offended."[31]

The implication of Ortega's account for the traditional story of the human condition is clear. From Ortega's perspective, the original actors are animals. We imitate them. Human actions and human history cannot be understood as the story of human agency alone. Our stories must also be the stories of animals. What had been a story about humans, to which we recently started thinking about adding animals as an appendix, now becomes a story in which animals have a central role and humans may enter in supporting roles. The epigraph of this essay points in the direction Ortega was traveling: "The white man has been only a short time in this country and knows very little about the animals; we have lived here thousands of years and were taught long ago by the animals themselves."[32] This does not mean that hunter-gatherers learned only by observing animal behavior. It refers to a time when humans and animals could speak with one another and share stories. Those stories had nonhuman animals not only as their subjects but also as their tellers.

An academic within the story of the human condition would consider this claim that animals are our teachers childish or puzzling. This is not the kind of shared community with animals that academics have in mind. But it is precisely the sort of claim made by many communities of hunter-gatherers. The two perspectives cannot be reconciled.

| Vacating the Human Condition |

Ortega claimed that hunting is a vacation from the human condition. Merely a vacation. "This is the reason men hunt. When you are fed up with the troublesome present, with being 'very twentieth-century,' you take your gun, whistle for your dog, go out to the mountain, and, without further ado, give yourself the pleasure during a few hours or a few days of being 'Paleolithic.'"[33] No worries, then. Hunting is just a vacation from the human condition.[34]

Ortega drew on the language of "vacation" because he was caught between the force of the story of the human condition on the one hand and his own criticisms of that story as it relates to hunting on the other hand. The appeal to a vacation was an attempt to have it both ways.

It is unclear, however, whether Ortega's notion of a vacation is coherent. First, one cannot take a vacation from the human condition. The story of the human condition offers a normative account of what makes us human: to be human is to be progressing from nature toward freedom in ways made possible by civilization's technology and political systems. A vacation is a temporary departure from the norm in ways allowed by the norm. But the human condition, as traditionally told, does not allow for suspension of those norms, not even temporarily. One does not simply take a vacation from being human or from belonging to the human moral community. One cannot put on or take off the human condition the way one changes from a business suit into a ghillie suit. The stories by which we order our lives, within which we love, work, and die, do not let us go, nor we them, with ease. To take a vacation from being subject to a set of norms is to deny the validity of those norms. Those who accept the received story of the human condition are right to think it is incompatible with hunting.

In addition, the word "vacation" downplays the force of Ortega's actual arguments. Ortega's arguments fail to reconcile the contradiction between hunting and the traditional story of the human condition. In its received form, the story of the human condition produces illusions and rests on false dichotomies. It offers flawed characterizations of academics, of hunters, of animals, and of hunting. It misconstrues the central conflicts that drive the plot. Ortega's alternative claims—that hunting is a natural occupation of humans, that academics and hunters engage their worlds in similar ways, and that recognition of the primacy of animal agency is necessary to understanding human actions—deny central positions of the story of the human condition. Ortega's views show that hunting offers a vantage point from which to advance criticisms and alternatives to civilization's founding myths. Hunting is legitimate, and it is a break with, not a temporary break from, the human condition. The implication of Ortega's argument is not that we should have the option of a vacation. The conclusion is that the story of the human condition is no longer an option; it must be vacated. Once we have seen the limits of that story, we cannot return to it afterward as if it nothing has changed.

In fact, we cannot help but return to it, not because we still think it is true but because it is so widely assumed that it still benefits us in specific ways and because we still have not found an alternative story. Ortega's argument entails that we should vacate this story, but the reality is that we have no place to vacate to.

It seems as though to vacate the human condition would require that we no longer be human. This is mind-boggling. It is true in the sense that it would mean we would no longer inhabit the story of the human condition. People may see us as we have seen others who didn't fit into our story. But the human condition is not a description of a matter of fact. It is a widely shared story of who and what belongs to our moral community. And yet, bewildering as these questions are, this is precisely what is required of an alert thinker, one who can recognize when prejudices, even prejudices that have lasted ten thousand years, have led us astray. Nothing is more traditional, habitual, or common-place than the story of human progress out of nature into the bright future of freedom. Nothing is less surprising than the claim that academics are urbane sophisticates, that hunters are backward rubes, and that animals have no stories of their own. Everyone knows these things. To step outside the human condition is to question these assumptions that constitute human history.

We have not even begun to reconstitute a perspective outside history. Ortega points us to the hunter, and there are accounts of anthropologists, a few firsthand accounts, and very few hunting communities still functioning today. The hunter has learned to see the world from the animal's perspective, to see, hear, smell, taste, and feel the animal world. The hunter can know what it is like to be a deer, or a wolf, or a bat. This is how the hunter takes up a position outside the human condition. The hunter imitates the animal.

Vacating the human condition requires that there be a community with an orienting story of some sort to replace it. The experience of hunting gives the hunter some basis for hope that something is there to catch us. Only if we vacate the human condition will we be in a position to recognize, as Ortega urged, the agency exercised by nonhuman animals and to hear the stories they tell of their actions. Only then may we be taught by the animals themselves.

Confessions of a Sublime Ape

Contemporary hunters defend their passion in a variety of ways. Clearly, the exaggerated masculine stereotype of the manly hick mountain man, which is fueled by the absurd antics of *Duck Dynasty,* Ted Nugent, and those of their ilk, provides no justification for hunting. A more salient proposition is that hunters have a profound understanding of the natural world and know their environment intimately, perhaps more so than any other outdoor enthusiast. To skillfully imitate a hen with mouth, slate, and box calls in order to coax a tom turkey from the next ridge to the gun or to pattern and kill a resident big buck, the hunter needs to "know" the animal, to think as it thinks, outdoorsmen will argue. However, this intimacy can be achieved without the killing, as Doug Peacock illustrates in his book *Grizzly Years,* which documents the time he spent living in close contact with grizzlies, unarmed, in the wilderness of the American West. Hunting is also sometimes defended as a source of sustenance. Hunters hunt to put food on the table. And while the fact that there is something deeply satisfying about eating game that one has harvested cannot be denied, in this day and age there are far more cost- and time-effective ways to procure dinner. Subsistence hunters are few and far between in the Western world. As Edward Abbey has argued in his antisport hunting essay "Blood Sport," from an ethical standpoint "killing [must be] justified by the need" and we are not hunting "in earnest"; therefore, "hunting sinks to the level of mere fun, 'harvesting animals,' *divertissement,* sadism, or sport."[1]

Perhaps we do hunt, as Abbey suggests, out of a selfish urge to engage in pure creature pleasure. We pursue our quarry to find moments of the sublime, to revive impressions within our psyche that are denied us by the world in which we find ourselves. Hunting in the modern world is an endeavor largely suited to satisfy visceral primitive impulses the contemporary urban/suburban reality forces us to repress. Scrabbling away at work, scrambling to acquire material plenty, enmeshed in a technocratic culture that strips us of our humanity, the world of steel, concrete, and plastic robs us of a piece of our soul. As Abbey argues in his novel *Good News,* humanity today suffers from "a failure of nerve" and "paralyzed emotions."[2] Crowded into "unreal" cities, Abbey asserts, humankind lives in "a landscape owned by corporations and dominated by gigantic machines—the ever-growing cities [assume] the shape of nightmare. Not a nightmare of horror but a nightmare of dreariness, a routine and customary tedium."[3] To hunt, then, is to pursue the sublime, thereby regaining freedom and a sense of self. The contemporary hunter/thinker takes to the field to accomplish what Annie Dillard advocates attempting: "to learn, or remember, how to live," she wrote in "Living like Weasels," to gain "something of the purity of living in the physical senses . . . [to get] out of your ever-loving mind and back to your careless senses."[4]

In the act of seeking and experiencing the sublime, humankind gains autonomy and confidence. The resultant emotion coming at the conclusion of a fearful or fearsome moment is what stimulates the latent sublimity in one's mind. Sublime impressions put one in touch with one's own inner power and allow one's mind and body to wander. Rambling the countryside and heaths, trekking the misty bogs and quagmires in pursuit of game, the hunter is unfettered and untethered. This notion of freedom and esteem won through adventures outside society is expressed in the memoirs and poetry of the Alaskan homesteader John Haines, who spent decades of his life self-sufficiently hunting, trapping, and fishing in the bush outside Richardson, Alaska. Haines explains in "Poem of the Forgotten" that he went into the wilderness "well quit of the world,"[5] and in his memoir *The Stars, the Snow, the Fire* he says that while there "my mind bent away from humanity . . . I entered for a time the old life of the forest, became part fur myself."[6] What Haines lost in terms of human connections while immersed in sublime wilderness he gained in self-confidence and personal liberty, admitting that his isolated hunting and trapping life gave him "a strange, mixed enjoyment" in having learned "so many intricate methods of death, brooded upon and perfected."[7] This powerful pull of the sublime is expressed throughout the hunting literature canon. This is the philosophical underpinning and justification of why people today continue to hunt. As Edmund Burke contends in his book *A Philosophical Enquiry into the Sublime and Beautiful,* the key concepts relating to the sublime are terror, pain, astonishment, solitude, silence, and obscurity. By focusing on these concepts, this essay illustrates how the hunt startles humankind out of banality and emancipates its inner ego.

There is a savagery to hunting that cannot be denied. Even if the hunt is a "fair chase" and the killing is done with respect, even when the killing is humane and fast, even when the animal is artfully processed and tastefully prepared, even when the gentleman-hunter adroitly lofts the barrel of his well-polished firearm skyward with great dignity and eloquence, there is a brutality to the affair. The hunter derives pleasure from the violence of the shotgun blast, the explosion of firearms, the gleaming hunting knife; there is a terrible excitement to it all. As Burke posits, "whatever is fitted . . . to excite the ideas of pain, and danger . . . whatever is any sort terrible . . . is a source of the sublime."[8] Pain and terror are transcendent emotions closely associated with the awe-inducing sublime. They are also emotions that the huntsman knows firsthand in his or her death dealings. In order to experience the sublime, the threat of danger or death must be present. And some hunts certainly possess this quality: hunting Kodiak brown bears with revolvers in a steep mountain thicket, hog-doggin' with a bowie knife (running pit bulls on feral pigs in the swamp pits of interior Florida), or standing down a charging rhinoceros or pachyderm with a high-powered rifle in African bush country certainly sparks a feeling of fearsome awe in the participants.

On the other hand, most contemporary hunts do not involve this element of personal danger. But the experience of the sublime is still open to hunters not in immediate peril through their ability to empathize with and contemplate the pain and terror of their quarry. The threat to and panic of the animals energizes, boosts adrenaline, and animates hunters' thoughts and emotions, leading them to a sublime state. Hunters know, as Burke knows, that the sounds of "animals in great pain or danger, are capable of conveying great ideas" and that "the angry tones of wild beasts are equally capable of causing a great and awful sensation."[9] Often, hunters experience the sublime vicariously through their victims, as their act of killing puts them in a unique, powerful, and thought-enhancing condition.

To dole out an animal's death is to act like God, and the Greeks knew well how the spirit of fear, terror, and pain evoked in the hunt aligns with notions of a savage deity. To have this ultimate power is a lesson in mortality and primality, and it evokes the sublime. In the "Homeric Hymn to Artemis," Artemis, "the chaste virgin of the noisy hunt, who delights in her shafts and strikes down the stag," is the embodiment of a frightful sublimity. She is worshipped and revered for her mastery—and her callousness.[10] A skilled huntress, she revels in the bloody harvest, the tumult, the terror, all of which exemplify her power: "the peaks of the lofty mountains tremble, the dark woods echo terribly to the shrieks of wild beasts, and both the earth and fish-filled sea are shaken. But she with dauntless heart looks everywhere to wreak destruction on the brood of animals."[11] Artemis, in all her savage glory, provides a model for hunters that still holds true today. She takes pride in her weaponry and uses it to deftly deal her death blow; she is mistress of her domain and stands proud upon her bloody pedestal. She is triumphant, singular, and terrible.

Michael C. Ryan

Of course, the quarry's terror and the huntsman's contemplation of it are brought about by the threat of pain. The exhausted rabbit squeals as it is cornered and the quivering hounds mash their snarling muzzles upon it. The wounded black bear cries as it bleeds out deep in the bush. The downed doe, knocked over in the pumpkin patch, defenseless, unable to flee, bleats as she is straddled, her ears pulled back, the razor-sharp blade applied to her throat. In these moments, the predating hunter understands Burke's claim that "Strength, violence, pain, and terror, are ideas that rush upon the mind together."[12]

Importantly, though, hunters are not sadists who get their kicks from the torment and suffering of animals. Hunters pride themselves on killing their game humanely and quickly. But hunters also understand that they are meting out pain upon other creatures, and they are not entirely hardened to this fact. Although it is not the hunters who directly experience the emotions and impulses of sublime fear or pain, their participation in these killing rites forces them to confront their own tenuous grip on mortality, the possibility of themselves unpredictably being seized up and rendered impotent, limp, useless, obsolete. Just as surely as the dying animal gasps its final breaths, its blank eyeballs staring up at the hunter, hunters know that someday others will circle around them to watch their rheumy-eyed death rattle as their souls drift off into the ether. It is through this empathetic and perhaps ironic recognition of the pain and terror and inevitability of death that hunters experience feelings of the sublime. While death and the contemplation of death are clearly not the same thing, hunters' active role in and observance of death nonetheless stir up impressions of the sublime buried in the psyche.

Haines acknowledges this in *The Stars, the Snow, the Fire*, when he describes the "blunted panic and bewilderment" of a moose after it has been shot.[13] But Haines has said that he is also "haunted" by the deaths of animals, an impression that is made clear in his poem "Victims," in which he imagines the suffocation of an animal he has snared: "parting the branches, the doomed / animal chokes on his own / breath, and sees, as in a red mist, / his own dripping carcass."[14] While it would be ethically irresponsible and do the sport damage to suggest that hunters revel in the pain they inflict and that they seek out game in order to enjoy their discomforting deaths, it can be argued that causing and observing—seeing, hearing, even smelling—an animal's pain and death *do* have an elevating effect on hunters: these moments of painful, transcendent rapture force them to confront and contemplate mortality and sublimity. What hunters gain through these experiences is a reminder of the human animal within— the primal, the elemental, the instinctive—that portion of the human psyche sublimated by social contracts and economic systems and cultural and familial imperatives. This is precisely how Haines attempts to explain the impact of his hunting and trapping on his thoughts and actions. Haines says that his intimate relationship with the animals he kills reminds him of his true, visceral nature:

"behind that immediate and apparent violence they are as well, and perhaps above all, images of a lost and intenser being . . . and still that lost being pursues us, no matter how remote and abstract our sensibilities have become. The mark of the forest is on us, never to be burned away."[15]

Burke asserts that the feeling of astonishment is the effect of the sublime in its highest degree. This feeling of amazement, wonder, or disbelief captures the essence of each hunter's being at the moment of the kill. In the quiet dusk of the forest, the archer strikes the buck deer true, the arrow slicing through the heart and lungs. The prey hunches, kicks, bolts; its hoofs pounding, it darts wildly into the brush, leaving what looks like a murder scene in its wake—trees and bushes spattered and splattered with blood from its blind death dash. A crash, branches breaking, some thrashing, then silence. The hunter is left transfixed, looking out over this terrific scene. The sound of hounds in their wild, headlong pursuit of their prey, what Faulkner describes as a sublime "moiling yapping" in *Go Down, Moses,* is heard echoing through the hollers. Exploding from the briars, the rabbit darts by the hunter, and all goes quiet and slow for the hunter as he swings his or her pump gun up and dials in the target. The gun plunges against the hunter's shoulder, and the rabbit is struck, pinwheeling to a sudden and immediate stop—what was just boisterous, animated, and adrenalized has been transfigured. And the marveling hunter stands "bathed in sweat and tumult / He slakes and kills, and eats meat / and knows blood."[16]

The canon of hunting literature often focuses on this sense of amazement, which comes from the thrill of the chase and the act of killing. James Dickey, in his poem "A Dog Sleeping at My Feet," articulates the intensity and alertness of the chase and describes how the hypnotized primal language of a predating beast/hunting dog can captivate him: "Before me the fox floats lightly / On fire with his holy scent. / All, all are running. / Marvelous is the pursuit, / Like a dazzle of nails through the ankles."[17] As the Christ imagery in this quotation suggests, in the pain and terror and tumult of the chase and kill there is a transcendent, fervid spirituality inherent to events like this. In *Go Down Moses,* Ike McCaslin experiences the feeling of astonishment after his first kill, "standing over the buck where it lay on the wet earth still in the attitude of speed, and not looking at all dead, standing over it shaking and jerking."[18] Similarly, the naturalist Aldo Leopold's first duck kill, as described in *A Sand County Almanac,* was a momentous occasion. After sitting in sublime pain from the cold on an uneventful, bitter Midwestern winter day, Leopold drops a duck and is left to marvel at the striking image of the bird in its death throes. "At sunset," Leopold wrote, "a lone black duck came out of the west, and without even a preliminary circling of the airhole, set his wings and pitched downward. I remember only an unspeakable delight when my first duck hit the snowy ice with a thud and lay there, belly up, red legs kicking."[19]

Michael C. Ryan

Haines perhaps best articulates that emotion and feeling of astonishment that comes with the taking of a sentient being's life. Upon approaching a slain moose, he captures Burke's idea that "Astonishment is that state of the soul, in which all emotions are suspended, with some degree of horror."[20] Haines looks down upon his quarry and "the open eye of the moose gazed blank and dull in the tree-stroked whiteness. . . . I felt, as I always do at such times, a strange and painful combination of emotions, if what one feels can be called emotion precisely—a mingling of awe, of regret, of elation and relief."[21] Haines, as well as the other writers quoted here, illustrates Burke's idea of the sublime as creating a "sort of delightful horror, a sort of tranquility tinged with terror."[22] Thus, the feeling of the sublime becomes intermixed and conflated with the fearful— the prey experiencing terror and death—and the fearsome—the reflective, adamant hunter absorbing energy from the kill.

To be sublime is to find the wildness of the woods. Burke contends that the sublime "comes upon us in the gloomy forest, in the howling wilderness."[23] In the forest landscape, where so many hunting endeavors take place, there can be found many of the qualities inherent in the sublime: silence, solitude, and obscurity. Utter silence is sublime, and Burke says that "absolute and entire solitude, that is, the total and perpetual exclusion from all society, is as great a positive pain as can be conceived."[24] Any dedicated bow hunter who has spent countless hours tucked away in the back corner of a wood lot understands the feelings of loneliness and aloneness that Burke argues stimulate feelings of the sublime. There is an unsettling quietude to the grey, predawn hours in the woods, where a sharp twig snap or the glow of a night animal's eyes bobbing about can startle the hunter out of his or her comfort zone. And great discomfort comes from sitting motionless and silent for long periods of time waiting for game to come down the trail. But there is also a meditative, Zen-like quality to such endeavors that sharpens one's mental, ocular, and auditory senses, making it a sort of "positive pain." Walt Harrington wrote of his experiences rabbit hunting with his father-in-law in his book *The Everlasting Stream*. In his reflections on one particular hunt, he discusses how a silent, solitary moment in the forest led to a sublime experience during which his senses were intensified and overwhelmed as he shot a cottontail scampering across his path. Harrington describes how "The silence in this gloomy wood probably helped unwittingly create in me the simultaneously sedate and intent cast of mind"; he then goes on to say that after quietly drawing up on and shooting the silently flushed rabbit, he "realized something fresh had happened, that I had entered a room outside of my experience . . . it felt not exactly good but all enveloping, a kind of sensory baptism . . . everything was quiet and clear and magnified."[25]

Staring out into obscurity, becoming lost in the shadowy, murky thicket and woodland, letting the mind and body freely ramble out into tangled, wild hinterlands has a sublime effect on the hunter. When the hunter is immersed in the dense wood, "all is dark, uncertain, confused, terrible, and sublime to the last degree."[26] And out of the obscure, snarled brush, where all was unknown, concealed, and uncertain, the rabbit bounded in front of Harrington, and he felled it, achieving a jolt of the sublime in the process. Similarly, in *Go Down, Moses,* Ike McCaslin's profound encounter with Old Ben, the mythic two-toed bear that is emblematic of the Mississippi wilderness, occurs in truly sublime fashion when the solitary bear silently comes into view out of the shadowy, yawny wilderness patchwork: "The wilderness coalesced. It rushed, soundless, and solidified . . . then he saw the bear. It did not emerge, appear. It was just there, immobile, fixed in the green and windless noon's hot dappling . . . dimensionless against the dappled obscurity."[27] Though Ike does not shoot the bear and he is not in position to bring it down—and though he realizes it would be a sin to kill such a powerful, revered symbol of wild freedom—the story of McCaslin's wilderness hunting indoctrination at the hands of Sam Fathers serves to illustrate the kinds of formative, sublime life events that ventures afield can present to the hunter. Thus, just like John Haines, who speaks "much of twilight, of dusk, of evening" because he knows of the tremendous, powerful draw of obscure sights and places, the hunter takes to the country hillsides and the wilderness wastes to find a "wild enchantment in the quiet, the loneliness, and the unknown.[28]

Thinking hunters are disciples of the hunt. They saunter about the landscape and know the liberty of thought and action. They know the importance of a well-placed shot and a well-dressed carcass. They know the moods and ways of the flora and fauna in the lands that they stalk. Hunters know the exact sentiment to which Faulkner was referring when he wrote about the "unforgettable sense of the big woods . . . profound, sentient, gigantic, and brooding, amid which he had been permitted to go to and fro at will."[29] Adventures afield inspire the primal soul of humankind. The sublime hunter knows what it means to wander, chase, kill, clean, skin, debone, process, and prepare, knows that each simple step in the hunting process has its intricacies and that, within these intricacies, aspects of the sublime—pain and terror, astonishment and awe, silence and obscurity—are prevalent and necessary.

BRIAN SEITZ

Hunting Time

Philosophy Afield

| Modern Times |

The conditions for the modern experience of time are dominated by technolog-ically organized assemblages that promote a sense of objectivity, universality, predictability, and familiarity that precedes either season or location, physical body or activity—which is to say that, on a fundamental level, time has be-come out of joint from material place and corporeal motion, in part because much of what passes for "motion" now consists of sitting in a machine. With the ascendance of the machine, noon mutated into *12*, an objective numerical designation that comes before and takes priority over that which falls outside the precise algorithms of the mechanism. In its determinative association with devices, time is organized by and simultaneously vanishes into chronometer-driven schedules, time zones, departure times, and so on.

In short, the sun is eclipsed by the clock. While technologized time condi-tions and shapes a massive domain of contemporary human experience—tick, tick, tick, tick, tick—it has little bearing on a whole other domain of experi-ence, the one illuminated by the sun.

Dawn can be gauged precisely by the clock but is neither synonymous with nor reducible to it, and—first philosophical note—the difference between them is not ensnared in the metaphysical opposition between subjective and objec-tive. Determined, that is, neither by a subjective choice nor by the objectivity of the clock, dawn is not 6:08 A.M., the moment announced by means of an alarm rather than the effects of an extra infusion of water the evening before, a traditional alarm that seeps into and eventually awakens consciousness from within the hunter's body, a reminder that it is *time to move*. Determined by our

173

relation to the sun, dawn is dawn, and it is when the hunter must start walking into the field or the woods. We choose to hunt, but dawn determines when we start walking.

The clock does not follow the hunter into the field in any conspicuous way. In the experience of hunting, time manifests itself in multifarious forms that together offer themselves for phenomenological consideration. By visiting overlaying aspects of modern and traditional hunts, I will take up forms of hunting time as if they were sequential, archaeological layers that congeal into two general, multifaceted formations, one of which is what the phenomenologists characterize as "everyday," the other of which is ontological. We moderns must begin with the everyday, with the clock and the calendar that get imposed on or imported into the field before we start walking into it. As is typical, it is only through the everyday that the ontological becomes available.

| Getting Coordinated |

The modern hunter has no choice but to commence the hunt in conformity with the calendrical formation, the everyday or typical time (Heidegger calls it "world time" or "objective time") that begins with state apparatuses determining dates and regulations for hunting seasons and mapping them onto the land divided into game zones, block management units, and other animated cartographic-bureaucratic grids that are in one sense abstract while also scientifically reflective of species variances and herd populations. For example, in regulating deer hunting, the Department of Environmental Conservation of the State of New York (my closest hunting ground) makes distinctions between archery season, Northern Zone early muzzle-loading season, "regular" modern firearms season, and late Southern Zone muzzle-loading season, as well as seasons for other game, such as bear, turkey, small game, waterfowl, and furbearers. (Such a delineated array would have bewildered traditional indigenous hunters, who were of necessity opportunistic.) Then there are dates in the form of deadlines for entering lotteries for special permits, for example doe tags, or game species whose healthy populations require a limited number of tags in a given district, such as antelope tags in Montana (another of my hunting grounds). These dates are predictable. They are not arbitrary, but their precision signifies a detachment from traditional hunting practices, even if this precision is a stiff echo of and thus bears some relationship to traditional practices, which themselves tended to follow mating patterns, reproductive cycles, and herd densities and movements.

Seasons established, the frame of possibilities provided to us, we hunters must then "make" or "carve out" time. This is the time associated with planning and preparing for the hunt, the time of anticipatory conversation—including negotiations with partners (archetypally but not essentially that means with spouses)—and of gathering and caring for gear. In the immediate and practical sphere, this form of time is what seems to make the hunt possible as it resolves the challenge of how to fit hunting into our busy schedules and nonhunting obligations. Yet it might in a sense also be considered fundamentally outside the hunt itself because the modern as distinct from traditional hunt exists in a special compartment, one associated with leisure activities rather than with the very conditions of existence. Scheduling of course includes the determination of travel time, and this usually involves driving time and sometimes entails plane reservations and even in extravagant and intricate cases a reservation for a plane to a city to a plane to a village to a plane to the field (lots of flight time for unguided drop-in caribou hunting, for example). All of these arrangements are nearly always scheduled in tight coordination with the calendar. That is, all of them are enmeshed in modern forms of the everyday or typical time.

Following planning and preparation, there is the transitional time associated with actual transport to the field. In some ways, this is simply an extension of typical time, occurring on a certain date, shoving off at a certain hour, and maintaining a certain relation to, for example, the speed limit, which is determined by machines, that is, by the relationship between the pickup truck and the clock. In prominent respects, this transitional time is thus routine. Yet, in other decisive respects, this time is a passageway and thus worthy of distinction since, along the way, hunters begin to situate themselves in the field or *to be spatially and temporally situated by it.* Hunters have always had to journey to the field and to game, and so this transition marks the beginning of a different, more fundamental—ontological—form of hunting time, even if the transit itself almost invariably occurs inside a machine. Whether passing from an urban or suburban environment or from a rural environment to an even more rural environment, this transition or overlap is the time when the hunt begins.

| Time Afield |

Then there is the dense experience of time in the field, where we move beyond transition and observe the full emergence of time's ontological aspects. To begin with, this time is coextensive with specific seasons; most hunting takes place in the fall (which is represented in an inelastic and thus only approximate form on the calendar, crude representation being the cost of precision). Whether we are taking a stand, stalking, or animated by the deliberate perambulation associated with "still hunting," time sometimes seems to disappear, displaced by the sky and the breeze and distinctive forms of patience. Put differently, time and the body tend "to move slowly" here, unless dramatic weather spins things differently, or until the game appears, which is often simultaneously both subtle and abrupt, gentle and utterly dramatic. Even when game never appears, there is often plenty else going on, including observations of other animals that few people other than hunters and lucky hikers ever see.

One gray day, sitting on top of a mountain just three hours from New York City, my gaze open to deer, my consciousness outside itself, I found that hunting time had shifted into a new dimension when I saw a movement that materialized into a mountain lion padding quietly through the trees; the wind was such that it never saw me in the time I saw it, which was probably a blessed fifteen seconds but seemed to last forever both then, on that snow-covered mountaintop, and now, in memory (yet another form of time), its tracks a connection to every other big cat in all of eternity. I mention this story to help illustrate the sense in which field time demands distinct consideration.

Wildly out of joint with modern times, we hunters are a dwindling breed, although if in the future we ever vanish, it will mean that everything else has, too. At odds with contemporary, industrialized culture and commercially packaged food, the hunter's choice to continue hunting is a strong one, and, once the hunter is committed, that choice is a passageway to a world that has fundamentally little to do with the present-day world.

The hunter passes out of that world and into the experience of field time and of *hunting as ritual* once he or she starts moving into the eternal space in which hunters have always walked. The second we get out of the pickup truck, we enter a different realm of experience. Load your rifle now, because as soon as you start walking, you are hunting and might encounter game: that slight movement ahead is a grouse imagining that it is hiding, so why not shoot it with your .30–30? Any traditional hunter would have taken the opportunity.

Undergirding and coextensive with the "slow" pace of field time, there is the deep time that links the hunter with (1) the very possibility of the hunt, a possibility now threatened by the environmental catastrophe distressing the field of the hunt, the signs of which are everywhere; and (2) the entire history of hunting, our link with the lives and practices of all ancient hunters. The hunt was what enabled us to exist and to become who and what we are, *meat on the fire* transformed into brain power. And so we are haunted by the ghosts of the human past. Hunting can sometimes seem like a solitary endeavor. And yet the hunter is never alone; all of the people not with him are there, including eons of dead hunters.

| Field Time to Eternity |

Archaeologists encounter material traces of ancient time in the field, the ontological ground of our hunting, reference to the past, the past not so long ago settled into the literal, physical earth. Here, preserved in the sediments,

Brian Seitz

archaeologists uncover both weapons and often dense layers of the skeletons of prey accumulated over millennia in the same location; sometimes these bones still hold the projectile points that penetrated and helped kill the creature, comprising an eternal and symbolic ensemble of flint and bone that once yielded meat. Perhaps more poignant are clearly deliberate arrangements of bones that once contained and protected ancient meat, carefully cached in the hope it would endure until it was next needed, a hope that the bones signal to us now. Hunting connects us to this time, when our ancestors needed to hunt game animals long extinct.

The hunter-philosopher José Ortega y Gasset observed that "The general lines of the hunt are identical today with those of five thousand years ago," although he might just as well have said twenty-five thousand years ago. Extending this thought: whether a stone pitched at a ptarmigan or a .257 Roberts fired at a pronghorn, it is, fundamentally, just different versions of similar routines. Tactical considerations do vary for a range of reasons—including range!—and hunting a woolly mammoth is not "the same" as hunting whitetail, but the strategic objectives and thus the dynamics of the hunt are as they have always been. Carrying a bow, my dead brother, masquerading as an antelope, reenacted or resurrected and thus embodied a hunter twelve thousand years ago, playing on the herd's curiosity, the dance something like the opposite of camouflage, another ancient approach: on one end the effort at simulation, at the other the effort at disappearance. (The hunter disappears in order to encourage the game to appear.) Hunters have used disguises and decoys forever. The aim has always been to get close enough to kill or capture the game animal. In that respect, the hunt is always the same. Beyond the same, to spear a fish today is *identical* to what it was thousands of years ago.

Once we have committed to the hunt, immersion into the eternal time of hunting is not a choice since, consciously or not, we may slip imperceptibly into it with each step in the field. And yet finding ourselves in that time, the time of the field, is synonymous with encountering the dead. Dead hunters, yes, but also extinct creatures that our indigenous North American ancestors once hunted and lived on—not just deer, elk, and antelope but also mammoths, mountain sheep, camels, indigenous horses, and other prey, including ancient forms of bison that, though gone, remain cousins and ancestors of modern American and European bison.

The time associated with, for example, the Madison Buffalo Jump in southwestern Montana encompasses two thousand years of use, two thousand years of repetition with a difference, different people performing the same ritual, each successful performance a different event. All of that time passed by, and nothing really changed, not until the modern European horses fundamentally altered the buffalo hunt, and then, a few days later, the Americans decided to exterminate the buffalo in order to exterminate the buffalo hunt, killing off a way of life that still exists in the cultural memory of the descendants of those hunter elders, a way of life that will always have existed.

In the deepest context, the time of hunting is the time of eternity. But there is, too, the time of mortality, of the end not of the prey but of the aging predator facing his own death. Time does not slow then, but the body does. As George Frison observes, "The aging hunter finds it increasingly difficult to climb steep slopes. . . . Brush patches and uneven terrain are avoided if possible, and quick bursts of running are no longer an option. Care is taken to locate obstacles such as rocks, tree limbs, and depressions that might cause bad knees to give way and lead to serious injury." Frison concludes that "The prehistoric hunter undoubtedly went through similar experiences," similar relative to the end of time or to the end of the time of the individual hunter. Indeed, this trope of inevitability is the very form of time featured in the Akira Kurosawa film *Dersu Uzala*. Based on a true story set in the early years of the twentieth century, the film tells of Dersu's days as a traditional Siberian hunter, which end when his eyesight starts going and he is forced to leave the forest for Vladivostok, where he is not allowed to fire off his gun, a hunter completely at odds with modern Russian times. Although he could no longer see to survive, the real Dersu chose to return to the forest, no doubt certain he was walking into his own demise; it is said that he was murdered for his rifle, murdered, that is, for his tool of death.

Werner Herzog's documentary *Happy People: A Year in the Taiga* displays time in several ways relevant to the motif of ancient time or eternity. Filmed in twenty-first-century central Siberia along the isolated Yenisei River, it follows a year in the life of a trapper, across the entire arc of the seasons, the vital arc of the traditional hunter's time; it is this full year that provides the narrative structure of the film.

While the trapper, Gennady, is Russian, the film makes a point of featuring local indigenous people, depicted as having largely forgotten their traditions, a jarring juxtaposition (if it is true). And yet, the Russian trapper lives out of joint with modern Russia.

Indigenous people disconnected from their past. A Russian disconnected from the present but deeply immersed and his life activities defined by the seasons. This is a singular set of modern hunting tensions related to time.

While Gennady uses a snowmobile and a chainsaw and carries both a rifle and a shotgun, he relies heavily on his axe and his knife for building both deadfall traps and the trapping huts in which he spends the bulk of the winter as he makes his rounds, accompanied by his dog (a timeless relation that refers back to the original interdependence of humans and wolves). And as has been the case since the beginning of time, a twenty-first-century Russian trapper is also a fisherman and a hunter-gatherer, a compound identity determined by the seasons and *what is out there in the field* rather than by the modern "choice" associated with time management: beyond the hubristic fantasy of management, this time unfolds of its own accord, this time follows nature, follows the animals following the seasons. Of oncoming winter, Gennady says, "You see that everything is going forward, as it should. . . . It's not you who is doing it, but you still feel a part of it. . . . Hunting brings you closer to the taiga than anything else." Hunting brings you closer to place and to real time, which is all of time, eternity, the time in which on a most fundamental plane nothing has changed. Except everything that has.

| From Now On |

Nature struggles everywhere now. Against the dominant trajectory of collapse, the planet is dotted with rewilding projects, many of which are embroiled in controversy, including projects to reintroduce wolves, to fence out sheep in order to let plants and the animals that follow them recover, or to rebuild a Pleistocene ecosystem, inspired by the imagination of a woolly mammoth reconstituted—cloned—through DNA taken from the flesh of creatures exposed by thawing tundra, an imagination or fantasy of the past revived, of long-extinct species brought back from the dead. The concatenation of these variegated undertakings, including those that seem mad, is vital to our imagination of and thus *hopes* for the future.

But equally important are efforts to rewild ourselves, to loosen the comforting and confining familiarities of a mechanical world, to cultivate our capacity for fundamental surprise. Driven by necessity, these are existential projects with which hunting is intimately associated and that, as I have suggested, connect us to eternity, to all of the past.

George Monbiot describes a salt marsh in Wales, where archaeologists have scraped away eight thousand years of sediments to reveal preserved, distinct human footprints; the tracks of other creatures are there, too, including deer tracks, which in their co-mingling with the human suggest traces of a hunt we not only can recognize but also are capable of reenacting today every time we start walking into the field.

When the hunter kills an animal, hunting time is not over, but time mutates again as activity shifts from sensing and seeking to the work of gutting, field dressing, and transporting the meat, which usually involves dragging, time decelerating in yet a different way during that drag. The drag leads us back into everyday time and to meat on the table. And yet, when we share and eat that meat and whether we are conscious of it or not, we participate in a material ritual that keeps us grounded in all of time. This is a practice that staves off future oblivion.

Frison, George, C. *Survival by Hunting: Prehistoric Human Predators and Animal Prey.* Berkeley: University of California Press, 2004.

Frison, George, C., ed., *Prehistoric Hunters of the High Plains,* 2nd ed. New York: Harcourt Brace Jovanovich, 1991.

Heidegger, Martin. *Being and Time,* trans. John Macquarrie and Edward Robinson. New York: Harper Perennial, 2008.

Herzog, Werner, dir.. *Happy People: A Year in the Taiga.* Studio Babelsberg, 2010.

Kurosawa, Akira, dir. *Dersu Uzala.* Mosfilm, 1975.

Monbiot, George. *Feral: Rewilding the Land, Sea, and Human Life.* London: Penguin Books, 2014.

Ortega y Gasset, José. *Meditations on Hunting,* trans. Howard B. Wescott. New York: Charles Scribner's Sons, 1985.

Brian Seitz

CHARLES J. LIST

Rebuilding the Wholesome Machinery of Excitement

Virtue and Hunting

At the beginning of the twentieth century, reflective hunters seemed to know exactly what the ideal hunter was. He (and he was male) was a man of a certain character: a person of integrity and honor, who was self-reliant and tough. Or, as one person defined the character of the gentleman-hunter, he had courage, perseverance, sagacity, strength, activity, and caution. This elitist ideal, so obviously anachronistic from our point of view, underwent significant transformations during the past century which explain its demise but does not answer the pressing question of what should replace it. That we need a replacement is evident given the corrupt image of hunters currently portrayed in both commercial hunting literature and popular media. This new image of the ideal hunter must be both ethically justifiable and culturally acceptable. The components of this ideal are implicit in the writing of some contemporary reflective hunters, but they need to be organized into a coherent and justifiable character. So, this essay will offer a reconstruction of the ideal hunter. First, I will examine the demise of the gentleman-hunter ideal, and especially the role played by the shifting semantics of "sport hunting." Second, I will critically explore a view that came to replace it, that hunting is an instinct. Third, I will collect and sort some necessary components for a reconstruction of the ideal. Fourth, I will organize these components into an ethically justifiable and culturally acceptable model.

The goal of this volume, as I understand it, is to explore the problems of being both an academic and a hunter. Initially I am tempted to say that it is actually pretty easy because as academics, we tend to have some free time and enough disposable income to purchase the necessities. But this isn't what is at stake. What is at issue is the kind of climate we face on campus when we hunters let on to the wrong person or group that we hunt. I distinctly remember the sour looks I got when I once naively owned up to hunting partridges and the dismissive comment "Oh, I could never do that!" This sort of response is even more surprising given that I teach in a fairly rural area, surrounded by lots of other people who hunt.

My academic area is philosophy, and especially environmental philosophy, and I've been lucky enough to be able to both hunt and write about it from the standpoint of a philosopher. In this regard, I recently had the opportunity to do some research at one of the leading private libraries devoted to field sports, the National Sporting Library and Museum, in Middleburg, Virginia. My research there was on the ways in which "virtue language" enters the vocabulary of reflective hunters, that is, hunters who also write about what they take themselves to be doing in a larger sense. I was interested in the prognosis of what I elsewhere call the "sportsman thesis" that field sports are capable of inculcating certain desirable virtues in participants. I discovered that this once commonly held belief had mostly disappeared over the course of the twentieth century, and I wanted to know why.

While at NSLM I read a sampling of the writings of reflective hunters and anglers distributed from about 1900 to 1980. These writers of course had a lot to say about why they did what they did, but little of it had anything to do with virtue development. Given the once widespread popular appeal of the connection between hunting and virtue, I became intrigued at the prospect of discovering what had become of this once powerful idea and what had replaced it. While answering this question in detail would take much more than I shall offer here, there is one connection that is worth exploring in some detail: the way in which "sport hunting," once defined in terms of the virtues of gentlemen, became subsequently reconstructed as hunting for pleasure, indeed as killing for pleasure. It is this picture that our nonhunting colleagues often have when we tell them we hunt. The transformation in the meaning of "sport hunting" and the ways reflective hunters might recover its central idea will be a central theme in what follows.

| The (Completely Understandable) Demise of the Gentleman-Hunter |

The following quotation from an anonymous nineteenth-century writer represents one version of what I call the sportsman thesis. This thesis has it that hunting, fishing, and other field sports are powerful sources of character development: "The pastimes of stream and woodland . . . are the characteristic exercises of many of the noblest properties of man's nature. They call into exertion courage, perseverance, sagacity, strength, activity, [and] caution; they are the wholesome machinery of excitement; of hope and fear, and joy and sorrow, regret and rejoicing; they are at once the appetite and the food of manhood. . . . *Instead of being antagonist[ic] meanings, the sportsman and the gentleman are [becoming] . . . synonymous terms.*[1] Here we find the essence of the gentleman-hunter, the virtues necessary for and the emotions occasioned by the hunt. The "pastimes of stream and woodland," fishing and hunting, are claimed to "exercise" a rather long list of virtues. There are several obvious problems here. First, the list of virtues is pretty spectacular. In addition to this hyperbole is the impending synonymy of the sportsman and the gentleman, an elitism that will not sit well with many hunters. The back story for this convergence of meanings is that, prior to the Civil War, hunters were considered backwoods rubes, having nothing to do with "genteel" society. However, after the war, hunting began to emerge as a way of developing some important virtues.

Hunting came to be seen as an activity suitable for gentlemen.[2] Of course, once this convergence of meaning of gentlemen as hunters became "sport hunting," this elite status did not sit well with egalitarian citizens who saw in gentlemen the remnants of long-rejected European nobility. So these American gentlemen sport hunters eventually found themselves in the bind of defending elitism in the face of democratic values and at the same time practicing an art that was considered primitive and brutish.

As a way of unpacking the complex idea of the character of a gentleman-hunter, I want to separate three components. These are implicit in the quotation above and serve as an organizational framework for what follows. First, there are various moral virtues mentioned, such as courage, perseverance, and sagacity or wisdom, by which I take the author to mean that these are character traits everyone would accept as desirable. Second, there is that component associated with excitement, those *feelings* one has as a hunter or angler: the joys, disappointments, and regrets one experiences. Finally, while not as obvious, there is the component of actions, of "activity and caution." Hunters and anglers within this elite culture had a code of personal behavior as well as a perceived duty to engage in appropriate civic action, a duty to improve hunting for others by restricting their own hunting and by using agricultural techniques for game husbandry and a duty to participate in the political processes connected to their activities.[3]

To jump ahead fifty years, the three ideas implicit in the concept of the gentleman-hunter were transformed around World War II primarily by the removal of any elitist connotations from the meaning of "sport hunting." As Andrea Smalley notes, "This wartime project of remaking sport hunting's image started with the redefinition of sportsmen. In the past, sportsmen differentiated themselves from 'the great mass of those who shoot' by class and by imitating European standards of sportsmanship. But the war prompted hunting magazines to claim that almost any man who had shot a gun was a sportsman, thus democratizing the image of post-war hunting. No longer did outdoor journals elevate the refined, elite sportsman of the late nineteenth century. Instead, they depicted hunters as part of the 'rough side' of American society. These were 'men who have grown up with guns, men who are fast wing-shots, men who can drill a running deer.'[4] Smalley puts it exactly right: the democratization of hunting was a crucial factor leading to the abandonment of the idea of the gentleman-hunter. Just having a gun and knowing how to use it was now sufficient to make one a hunter. The effects of this "redefinition of sportsman" are important for understanding the philosophical and ethical problems that continue to plague hunting. One important consequence is that sport hunting lost one unifying goal: the development of moral virtue. That is, the replacement of gentleman-hunters with hunters from the "rough side" seemed to entail the rejection of the acquisition of courage or perseverance. I say "seemed to entail" because, as we'll see, I don't think we are really forced to this conclusion. But it is easy enough to see how one might go in this direction. After all, if sport hunting is seen partially as an attempt to acquire gentlemanly virtues and if the very idea of a gentlemen is compromised, then so is the goal of virtue development.

Another factor that contributed to the demise of the gentleman-hunter, as Daniel Herman points out in *Hunting and the American Imagination,* was the unstable concept of civic gentility:

> Middle-class urbanites no longer embrace hunting as they once did in part because gentility has been redefined. Though Protestant and Enlightenment conceptions of the ideal citizen—the man of rationality and restraint—were eclipsed in the nineteenth century, they returned in the late twentieth. To be middle class in modern America is, generally speaking, to be a restrained and domesticated citizen, not to be a chivalrous slayer of animals.[5]

Civic responsibility for game and fish as active husbandry, another component of the gentleman-hunter ideal, was replaced by a different kind of citizenship, a restrained domesticity, entailing perhaps voting right or joining some conservation organizations but not taking direct responsibility for the improvement of fish and game populations. This would be left to state and federal institutions, with their access to the best science and technology of the day.

One final cause of the demise of the gentleman-hunter ideal is that, in their efforts to reduce market hunting and thereby preserve cherished game species, gentlemen hunters condemned hunting for "the pot." This explicit disdain for the food-gathering aspect of hunting was to become an easily widened crack in the façade of sport hunting. This dangerous line of thought established a familiar but in my view misleading distinction. The classification of kinds of human hunting into subsistence, sport, and commercial currently has wide appeal and forms the background for many policies and arguments about hunting. As people typically think about it, they would say there is hunting for survival (subsistence), hunting for profit (commercial), and hunting for pleasure (sport). Sport hunters, according to this way of thinking, do not need the nutritional supplements to their diets, even though they sometimes eat what they kill. Nor do they profit economically from their hunting. On the contrary, it costs them a lot of time and money to take the game they do. Given this way of looking at things, it seems sport hunters can now be motivated only by pleasure-seeking, and hunting itself is reduced to killing wild animals.

Once sport hunting lost its connection to the nuanced sensibilities and emotions once idealized, nonhunters could conclude only that these hunters killed simply for the pleasure of it—a difficult position to defend, to say the least. Sport hunting, by default, became hunting for pleasure. Equally important, hunting itself was of necessity redefined as competent use of a firearm to kill animals, to "drill a running deer," as Smalley relates. So sport hunting became, after this redefinition, killing for pleasure, killing for fun. This is the trap that reflective hunters currently face.

| The Well-laid Trap of "Sport Hunting" and Struggles to Escape |

In this section I want to explore the conception of sport hunting that ultimately came to replace the gentleman-hunter ideal. This line of thought begins with the gentleman-hunter ideal and then tracks the evolution of one substitute for it.

So let's characterize the gentleman-hunter in this way: for him, sport hunting was performing a difficult activity in the pursuit of character development, including moral virtue, civic engagement, and a refined sensibility. His hunting was intentionally made difficult by the self-imposition of rules and traditions that required fair chase, chivalry, and a specialized vocabulary.[6] The "sport" in sport hunting was provided by this and also the attempt to become a "sportsman," one who had the requisite capacities. Now, as I've mentioned, several things occurred over roughly the same period. First, the number of hunters after World War II vastly increased. Firearms became inexpensive and so did the ability to transport guns, dogs, and other hunters by automobile. The "difficult activity" of hunting became much easier as gadgets and other commercial hunting aids were introduced and heavily marketed. Second and perhaps related to this, the ideal of hunting as character development began to crack under the pressures already identified: its elitism, its conflict with other traditional American ideals, and the acceptance of seemingly simple distinctions among sport, subsistence, and commercial hunting.[7] Thus, both hunting as a complex undertaking and sport as a source of character development underwent major modification. And the question became, what was to replace them? Once "sport" was disconnected from character and hunting became relatively easy, the door was open for critics to proclaim that sport hunting was killing for fun. That is, the only plausible motive for sport hunting, once virtue development was stripped away, seemed to be pleasure.

Roger Caras, in his 1970 book, *Death as a Way of Life,* begins his examination of hunting by accepting the killing-for-fun formula. He seeks to explain "the phenomenon of men taking time off from essential economic activity to engage in the often strenuous and even dangerous task of killing animals for the sheer pleasure of doing it."[8] Clearly Caras believes sport hunting is killing for fun or, to be more precise, that hunting is animal killing and the "sport" motive in sport hunting can be attributed only to pleasure seeking. Once he accepts this conclusion, what is of interest is his explanation for this phenomenon. He believes, as do many others, that "the will to hunt, the desire to hunt, lies deep. It is, and I do believe this, inherent in man."[9] This deep desire, he believes, is a result of the critical reliance of early humans on hunting and the pleasure "nature rewarded" them for their killing behavior. This claim, which is called by others the "hunting hypothesis," figures importantly in debates about the morality of hunting. Caras believes that our Paleolithic ancestors, the "man-apes," learned hunting by "patterns of play" during their childhood. He elaborates: "However, somewhere in history, or rather before it, a strange thing began to happen . . . at some stage in our development grown men, too, started killing for fun rather than out of necessity. Since men who could find the time to hunt for fun were not likely to be men who had to hunt for a living, their activities could hardly be considered educational."[10] When Caras writes of grown men "killing for fun," he explains this phenomenon by asserting that it must inherently feel "good to kill" because "nature gave killing a measure of pleasure."[11]

With this we see not only the transformation of sport hunting from that ideal pastime inherent in the gentleman-sportsman to the manifestation of the brutal slogan "killing for fun" but also the proffered explanation that we have an instinct to kill. While it is undoubtedly true that hunting is sometimes a pleasurable activity, these pleasures are various and are associated with the complex activities inherent in the hunt, only one of which is the kill. To claim, as Caras does, that it's the kill that is the source of pleasure in the hunt is like saying it's the color that is the source of pleasure in a glass of wine. Drinking a glass of wine has associated with it a host of relationships and events that collectively may give one pleasure. So, the question that needs to be addressed is how the complex activities that constitute hunting, only one of which is the kill, are associated with the kind of pleasures in the hunt. As to Caras's hypothesis that "nature gave killing a measure of pleasure," we might wonder what his evidence is for saying so, given that he is clearly projecting a contemporary and, in my view, mistaken understanding of hunting back into the distant past. In the years since Caras and many others first endorsed the hunting hypothesis, anthropologists and others have decidedly rejected this idea that humans are what they are because they were first hunters. And if this is so, the claim that nature made killing pleasurable, while still possibly true, becomes at best only a partial explanation for the fact that humans continue to hunt, for sport or subsistence.

So Caras's explanation for the claim that sport hunting is killing for fun is seen to be unsupported because to say that killing animals is an inherently pleasurable activity is to leave unspecified both the kinds of pleasures in the hunt and the ways these pleasures are related to the hunt. It also is doubtful that the hypothesis of "natural killing pleasure" has any basis. Most important, the claim that gets the whole argument going, that hunting is (wild) animal killing, is inaccurate. To say hunting is killing for fun might be a convenient bumper-sticker slogan for one's attitudes, but it has no rational justification as an accurate characterization of hunting.

Yet the hunting hypothesis, the idea that hunting is an instinct, persists. For example, Ann Causey, in her 1989 article "On the Morality of Hunting," presents a view that is in important respects similar to Caras's but that functions as a defense of a kind of sport hunting. She also reverts to the "hunting hypothesis" that humans are inherently hunters as a way of explaining the pleasures of hunting. She says that "the desire to hunt is the modern vestige of an evolutionary trait of utmost adaptive significance to early man."[12] But the instinct she identifies is not, as for Caras, the instinct to *kill*; rather, it is the instinct to *hunt*. As such, she claims: "Sport hunters participate in hunting for the pleasure of the hunt itself and not for any particular result of that effort. . . . The drive in sport hunting is to be a link in the chain of nature, connected as predator to prey, and thus to participate directly in natural processes and phenomena which are hidden from the casual observer."[13] So Causey, like Caras before, finds an instinct or "urge" at the bottom of the sport-hunting well. Unlike Caras, Causey does not draw a misanthropic conclusion from this instinct, that humans are born killers, but rather tries to explain how it more closely connects us with nature in this time of technological and cultural isolation. This is a fairly popular theory, and it can be found in defenders of the "biophilia hypothesis" as well as among other defenders of hunting such as Paul Shepard, David Petersen, and Allen Jones. But it is not at all clear that there persists such an instinct to hunt, although there may be one to interact with nature, and surely hunting had a lot to do with our evolution.[14] If there were a real disposition to hunt, it would be decidedly odd that so many of our friends and neighbors manage to fight it so successfully. After an extensive review of the evidence for the hunting hypothesis, Matt Cartmill finds it a symbolically suggestive myth but a factually unsupported idea.[15]

Even if there were such an instinct, it would supply only an *explanation* for why we desire hunting and not a *justification* of why it is valuable. Ethically, knowing why we are inclined to do something does not justify that action.

Rather, what is demanded is a justification in terms of accepted ethical ideals. For example, a child's bad behavior may be explained by a bad home life, but that doesn't make the behavior any less wrong, although it may excuse it. The supposition of such an instinct, true or not, does not advance the search for moral justification for sport hunting.

Perhaps part of what is missing from what I called the brutal formula of sport hunting as killing for fun can be found in widely cited passage from Ortega y Gasset. Ortega also accepts the hunting hypothesis, but his understanding of what hunting is provides a clue as to how we might escape the sport hunting trap. He says: "To the sportsman the death of the game is not what interests him; that is not his purpose. What interests him is everything that he had to do to achieve that death—that is, the hunt. Therefore, what was before only a means to an end is now an end in itself. Death is essential because without it there would be no authentic hunting. The killing of the animal is the natural end of the hunt and that goal of hunting itself, *not* of the hunter."[16]

When Ortega y Gasset wrote that what interests the sportsman is "everything that he had to do to achieve that death," he was inviting us to think about the complexity of the activity as well as the various motives we may have for engaging in it. This includes an interest in the development of competence in many skills, from marksmanship to woodcraft, perhaps in developing virtues from self-control to courage, and in developing cognitive abilities from habitat reading to the natural history of the game. The motivations of sport hunters, then, are understandable only when placed in this complex set of practical conditions.

The way forward is to reject the reduction of sport hunting to killing for pleasure, which then requires an explanation like the hunting hypothesis, and instead to reconstruct an ideal that is based in the complexity of hunting and not in instinct.

| Reconstructing an Ideal |

I believe I have now established that there is a need to reanimate the sportsman thesis: hunting can be chosen as a way of developing character. Without this alternative, what is called sport hunting has been reduced to killing for pleasure or hunting for pleasure. I have argued that two movements took place in the twentieth century. First, hunting got defined as killing wild animals, an extreme narrowing of the actual complexity of hunting—that set of skills and techniques necessary for the acquisition of animals for food or other human uses, killing being one means of achieving that goal. Second, the motives or reasons for choosing hunting were similarly reduced to fun, money, or survival, and sport hunting then was slotted in as fun hunting, or fun killing. This double movement placed most reflective hunters in the untenable position of

Charles J. List

attempting to find some rationale to justify this (bizarre) activity, and while there have been some very creative attempts to do just this, the one that I examined, the one that got lots of attention, was the hunting hypothesis, that hunting is an instinct. But as I've shown, this simply will not do, both because the hypothesis itself is probably wrong and because, even if it were true, it still would not offer a *justification* for hunting but only an *explanation* of its persistence.

One thing that will help in thinking clearly about these matters is to keep *hunting* as an incredibly complex and ancient practice separate from contemporary *hunter's motives* or reasons for choosing hunting. We do this all the time in other cases: baseball as a game is different from the reasons people choose to play it or watch it; baking is an activity with a history and sets of standards independent of the reasons people choose to bake. Hunting is an ancient practice with evolving sets of standards, techniques, skills, and technologies, and hunters can choose to participate for a host of reasons. The practice of hunting itself is simply the way wild animals are acquired, regardless of the motive: by net or hook, trap or bow, shotgun or spear.

The motives for participation in any practice may be divided into three overlapping kinds, according to Aristotle: the pleasant, the useful, and the noble. It is "the noble" that concerns us here in regard to the sportsman thesis. The tricky part is that in hunting, as in other practices, the noble—the choice to participate in a practice in the quest for excellence of character—can also be pleasurable as well as useful. Thus, baking a fine loaf of bread is not only useful for those who wish to eat it but pleasant as well. Playing a beautiful passage in a musical score may be done for ennobling self-chosen purposes, but it is also pleasurable, if not to the listeners then to the artist. Even if hunting is chosen primarily for character development, it as such may also give pleasure to the hunter—for example, the pleasure that accompanies the practical use of the animal as food. And when hunting is chosen for more practical reasons, surely pleasure may also be derived, and perhaps even a dose of character development. When it comes to hunters' motives, they may often be mixed, but the noble, or choosing an activity for the development of excellence, must be an allowable choice.

Another name for "excellence" is "virtue." A virtue is a disposition or habit we acquire to do the right things at the right times. A vice is the contrary. We've seen that the august list of moral virtues associated with hunting, in the days of the sportsman-gentleman, were almost laughably grand, and besides they didn't really seem associated with actual hunting in any conceptually tight way. What we need, to construct a contemporary hunter paragon, is a set of virtues that together form an integrated character, closely tied to hunting, that also provides a suitable ideal sufficient for even nonhunters to encourage the practice to continue. That is, we'll hope others will accept the possibility of the inculcation of these virtues as sufficient to let hunting go on into the future.

One's character, which develops slowly over the course of one's life, is not chosen out of thin air but rather often reflects those paragons of virtue we wish to emulate. There are, as I have indicated, three interrelated components of character already implicit in the gentleman-hunter ideal: first, the capacity to control and refine emotions connected to the hunt; second, those moral virtues that are desired traits or excellences; third, the actions hunters perform in both the private and the public spheres as a result of character.

As a way of getting some traction on the problem of constructing a twenty-first-century paragon with these components, we can do no better than to contrast two historical images of the ideal hunter along these lines. First, there is the "American Native" embodied by Teddy Roosevelt, an ideal that retains some of the hunter-gentleman. As Herman says: "As naturalist, sport hunter, and devotee of the cult of Boone, Roosevelt was the supreme American Native, the indigenous man who seemed to incarnate the Spartan, manly virtues of American nature."[17] Second, David Peterson, in *Heartsblood: Hunting, Spirituality, and Wildness in America,* proposes as his ideal Dersu Uzala, whom he calls "A Hunter/Conservationist Paradigm."[18] Dersu, around the same time Roosevelt was taking on the responsibilities of president at the beginning of the twentieth century, continued to live the life of a hunter-gatherer in Asia. While similar in some respects to the "American Native" paragon identified by Herman, he displayed clear differences as well. Dersu, by contrast to Roosevelt, was an "animistic archetype," in Petersen's words, of "how, for tens of thousands of generations we all lived and thought, back when every human on earth was a professional hunter and gatherer."[19] As Petersen understood it, animism is a "zoomorphic (animal oriented) deeply spiritual worldview that sees all of nature as sentient and significant."[20] Now I doubt that TR was an animist, but he was a "naturalist," sharing with Dersu a deep knowledge of the natural processes at work around him and thereby an emotional connection to the natural world.

I don't think we need to go to the extreme of animism to create an adequate ideal. It is probably asking too much of contemporary materialistic hunters to suggest that they treat the natural world—every rock, tree, and stream—as alive with human-like spirits. However, the core of Dersu's animism and perhaps of Roosevelt's nature loving are their emotional connections to nature where nature is believed to be a holistic, ecological system. Such a view enables an emotional connection between hunters and the land, including the animals hunted, because hunters' community is expanded beyond the human to include the *biotic* community. This holistic view of hunting, which Petersen calls "nature hunting," requires a belief not that nature is sentient, as animism or the Gaia hypothesis would have it, but rather that humans and ecosystems are intimately connected, a view that is much like Aldo Leopold's land ethic.

In addition to Dersu's deep emotional connections to nature, we should also note the evident expertise he displayed when dealing with the situations that arose daily with correct actions flowing from his character. When one reads *Dersu the Trapper* one is impressed not only by his knowledge of the natural world but also by his skillfulness in making his way through it: his ability to make useful items, to repair what he had, to shoot accurately, to set the traps in the right places. These skillful actions, which are sometimes summed up as "woodcraft," are an aspect of Dersu's character. Roosevelt also displayed this facility in his actions both while hunting and, in contrast to Dersu, in the public sphere. His public policies flowed from his character as a hunter, as did his private skills in the field.

Without accepting the buckskin-clad animism of Dersu or the elite, antiquated, but manly and Spartan virtues of Roosevelt, we can nevertheless derive from these ideals a contemporary model.

First, there is a necessary emotional connection with the wild that derives from the feeling that we are connected with all living and nonliving things in a single holistic ecosystem. This is not necessarily a spiritual connection, as it is in animism, but it is powerful. It is also, by the way, supported by the best ecological science of the day. While some hunters will be guided by a more religious conviction, or perhaps a kind of "mindfulness,"[21] the emotional strength of the connection cannot be denied. But one thing is necessary for the attainment of this connection. As Petersen wrote: "To attain the personal epiphanies, aesthetic bliss, visceral emotions, and introspection that inform true hunting—nature hunting, spiritual hunting—I need, first and foremost, the solitude, silence, and beauty of wildly natural surroundings."[22] If wildly natural surroundings are necessary to attain this emotional state and if this virtue is what is desired, surely it follows that we hunters must do everything we can to preserve such conditions.

Second and related to the deep emotional connections established by hunting, hunters should aspire to inculcate certain moral virtues. These must replace those elitist and sexist goals of gentleman-hunters. One, which seems especially pertinent to me in the context of hunting, has long been recognized in other areas of moral competence: environmental temperance or moderation. This virtue, when moved into the context of hunting, requires close control over competitive desires, limits on the acquisition of game, and a "go light" attitude. Environmental temperance is, I think, what makes Dersu's mode of life so appealing: he is capable of getting by with nothing but "a small square of tent cloth, his bed a goatskin, his clothing mostly buckskin, and all his worldly plunder rides easily in a handmade birch-bark pack."[23] The contrast between this and the fully loaded SUV could not be starker.

Finally, both Dersu and Roosevelt were excellent woodsmen, an appellation for those who have all the skills required to do the right thing at the right time. This skill, which is a case of what philosophers call "practical wisdom," is related both to one's knowledge of the natural world and also to one's emotional attachment to it. The ideal hunter will have this capacity not just in the woods or in the wild but also in facing those constant civic challenges to hunting in the forms of private lands, habitat loss, invasive species, and so on. These are problems hunters must do something about, and their actions must be conditioned by both well-formed knowledge and well-honed emotions. This is something Dersu could not have anticipated, but Roosevelt clearly did: the demand for hunters to be civically active in order to preserve those conditions necessary for the hunt to continue.

I have argued that hunters need a new ideal because sport hunters have been placed in the untenable position of defending a boiled-down and brutal characterization of their motives for hunting. The historical transition from gentleman-hunters to killing for fun has been sketched. So too has the most prominent response to this predicament: hunting as instinct. I do not think we should rely on this hypothesis because at best it explains why some of us need to hunt but in no way offers an ethical justification for hunting. What is needed is to refit hunters into the universal quest for excellence of character, a position that has a long ethical pedigree.

My sketch of the ideal hunter obviously lacks many details. Perhaps we should fill these in as we compare ourselves to it. One thing to keep in mind is that ideals need not be mere abstractions but are often more or less realized in the people around us—our family members, friends, and hunting companions. Aspects of character are present in the stories we tell each other that connect our hunting from one year to the next and tie together our lives as hunters. We cannot, however, be complacent in this, because the quest for excellence of character places severe demands on hunters to participate civically, to display temperance and moderation, and to genuinely care about the biotic community of which we are members.

We should also keep in mind that hunting can never be purely a quest for character, because it is by nature a practical art of acquisition; it always has a utilitarian element. Once animals are acquired, we must make good use of them. In this way we both acquire useful goods and, with effort, good characters.

Appendix

An Annotated List of Recommended Hunting Texts

This list is for those interested in reading further in the subject matter of this book and for those teachers interested in using such material in their courses. It is divided into poetry and fiction (classical to contemporary) and modern nonfiction (beginning with Thoreau) written by academics and other intellectuals.

Of course this list is not meant to be exhaustive. The main criteria for selection are literary quality, intellectual depth, and availability to readers. Most of the books can be found in decent university libraries or (in the case of older, shorter texts) on the Internet. It includes a minimum of journalism, how-to books, academic monographs, fishing literature, and writing from other countries.

I'd like to thank the various contributors to this volume for their many helpful suggestions.

Literature

Ovid, *Metamorphoses,* 1st century C.E. Book Three tells the story of the deer hunter Actaeon, who upon accidentally seeing the goddess Diana bathing is turned into a stag and pursued as quarry.

Sir Gawain and the Green Knight, 14th century. This alliterative poem follows one of King Arthur's knights as he tests his courage against the mysterious Green Knight. Part III is an early literary example of the intertwining of hunting and sexuality as Gawain is the target of a noble lady's overtures while her lordly husband leads hunts for deer, boar, and fox, all of which are described in detail.

Sir Thomas Wyatt, "Whoso List to Hunt, I know where is an Hind," 1542. In this influential sonnet written during the reign of Henry VIII, Wyatt uses the symbolism of the hunt to describe his forbidden interest in Anne Boleyn.

Andrew Marvell, "The Nymph Complaining for the Death of Her Fawn," ca. 1650. In this poem, Marvell's Civil War–era political and metaphysical ruminations begin with the wanton killing of a fawn by a group of soldiers.

Sir Walter Scott, *Lady of the Lake,* 1810. Along with Scott's historical novels *Waverley* and *Rob Roy,* this poem helped inspire the Scottish Highland revival of the nineteenth century. Canto 1 focuses on a stag hunt.

Ivan Turgenev, *A Sportsman's Sketches,* 1852. This classic of Russian realism had a strong influence on Hemingway. Several sketches revolve around hunting within the context of Russian serfdom, while the epilogue, "The Forest and the Steppe," is an unabashed celebration of the pleasures of bird hunting.

Sarah Orne Jewett, "A White Heron," 1886. A young girl growing up in rural New England must choose between her love of nature and the attentions of an Audubon-type ornithologist.

Franz Kafka, "The Hunter Graccus," 1917. Readers familiar with Kafka's piercing blend of grotesque inventiveness and flat prose will appreciate this short fable of the hunter's relation to modern life.

Felix Salten, *Bambi, a Life in the Woods,* 1923. Originally written for readers of all ages when first published in Austria, the novel is much richer than the later Disney movie in both its anthropomorphic depiction of animal life and its complex understanding of the relationship between wild animals and human hunters.

D. H. Lawrence, "The Fox," 1923. Lawrence is known for his emphasis on the importance of attending to the physical and the instinctual in modern life. In this novella, the predator/prey relationship serves as a metaphor for romantic relationships. Readers might also be interested in Lawrence's brief, satirical essay "Man Is a Hunter."

Ernest Hemingway, "Big Two-Hearted River," 1925. This two-part story follows Nick Adams on a fishing trip in upper Michigan. Hemingway's narrative suggestively links Nick's fishing and camping to his attempts to recover from an unspecified psychic trauma.

———, "The Short Happy Life of Francis Macomber," 1936. On African safari with his wife and a renowned hunting guide, the title character tests his "grace under pressure" hunting lion and water buffalo. In this mid-period story Hemingway's latent themes/personal insecurities concerning masculinity are much more explicit than in the early work.

Siegfried Sassoon, *Memoirs of a Fox-Hunting Man,* 1928. In this first in a well-written three-volume series of slightly fictionalized memoirs, Sassoon, best known for his First World War poetry and protest, describes his sheltered and naïve early life fox hunting and playing cricket in southern England before the war. The volume concludes with Sassoon volunteering for military service and serving in France, concluding with the battle of the Somme in 1916.

Caroline Gordon, *Aleck Maury, Sportsman,* 1934. This lyrical novel from a member of the southern-agrarian literary clique the Fugitives focuses on an early twentieth-century classics professor from Virginia who strives to balance his teaching duties and family responsibilities with his love of fishing and hunting.

William Faulkner, "The Bear," 1942. This novella links hunting and manhood in the context of nineteenth- and early twentieth-century Southern culture. A fine example of Faulknerian mythos, "The Bear" is one of seven stories collected in *Go Down Moses* and is available in a slightly edited form in the *Big Woods,* a collection of four hunting stories.

Keith Douglas, "Aristocrats," 1943. Douglas went AWOL from a staff position in the British army to rejoin his regiment on the front lines during the North Africa campaign in World War II. In "Aristocrats," he ironically uses the language of fox hunting to describe the aristocratic officers who led the Sherwood Rangers, a former cavalry unit.

William Humphrey, *Home from the Hill,* 1957. Set in the east Texas country of Humphrey's birth, this novel foregrounds a connection between hunting and sexuality in the tragic relationship between a wayward father and a faithful son. While somewhat dated, Humphrey's novel at times approaches the power of Faulknerian mythos. Humphrey was on the English faculty of Bard College in the 1940s and 1950s and later taught for short stints at MIT, Smith, and Princeton.

Wilson Rawls, *Where the Red Fern Grows,* 1961. This classic of adolescent literature follows the adventures of a poor country boy and his two hunting dogs in the Ozarks. The dramatic and touching ups and downs of boyhood and hunting are modulated by the novel's Christian underpinnings.

Sylvia Plath, "The Rabbit Catcher," 1962. In Plath's inimitable style, this poem (included in *Ariel, the Restored Edition,* 2004) uses rabbit trapping as metaphor for marriage. Well after her death, Plath's husband, Ted Hughes, wrote a response poem of the same title, included in *Birthday Letters* (1998).

James Dickey, "The Heaven of Animals" and "The Summons," 1962. These poems, as well as a few others in Dickey's 1962 collection *Drowning with Others,* imagine hunting from the point of view of both hunter and hunted in powerful, sinuous lines.

———, *Deliverance,* 1970. Four suburbanites' wilderness trip from hell. But this novel is much more than the lurid scenes you remember from the movie: one part blistering poetry of the body-mind relation (with an emphasis on bow hunting) and one part lean, Hemingwayesque delineation of action, Dickey's writing carries the reader through the narrative like a canoe down a raging river.

Pinckney Benedict, "Booze," 1987. This accomplished short story (from Benedict's collection *Town Smokes*), set in Appalachia, focuses on a boy's search for a massive, quasi-mythical wild hog that is harassing his family farm. As Faulkner did in "The Bear," Pinckney uses suspense to weave together the hunt and the young narrator's incipient maturity in an unpromising natural and social environment. Benedict is currently teaching creative writing at Southern Illinois University.

Cormac McCarthy, *The Crossing,* 1994. The follow-up to the acclaimed *All the Pretty Horses,* the novel showcases McCarthy's powerful style and mythical themes. Part I, a novella of sorts, follows the protagonist as he tracks, traps, and then rescues a wolf preying on his family's cattle herd in Depression-era New Mexico.

Pam Houston, "Dall," 1996. This compelling story follows Houston's hunt for Dall sheep in rugged Alaska with her hunting guide boyfriend and is included in Houston's edited volume *Women on Hunting.* Other interesting pieces in this multigenre collection include Joyce Carol Oates's short story "The Buck," Annie Dillard's meditation on stalking, Rosellen Brown's poems on hunting and hunters, Jane Smiley's essay on fox hunting, and Betty Fussell's piece on cooking and eating meat.

Rick Bass, "The Myths of Bears," 1997. Bass is an award-winning writer, activist, and professor in the MFA programs at the University of Southern Maine and at Iowa State University. The novella "The Myths of Bears," collected in *The Sky, the Stars, the Wilderness,* powerfully and inventively parallels the symbiotic relationship between husband and wife with that of predator and prey.

Tom Franklin, *Poachers*, 1999. The excellent, noirish title story of this collection, set in rural Alabama, pits an implacable game warden against three brothers to whom the usual game rules don't apply. Franklin currently teaches creative writing at the University of Mississippi.

Carol Frost, "To Kill a Deer," 2000. Frost is a hunter and professor of creative writing at Rollins College. "To Kill a Deer" recounts the speaker's hunting, killing, and dressing of a doe in vivid, concrete imagery. Collected in *Love and Scorn: New and Collected Poems*.

Rudolfo Anaya, "Devil Deer," 2006. Environmental damage caused by a nuclear facility threatens the deer-hunting traditions of a Latino community in New Mexico. Collected in *The Man Who Could Fly and Other Stories*. Anaya taught creative writing at the University of New Mexico before retiring to write full time.

Benjamin Percy, *The Wilding*, 2010. This stirring novel by the writer-in-residence at St. Olaf College follows a high school English teacher on a hunting and camping trip to one of the last remaining areas of wilderness in central Oregon with his difficult father and his diffident son.

Thorpe Moeckel, *Venison*, 2010. This book-length poem is by a hunter and professor of creative writing at Hollins University.

Thomas McIntyre, *The Snow Leopard's Tale*, 2012. In this finely wrought novella set in the Chinese highlands by a nature writer and journalist, the metamorphosis of his feline protagonist articulates the subtle relation between the instinct consciousness of animals and the workings of human civilization.

H. William Rice, *The Lost Woods*, 2014. Rice is professor and chair of the English Department at Kennesaw State University. While each of these short stories ably depicts the specific practices and cultural contexts of hunting deer, quail, turkey, and ducks, among other species, in weaving them together to trace an extended family's hunting over several generations in the South Carolina piedmont Rice provides a deeply stirring account of the vexed relationship between rural life and modern development.

Nonfiction

Henry David Thoreau, *Walden*, 1854. A former hunter as well as a pioneering environmentalist, Thoreau, in the chapter "Higher Laws," offers a critique of hunting as largely based on animal instinct that should be transcended in favor of a "higher" spirituality.

Theodore Roosevelt, *Hunting Trips of a Ranchman*, 1885. Before entering politics, Roosevelt was a noted big-game hunter and rancher on the western prairies. He later spearheaded the modern conservation movement. Literary scholars may be particularly interested in Roosevelt's role in the "nature fakers" controversy—in 1907, while serving as president, he criticized writers such as Jack London for a supposed lack of realism.

Vladimir Arsenyev, *Dersu Uzala*, 1923. This book describes the author's travels in far-eastern Russia at the turn of the twentieth century, with a focus on the hunting ability and animist philosophy of his Nanai guide, Dersu Uzala.

Ernest Hemingway, *Green Hills of Africa*, 1935. This narrative of Hemingway on African safari (with wife no. 2 in tow) is essentially a nonfictional counterpart to his story "The Short Happy Life of Francis Macomber" in its emphasis on the ethics of hunting in the context of concerns about masculinity. Descriptions of big-game hunts are interspersed with Hemingway's comments on various American and European writers.

Jack O'Connor, *Classic O'Connor*, ed. Jim Casada, 2010. O'Connor, a renowned big-game hunter and firearms expert, taught journalism at the University of Arizona for more than a decade before turning to writing full time. This collection of "adventures" written for outdoors magazines stretches from the 1930s to the 1970s and will appeal mostly to those interested in trophy hunting and guns.

Havilah Babcock, *The Best of Babcock*, 1985. Babcock would sometimes play hooky from his duties as English professor and department chair at the University of South Carolina or sometimes skip out on academic conference sessions to pursue his passion for bird hunting and fishing. In this collection of pieces originally published in outdoor magazines from the 1930s to the 1960s, Babcock's unique mix of storycraft, hunting wisdom, and (often self-deprecating) humor are on ample display.

José Ortega y Gasset, *Meditations on Hunting*, 1942. In this influential treatise, Ortega, a philosopher and professor, argues that hunting constitutes a necessary return to nature. See Gregory Clark's essay in this volume for a more complex rendering.

Aldo Leopold, *A Sand County Almanac*, 1949. Professor of game management at the University of Wisconsin, Leopold was that rare combination of hunter and intellectual. A landmark of environmental literature, this engaging, elegiac book combines sharply drawn observational sketches and meaty essays on ecology.

Vance Bourjailly, *The Unnatural Enemy*, 1963. A novelist, journalist, and professor at the Iowa Writers Workshop, Bourjailly writes about bird hunting with verve, humor, and humility. Several essays in this book originally appeared in the *New Yorker* and *Esquire*.

John Madson, *Out Home*, 2008. In this collection of essays from the 1960s and 1970s, Madson, a conservationist and journalist, ranges from elegies for the Midwestern prairies to celebrations of the joys of hunting and hiking, often with wife and kids in tow. Madson's prose is folksy yet sharp.

Edward Hoagland, "War in the Woods," 1971. A prolific nature writer and noted essayist, Hoagland captures the personalities and local culture at play while observing bear hunting in rural New England. Collected in *Hoagland on Nature: Essays*.

Susan Griffin, "The Hunt," 1978. This text from a noted feminist writer and lecturer is an excerpt from *Women and Nature: the Roaring Inside Her*, an influential and complex eco-feminist treatise on the parallel subjugation of women and nature.

Robert Wegner, *Deer and Deer Hunting*, 1984. An authoritative and wide-ranging study of whitetail deer hunting, with chapters on noted practitioners and writers on the subject, followed by sections on deer biology and hunting ethics. Wegner earned a Ph.D. in cultural history and taught for a time at the University of Wisconsin before becoming a full-time author and editor. Though published more than three decades ago, Wegner's extensive annotated bibliography includes a number of volumes worth consulting.

Rick Bass, *The Deer Pasture*, 1985. Part Mark Twain (in Tom Sawyer mode) and part Garrison Keillor (all of the rural past is "above average"), this series of reminiscences of life in the Texas Hill country is a good read for those who relish the challenge of the chase and the good times in between.

James Kilgo, *Deep Enough for Ivorybills,* 1988. A longtime English professor at the University of Georgia, Kilgo reconnects with his roots in rural South Carolina through hunting and fishing with friends and colleagues in the Savannah River swamp. *Deep Enough* is a series of related, sharply etched essays—all versions of what Kilgo refers to as the *songfeast*—in which fellowship with fellow aficionados of the outdoors is as prized as the satisfaction of a good hunt.

Stephen Bodio, *Querencia,* 1990. Lifelong vagabonds, Bodio and Betsy find a home in the austere beauty of the New Mexico mountains. Hunting, falconry, new friends (human and non), and the spiritual beauty of the landscape are memorably conveyed in Bodio's lean but deeply felt prose. Bodio taught writing for many years at Sterling College and edited *The Sportsman's Library,* an anthology of both notable and obscure writers on hunting and fishing.

Jim Harrison, *Just Before Dark,* 1991. Harrison briefly worked as a professor of English at Stony Brook University before turning to writing full time. This book's second half focuses on hunting and fishing. "A Sporting Life" is a particularly good example of Harrison's easygoing philosophy of the outdoors.

Stuart A. Marks, *Southern Hunting in Black and White: Nature, History, and Ritual in a Carolina Community,* 1991. A professor of anthropology at St. Andrews University who grew up hunting, Marks offers a fascinating analysis of individual hunters' motivations and the sociohistorical context of their hunting. On the basis of interviews with a variety of hunters and field studies of hunting in Scotland County, North Carolina, Marks draws conclusions that pertain to the rural South in general.

Archibald Rutledge, *America's Greatest Game Bird: Archibald Rutledge's Turkey-Hunting Tales,* ed. Jim Casada, 1994. Rutledge taught English at Mercersburg Academy in Pennsylvania for more than three decades before returning to his family plantation in the South Carolina lowcountry and served as that state's first poet laureate. Chiefly written between 1920 and 1950, these autobiographical pieces combine a folksy lyricism (appropriate to the pre–civil rights South) with detailed renderings of the wild turkey's characteristics. Rutledge also played an important early voice in conservation, helping to revive the wild turkey population.

David Petersen, ed., *A Hunter's Heart: Honest Essays on Blood Sport,* 1996. A collection of narrative and analytical pieces, this book offers a useful introduction to the ethics of hunting. Writers include Edward Abbey, Tom McGuane, Peter Mathiessen, David Peterson, Mary Zeiss Stange, Jim Fergus, and Terry Tempest Williams.

Richard Nelson, *Heart and Blood: Living with Deer in America,* 1997. Author of several books on northwest Native American hunting, Nelson offers a lyrical and informed argument for the ecological importance of deer hunting through a series of case studies examining the complex relation between deer and human civilization in places such as Fire Island, New York; Angel Island, California; southern Wisconsin; upstate New York; the Texas Hill country; and coastal Alaska.

Christopher Camuto, *Hunting from Home: A Year Afield in the Blue Ridge Mountains,* 2000. An English professor at Bucknell University, Camuto is both a serious thinker and a hunter. Chapters on grouse hunting with his dog and deer hunting with bow and muzzleloader are combined with expositions of his hunting and environmental philosophy.

Walt Harrington, *The Everlasting Stream*, 2002. Formerly a *Washington Post* journalist and presently professor at the University of Illinois, Harrington recounts learning to hunt with his African American in-laws in rural Kentucky. Along the way, Harrington offers insightful observations about masculinity, friendship, and the ethics of hunting.

David Foster Wallace, "Consider the Lobster," 2004. This thought-provoking essay by the noted (and late) fiction writer centers on his visit to a lobster festival in Maine and is good fodder for a discussion of the ethics of animal consumption.

Michael Pollan, *The Omnivore's Dilemma: A Natural History of Four Meals*, 2006. In the last third of this wide-ranging, articulate work devoted to natural and unnatural contemporary food chains, Pollan, a food writer, takes up hunting in order to explore the ethical, ecological, and nutritional value of providing one's own meat.

Brian Luke, *Brutal: Manhood and the Exploitation of Animals*, 2007. A former philosophy professor, Luke argues that human hunting is not natural or a part of evolution but a lynchpin of patriarchal masculinity.

Jeffrey P. Cain, "Blood Culture and the Problem of Decadence," in *Wild Games: Hunting and Fishing Traditions in North America*, 2009. An English professor and hunter, Cain, in this cogent essay, examines the commercialization of hunting as epitomized by the popular outdoor retailer Cabela's. He argues that such commercialization encourages inauthentic hunting. Other essays in this collection focus on the folklore of deer hunting, poaching and ethnicity, and sport hunting.

Robert DeMott and Dave Smith, eds., *Afield: American Writers on Bird Dogs*, 2010. It might be said that, rather than using dogs to hunt birds, hunters pursue birds in order to be with their bird dogs. A sparkling introduction on the relationsip between hunting and writing sets the stage for essays by Richard Ford, Jim Harrison, Thomas McGuane, and others.

Lily Raff McCaulou, *Call of the Mild: Learning to Hunt My Own Dinner*, 2012. McCaulou moved from the East Coast to central Oregon to take a journalism job and ended up a devoted hunter in the process. An engaging introduction to hunting for nonhunters, the book also offers helpful discussions of related issues such as ethics, food, gender, and the environment.

Steven Rinella, *Meat Eater: Adventures from the Life of an American Hunter*, 2012. Rinella, a lifelong hunter and Sportsman Channel host, offers chapters on hunting various species, with "Tasting Notes" on each species (squirrel, bear, deer, beaver, even mountain lion).

Paula Young Lee, *Deer Hunting in Paris: A Memoir of God, Guns and Game Meat*, 2013. A memoir of learning to hunt in Paris, Maine, this book by a historian and sometime academic is an engaging example of current do-it-yourself food culture.

Notes

Introduction

1. "2011 National Survey of Fishing, Hunting, and Wildlife-Associated Recreation," U.S. Fish and Wildlife Service, http://www.census.gov/prod/2012pubs/fhw11-nat.pdf (accessed February 8, 2016).

2. "Occupational Outlook Handbook: Postsecondary Teachers," Bureau of Labor Statistics, http://www.bls.gov/ooh/education-training-and-library/postsecondary-teachers .htm (accessed February 8, 2016).

3. "Employees in Postsecondary Institutions, Fall 2009, and Salaries of Full-Time Instructional Staff, 2009-10," National Center for Educational Statistics, http://nces.ed.gov/ pubs2011/2011150.pdf (accessed February 8, 2016).

4. "2011 National Survey."

Gun and Gown

1. Tovar Cerulli, "Meat and Meanings: Adult-Onset Hunters' Cultural Discourses of the Hunt" (master's thesis, University of Massachusetts, 2011), http://tovarcerulli.com/ wp-content/uploads/2012/01/Cerulli_Thesis_Meat-and-Meanings.pdf (accessed February 8, 2016).

Becoming-Academic and Becoming-Animal

1. All names are pseudonyms. To ensure anonymity, the people depicted in this ethnography are composites of a variety of individuals observed while conducting research.

2. Finn Lynge, *Arctic Wars, Animal Rights, Endangered Peoples,* trans. Marianne Stenbaek (Boston: University Press of New England, 1992).

3. William Cronon, "The Trouble with Wilderness: or, Getting Back to the Wrong Nature," in *Rethinking the Human Place in Nature,* ed. William Cronon (New York: Norton, 1995), 69–90.

4. Gilles Deleuze and Felix Guattari, *A Thousand Plateaus: Capitalism and Schizophrenia* (Minneapolis: University of Minnesota Press, 1987).

5. Annette Watson and Orville H. Huntington, "They're Here, I Can Feel Them: The Epistemic Spaces of Indigenous and Western Knowledges," *Social and Cultural Geography* 9, no. 3 (2008): 257–281.

6. Sean Patrick Farrell, "The Urban Deerslayer," *New York Times,* November 24, 2009, http://www.nytimes.com/2 (accessed January 15, 2016).

Out of the Closet

1. Henry David Thoreau, *Walden, or Life in the Woods* (New York: Random House, 1991), 172.

2. Aldo Leopold, *A Sand County Almanac* (New York: Oxford University Press, 1966), 176, 55, 57–58.

3. Ernest Hemingway, *The Old Man and the Sea* (New York: Charles Scribner's Sons, 1952), 75.

4. Dana Lamb, *The Fishing's Only Part of It* (Clinton, N.J.: Amwell Press, 1982), 170.

The Knife, the Deer, and the Student

1. Robert Remington, "U of Alberta Professor Says: Let Us Prey," *National Post* (Toronto, Canada), November 14, 2001, http://sports.espn.go.com/espn/print?id=1278134 &type=story (accessed January 15, 2016).

A View from the Saddle

1. John C. McKinney, *Constructive Typology and Social Theory* (New York: Appleton-Century-Crofts, 1966), 71.

2. Raymond Carr, *English Fox Hunting: A History* (London: Weidenfield and Nicholson, 1976).

3. Michael Clayton, *Endangered Species: Foxhunting—the History, the Passion and the Fight for Survival* (Shrewsbury: Swan Hill Press, 2004).

4. Emma Griffin, *Blood Sport: Hunting in Britain since 1066* (New Haven: Yale University Press, 2007), 238.

5. Lionel Edwards, *The Wiles of the Fox* (London: The Medici Society and The Sporting Gallery, 1932), 8.

6. Clayton, *Endangered Species.*

7. J. A. Ewald et al., "Fox-Hunting in England and Wales: Its Contribution to the Management of Woodland and Other Habitats," *Biodiversity and Conservation* 15 (2006): 4309–4334.

8. J. Finch, "'What More Were the Pastures of Leicester to Me?' Hunting, Landscape Character, and the Politics of Place," *International Journal of Cultural Property* 14 (2007): 361–383.

9. Mary T. Hufford, *Chaseworld: Foxhunting and Storytelling in New Jersey's Pine Barrens* (Philadelphia: University of Pennsylvania Press, 1992).

10. Chris Philo and Chris Wilbert, eds., *Animal Spaces, Beastly Places: New Geographies of Human–Animal Relations* (London: Routledge, 2000).

11. Alison Acton, "Getting By with a Little Help from My Hunter: Riding to Hounds in English Foxhound Packs," in *Hunting—Philosophy for Everyone: In Search of the Wild Life,* ed. Nathan Kowalsky (West Sussex: Wiley-Blackwell, 2010), 80–92.

12. Donna Haraway, *When Species Meet* (Minneapolis: University of Minnesota Press, 2008), 224.

13. Roger Scruton, *On Hunting* (London: Yellow Jersey Press, 1998), 60–61.

14. Ibid., 93.

15. Yoi Over, *Bells of the Chase* (London: Hutchinson and Co., n.d), 17.

16. Paul Milbourne, "The Complexities of Hunting in Rural England and Wales," *Sociologia Ruralis* 43, no. 3 (July 2003): 289–308.

17. Eric A. Eliason, "Foxhunting Folkways under Fire and the Crisis of Traditional Moral Knowledge," *Western Folkways* 63, no. 1/2 (Winter–Spring 2004): 150.

18. Garry Marvin, "Inedibility, Unspeakability, and Structures of Pursuit in the English Foxhunt," in *Representing Animals*, ed. Nigel Rothfels (Bloomington: Indiana University Press, 2002), 139.

19. Donna Landry, *Invention of the Countryside: Hunting, Walking and Ecology in English Literature 1671–1831* (Hampshire: Palgrave, 2001).

20. Keith Thomas, *Man and the Natural World. Changing Attitudes in England 1500–1800* (New York: Oxford University Press, 1983), 182.

21. G. E. Mingay, *Parliamentary Enclosure in England* (London: Longman, 1997).

22. Roger Scruton, "Landscape: The View of the Hunters and the Farmers," *Open Democracy* (June 25, 2002), https://www.opendemocracy.net/ecology-hunting/article_415.jsp (accessed February 12, 2016).

23. Robert Smith Surtees, *The Analysis of the Hunting Field* (New York: Appleton, 1904), 155.

24. Jane Ridley, *Foxhunting* (New York: HarperCollins, 1990), 115.

25. Roger Longrigg, *The History of Foxhunting* (London: Macmillan, 1975).

26. Tom McGurk, "Greens Must Not Be Allowed to Sabotage Our Ancient Rituals," *Sunday Business Post,* December 30, 2007, http://www.businesspost.ie/greens-must-not-be-allowed-to-sabotage-our-ancient-rituals-2/ (accessed February 12, 2016).

27. Stuart R. Harrop, "The Hunting Act 2004: Cruelty, Countryside, Conservation, Culture or a Class Act?" *Environmental Law Review* 7 (2005): 201–205; Allyson May, *The Fox-Hunting Controversy* (New York City: Routledge, 2013).

28. Adam Boulton, *Tony's Ten Years: Memories of the Blair Administration* (London: Pocket Books, 2009), 197.

29. Ibid.; Andy McSmith, "Prescott 'Redoubles' Determination to Abolish Foxhunting," *The Telegraph,* September 26, 2000, http://www.telegraph.co.uk/news/uknews/1356821/Prescott-redoubles-determination-to-abolish-foxhunting.html (accessed February 12, 2016).

30. DPP v. Anthony Wright. In the High Court of Justice Queen's Bench Division, Case No. Co/2553/2008, February 4, 2009.

31. Martin Kettle, "World Exclusive Tony Blair Interview," *The Guardian,* August 31, 2010, http://www.theguardian.com/politics/2010/sep/01/tony-blair-a-journey-interview (accessed February 12, 2016).

32. Charlie Pye-Smith, *Rural Rites: Hunting and the Politics of Prejudice* (House of Commons, London: All Party Parliamentary Middle Way Group, 2006), 40.

33. Anthony Giddens, *Runaway World* (London: Profile Books, 2002).

34. Marvin, "Inedibility," 140.

35. Eliason, "Foxhunting Folkways," 158.

36. Tim Ingold, *Perception of the Environment: Essays on Livelihood, Dwelling and Skill* (London: Routledge, 2000); José Ortega y Gasset, *Meditations on Hunting,* trans. Howard B. Wescott (Belgrade, Mont.: Wilderness Adventures Press, 1995).

37. May, *The Fox-Hunting Controversy.*

38. Hugh Brody, "The Hunter's View of Landscape: A Response to Roger Scruton,"

Open Democracy (August 20, 2002), https://www.opendemocracy.net/ecology-hunting/article_430.jsp (accessed February 12, 2016).

39. Stuart R. Harrop and D. F. Harrop, "The Conservation of Biodiversity, the Regulation of Its Management and the Current and Prospective Regulation of Hunting with Hounds," *Submission to the Committee of Inquiry into the Impact of Hunting with Dogs,* 2000.

40. Lord Burns, "Debate on the Hunting Bill," *Hansard,* March 12, 2001, 533, http://www.publications.parliament.uk/pa/ld200001/ldhansrd/vo010312/text/10312-06.htm#10312-06_para26 (accessed February 12, 2016).

41. Kaoru Fukuda, "Different Views of Animals and Cruelty to Animals: Cases in Fox-Hunting and Pet-Keeping in Britain," *Anthropology Today* 13, no. 5 (October 1997): 2–6.

42. May, *The Fox-Hunting Controversy.*

43. James Barrington, "A Plea for the Wild," *Open Democracy* (September 22, 2004), https://www.opendemocracy.net/ecology-hunting/article_2103.jsp (accessed February 12, 2016).

44. Sandra E. Baker and David W. MacDonald, "Foxes and Foxhunting on Farms in Wiltshire: A Case Study," *Journal of Rural Studies* 16 (2000): 185–201.

45. Mark Thomas, "Mark Thomas Warns the Toffs That Polo Is Next," *New Statesman,* September 27, 2004, http://www.newstatesman.com/node/148933 (accessed February 12, 2016).

46. John Prescott, "John Prescott on Fox-Hunting: Kill Off This Plan—Not the Foxes," *Mirror,* March 23, 2014, http://www.mirror.co.uk/news/uk-news/john-prescott-fox-hunting-kill-3273633 (accessed February 12, 2016).

47. Hufford, *Chaseworld*; Venetia Newall, "The Unspeakable in Pursuit of the Uneatable: Some Comments on Fox Hunting," *Folklore* 94, no.1 (1983): 86–90.

48. Barrington, "A Plea for the Wild."

49. "History," Banwen Miners Hunt, http://www.banwenminershunt.co.uk/page7.htm (accessed February 12, 2016).

50. Milbourne, "The Complexities of Hunting."

Duck Dynasty

1. TV by the Numbers, "Duck Dynasty Season 4 Premiere Garners 11.8 Million Viewers, Sets Records," *TV by the Numbers,* August 15, 2013, http://tvbythenumbers.zap2it.com/2013/08/15/duck-dynasty-season-4-premire-garners-11-8-million-viewers-becoming-the-number-1-nofiction-telecast-in-cable-history/ (accessed February 8, 2016).

2. Chris Starrs, "Jeff Foxworthy (b. 1958)," *New Georgia Encyclopedia,* http://www.georgiaencyclopedia.org/articles/arts-culture/jeff-foxworthy-b-1958 (accessed February 8, 2016).

3. Mark Damian Duda, Martin F. Jones, and Andrea Criscione, *The Sportsman's Voice: Hunting and Fishing in America* (State College, Pa.: Venture Publishing, 2010). See also Richelle Winkler and Keith Warnke, "The Future of Hunting: An Age-Period-Cohort Analysis of Deer Hunter Decline," *Population and Environment* 34, no. 4 (2013): 460–480.

4. Paul Shepard, *The Tender Carnivore* (New York: Charles Scribner's Sons, 1973), 122–123.

5. M. N. Peterson, "An Approach for Demonstrating the Social Legitimacy of Hunting," *Wildlife Society Bulletin* 32, no. 2 (2004): 310–321, 313.

6. M. N. Peterson et al., "How Hunting Strengthens Social Awareness of Coupled Human and Natural Systems," *Wildlife Biology in Practice* 6, no. 2 (2010): 127–143.

7. Jeffrey P. Cain, "Blood Culture and the Problem of Decadence," in *Wild Games: Hunting and Fishing Traditions in North America,* ed. Dennis Cutchins and Eric A. Eliason (Knoxville: University of Tennessee Press, 2009).

8. Ibid., 47.

Snake Bit on the Ogeechee

1. Hal Herzog, *Some We Love, Some We Hate, Some We Eat* (New York: HarperCollins, 2010), 44.

2. Harry W. Greene, *Snakes: The Evolution of Mystery in Nature* (Berkeley: University of California Press, 1997).

3. Archie Carr, *The Windward Road* (New York: Knopf, 1956).

4. Herzog, *Some We Love,* 44.

5. Roger Conant and Joseph T. Collins, *Reptiles and Amphibians of Eastern/Central North America* (Boston: Houghton Mifflin, 1998), 401.

6. "Venomous Snakes FAQs," Department of Wildlife Ecology and Conservation, University of Florida, http://ufwildlife.ifas.ufl.edu/venomous snake faqs.shtml (accessed February 15, 2016).

7. Greene, *Snakes,* 77–91.

8. Emily Dickinson, "Snake," *The Literature Network,* http://www.onlineliterature .com/dickinson/455/ (accessed February 15, 2016).

9. James Dickey, "Reincarnation," in *Buckdancer's Choice* (Middleton, Conn.: Wesleyan University Press, 1965), 29.

10. James Dickey, *The Enemy from Eden* (Northridge, Calif.: Lord John Press, 1978), 2.

11. Edward Abbey, *Desert Solitaire* (New York: Simon and Schuster, 1968), 20.

12. Ibid., 23, 24.

13. Ibid., 25.

14. Margaret Atwood, *Selected Poems II: Poems Selected and New 1976–1986* (Boston: Houghton Mifflin 1987), 92.

15. Ibid., 88.

16. Ibid., 88.

17. Ibid., 89.

18. Ibid., 90, 95, 93.

19. Greene, *Snakes,* 303, 304.

20. Ibid., 305.

21. Atwood, *Selected Poems II,* 89.

Squirrel Hunting and the View from Here

1. José Ortega y Gasset, *Meditations on Hunting,* trans. Howard B. Wescott (Belgrade, Mont.: Wilderness Adventures, 1995), 129.

2. Archibald Rutledge, *An American Hunter* (New York: Frederick A. Stokes, 1937), quoted in Chuck Wechsler and Jim Casada, eds., *Passages: The Greatest Quotations from Sporting Literature* (Columbia, S.C.: Sporting Classics, 2011), n.p.

3. David Hume, *A Treatise of Human Nature* (Oxford: Oxford University Press), 451–452.

4. Thomas Wyatt, "Whoso List to Hunt," in *The Norton Anthology of Poetry*, ed. Alexander W. Allison et al. (New York: W. W. Norton, 1983), 90.

5. Sherod Santos, ed., *Greek Lyric Poetry: A New Translation* (New York: Norton, 2005), 139.

6. Susan Wolf, "Moral Saints," *Journal of Philosophy* 79, no. 8 (1982): 419–439. *JSTOR*, links.jstor.org/sici=0022-362X%28198208%2979%3A8%3C419%3AMS%3E2.0.CO%3 B2-0, 419.

7. Ibid., 423.

8. Ibid., 422.

9. Ibid., 422.

10. Susan Wolf, "Morality and the View from Here," *Journal of Ethics* 3, no. 3 (1999): 203–223. *JSTOR*, www.jstor.org/stable/25115614, 212.

11. Ibid., 203, 223.

12. Frans de Waal, *The Atheist and the Bonobo: In Search of Humanism among the Primates* (New York: W. W. Norton, 2013), 184.

13. Wolf, "Morality," 219.

Hunting Ethics

1. Aldo Leopold, *A Sand County Almanac and Sketches Here and There*, Special Commemorative ed. (New York: Oxford University Press, 1987), vii.

2. Roderick Nash, *Wilderness and the American Mind*, 4th ed. (New Haven: Yale University Press, 2001), 147–150.

3. Ibid., 150.

4. Theodore Roosevelt, "The American Wilderness," in *The Great New Wilderness Debate*, ed. J. Baird Callicott and Michael P. Nelson (Athens: University of Georgia Press, 1998), 74.

5. "Fair Chase Statement," Boone and Crockett Club, 2016, http://www.boone-crockett.org/huntingEthics/ethics_fairchase.asp (accessed January 15, 2016).

6. Leopold, *A Sand County Almanac*, 177–178.

7. Ibid., 178.

8. Ibid.

9. Ibid., 179.

10. Ibid., 178.

11. Alasdair MacIntyre, *After Virtue*, 3rd ed. (South Bend: University of Notre Dame Press, 2007), 187.

12. Theodore Roosevelt, "Letter to Francis V. Greene, on September 23, 1897," Theodore Roosevelt Papers, Library of Congress.

13. Gary Varner, *In Nature's Interests: Interests, Animal Rights, and Environmental Ethics* (Oxford: Oxford University Press, 1998), 98–120.

14. Leopold, *A Sand County Almanac*, 179.

Vacating the Human Condition

1. José Ortega y Gasset, *Meditations on Hunting*, trans. Howard B. Wescott (Belgrade, Mont.: Wilderness Adventures Press, 1995), 121.

2. Ibid., 38–39.

3. Ibid., 40.

4. Ibid., 125.

5. Ibid., 69.

6. Ibid., 140.

7. Ibid., 70.

8. Ibid., 71.

9. Ibid., 140.

10. Ibid., 140, 139.

11. Ibid., 140.

12. Ibid., 30.

13. Ibid., 137.

14. Ibid., 137.

15. Ibid., 139.

16. Ibid., 35, 113.

17. Ibid., 113.

18. Ibid., 132.

19. Ibid., 138–139.

20. Ibid., 59.

21. Ibid., 59.

22. Ibid., 59.

23. Ibid., 106.

24. Ibid., 59.

25. Ibid., 60.

26. Ibid., 64.

27. Ibid., 64.

28. Ibid., 65.

29. Ibid., 138.

30. Ibid., 106.

31. Ibid., 121.

32. A Carrier Indian from British Columbia, quoted in David Abram, *Becoming Animal: An Earthly Cosmology* (New York: Pantheon Books, 2010), 259.

33. Ortega, *Meditations*, 125.

34. Ibid., 121.

Confessions of a Sublime Ape

1. Edward Abbey, *One Life at a Time, Please* (New York: Holt, 1987), 39.

2. Edward Abbey, *The Serpents of Paradise* (New York: Holt, 2000), 288.

3. Ibid., 287.

4. Annie Dillard, "Living like Weasels," in *Literature and the Environment: A Reader on Nature and Culture,* ed. Lorraine Anders, Scott Slovic, and John P. O'Grady (New York: Longman, 1999), 7.

5. John Haines, *Winter News* (Middletown, Conn.: Wesleyan University Press, 1982), 13.

6. John Haines, *The Stars, the Snow, the Fire* (St. Paul, Minn.: Graywolf, 2000), 28.

7. Ibid., 28, 22.

8. Edmund Burke, *A Philosophical Enquiry into the Sublime and Beautiful and Other Pre-Revolutionary Writings* (New York: Penguin, 1998), 86.

9. Ibid., 125.

10. Mark P. O. Morford and Robert J. Lenardon, eds., "Homeric Hymn to Artemis," in *Classical Mythology*, 5th ed. (Oxford: Oxford University Press, 1994), 141.

11. Ibid., 141.

12. Burke, *A Philosophical Enquiry*, 165.

13. Haines, *The Stars*, 124.

14. Haines, *Winter News*, 27.

15. Haines, *The Stars*, 158.

16. Haines, *Winter News*, 32.

17. James Dickey, "A Dog Sleeping at My Feet," in *Literature and the Environment: A Reader on Nature and Culture*, ed. Lorraine Anders, Scott Slovic, and John P. O'Grady (New York: Longman, 1999), 115–117.

18. William Faulkner, *Go Down, Moses* (New York: Vintage, 1970), 158.

19. Aldo Leopold, *A Sand County Almanac and Sketches Here and There* (Oxford: Oxford University Press, 1949), 121.

20. Burke, *A Philosophical Inquiry*, 101.

21. Haines, *The Stars*, 124.

22. Burke, *A Philosophical Inquiry*, 165.

23. Ibid., 109.

24. Ibid., 90.

25. Walt Harrington, *The Everlasting Stream* (New York: Grove, 2002), 102.

26. Burke, *A Philosophical Inquiry*, 103.

27. Faulkner, *Go Down*, 200.

28. Haines, *The Stars*, 155, 125.

29. Faulkner, *Go Down*, 169.

Rebuilding the Wholesome Machinery of Excitement

1. "What Constitutes a True Sportsman," *American Sportsman*, November 1872, cited by John F. Reiger, *American Sportsmen and the Origin of Conservation*, 3rd ed. (Corvallis: Oregon State University Press, 2001), 29. Italics mine.

2. Daniel Herman, *Hunting and the American Imagination* (Washington, D. C.: Smithsonian Institution Press, 2001). See especially chapter 10.

3. Darcy Ingram, *Wildlife Conservation, and Conflict in Quebec, 1840–1914* (Vancouver: University of British Columbia Press, 2013).

4. Andrea L. Smalley, "'I Just Like to Kill Things': Women, Men and the Gender of Sport Hunting in the United States, 1940–1973," *Gender and History* 17, no. 1 (2005): 192.

5. Herman, *Hunting and the American Imagination*, 272, 277.

6. Matt Cartmill, *A View to a Death in the Morning: Hunting and Nature through History* (Cambridge, Mass.: Harvard University Press, 1993), 63, 64 .

7. Smalley, "'I Just Like to Kill Things,'" 203.

8. Roger Caras, *Death as a Way of Life* (Boston: Little Brown, 1970), 11–12.

9. Ibid., 45.

10. Ibid., 8–9.

11. Ibid., 17.

12. Ann Causey, "On the Morality of Hunting," *Environmental Ethics* 11 (1989): 330.

13. Ibid., 332.

14. Valerius Geist, "The Carnivorous Herbivore: Hunting and Culture in Human Evolution," in *Hunting: Philosophy for Everyone,* ed. Nathan Kowalsky (West Sussex, UK: Wiley-Blackwell, 2010), 121–133.

15. Cartmill, *A View to a Death.*

16. José Ortega y Gasset, *Meditations on Hunting,* trans. Howard B. Wescott (Belgrade, Mont.: Wilderness Adventure Press, 1995), 110. Italics mine.

17. Herman, *Hunting,* 225.

18. David Petersen, *Heartsblood: Hunting, Spirituality, and Wildness in America* (Washington, D.C.: Island Press, 2000).

19. Ibid., 22.

20. Ibid., 23.

21. Ted Kerasote, *Heart of Home* (New York: Villard, 1997).

22. Petersen, *Heartsblood,* 82.

23. Ibid., 22.

Contributors

ALISON ACTON is a lecturer in social science and a freelance academic who conducts much of her anthropological fieldwork while hunting on horseback. Her focus is on the relationship between landscape, humans, animals, and hunting. She has contributed to the anthology *Hunting: Philosophy for Everyone* (2010) and also had papers published in the journals *Anthrozoos* and *Landscape Research* and has been featured on the BBC Radio 4 program *Thinking Allowed.*

DAVID BRUZINA teaches ESOL, composition, and literature courses in the English Department at the University of South Carolina Aiken. His poems have appeared in a number of literary journals including *Green Mountains Review, Waccamaw,* and *StorySouth.* A native of Kentucky, he taught at various universities in Ohio, Virginia, and North Carolina before settling in South Carolina, where he now hunts, fishes, gardens, and writes.

TOVAR CERULLI is author of *The Mindful Carnivore: A Vegetarian's Hunt for Sustenance* (2012). He recently completed a Ph.D. in communication at the University of Massachusetts at Amherst, where his research focused on Euro-American and Ojibwe hunting communities' ways of talking about wolves. A consultant dedicated to fostering conservation endeavors in which diverse views are valued, he lives in Vermont.

GREGORY A. CLARK is chair of the philosophy department at North Park University. He was born and raised in central Illinois but now lives in a Mennonite community in Chicago. His publications explore conflicts between urban and rural values. He teaches experiential courses such as "Philosophy of Nature," "Zen and Archery," "Walking," "Intentional Christian Community," "The Zombie Apocalypse," and "Spirit in the Wilderness." His writing has appeared in Seattle Pacific University's *Lingua* art journal and *Etc.* magazine.

LEE FOOTE'S activities declarify his identity: father, husband, banjoist, dog trainer, author, gardener, wetland ecologist, hunter, motorcyclist, volunteer, churchgoer. He works, however, as a professor of renewable resources and director of the 240-acre Devonian Botanic Garden at the University of Alberta in Edmonton. He writes for several magazines, is active in conservation organizations, and maintains active teaching and research programs. His most recent book is *Oral Exams* (2015).

DAVID GRAHAM HENDERSON teaches philosophy and environmental thought at Western Carolina University. Born and raised in the piney woods of Texas, he now lives in the Great Balsam Mountains of North Carolina, with his wife and children. Having earned a master's degree in wildlife science and a doctorate in philosophy, he works to keep his teaching and writing about the American wilderness experience grounded in as much personal wilderness experience as he can get.

DOUGLAS HIGBEE is associate professor of English and Anonymous Endowed Chair in the Humanities at the University of South Carolina Aiken. He is editor of *Military Culture and Education* (2010) and coeditor of *Teaching Representations of the First World War* (2017). He is the author of several articles on twentieth-century war poetry, including Siegfried Sassoon, Ivor Gurney, and Brian Turner.

CHARLES J. LIST is professor of philosophy at SUNY Plattsburgh in Plattsburgh, New York. He is the author of *Hunting, Fishing, and Environmental Virtue: Reconnecting Sportsmanship and Conservation* (2013) and has published numerous articles on the ethics of hunting, most recently "Local Food and the New Hunter," forthcoming in *The Oxford Handbook of Food Ethics*. He is a past Daniels Fellow at the National Sporting Library and Museum in Middleburg, Virginia, and continues to hunt and fish in the Champlain Valley and in the Adirondacks.

JEREMY LLOYD serves on the faculty of Great Smoky Mountains Institute at Tremont, a residential environmental learning center based in Great Smoky Mountains National Park, where he directs university programs, summer camps, and hiking and wilderness expeditions. He also teaches several courses in the Southern Appalachian Naturalist Certification Program. His work has appeared in *Sierra, Gray's Sporting Journal, The Sun, Fourth Genre, North Carolina Literary Review,* and other publications. Originally from Western Pennsylvania, he lives with his family in east Tennessee.

PHILIP MASON is assistant professor in the Department of Sociology, Geography, and Anthropology at the University of South Carolina Aiken. His research usually encompasses the relationship between religion and health or stratification among rural–urban locals. His work has been published in *Review of Religious Research, Population Research and Policy Review,* and *Journal of Maps,* among other outlets. Originally from Utah, Philip was an avid skier and climber, but since moving to the South he has become a novice hunter. In between his familial and academic duties, he hopes to harvest his first whitetail buck on local public swampland.

DONALD A. MUNSON is professor of biology and Joseph H. McLain Professor of Environmental Studies, Emeritus, at Washington College. He spent thirty-seven years on its faculty, where he chaired the Biology Department for twelve years and created and then directed the Environmental Studies Program for fifteen years. He has more than sixty-five publications/presentations and two Outstanding Teaching Awards to his credit. In his retirement he hunts and fishes on the Chesapeake Bay and in Montana, the Catskills, and the Adirondacks.

MICHAEL C. RYAN received his Ph.D. in American literature from Ohio University and is a language arts teacher and wrestling coach at Lancaster High School in south-central Ohio. He farms and hunts the cusp of the Appalachian foothills and regularly writes hunting and fishing articles for the agricultural magazine *Ohio's Country Journal*. His most recent scholarly article, on environmental literature of the Midwest, was recently published in *Dictionary of Midwestern Literature, Volume II* (2016).

BRIAN SEITZ is professor of philosophy at Babson College. He is the author of *The Trace of Representation* and *Intersubjectivity and the Double: Troubled Matters* (2016) and coauthor, with Thomas Thorp, of *The Iroquois and the Athenians: A Political Ontology* (2013). He is also coeditor, with Ron Scapp, of *Fashion Statements* (2010), *Etiquette* (2012), *Living with Class* (2013), and *Eating Culture* (1998). Seitz also has authored numerous articles in social and political philosophy and environmental philosophy.

DAVID SELIGMAN is professor emeritus of philosophy at Ripon College in Wisconsin, where he taught ethics, social and political philosophy, and environmental philosophy and served as vice president/dean of faculty and director of the Ethical Leadership Program. An avid fly fisherman and devoted hunter, he lives in Wisconsin with his wife and his spaniels and continues to reflect upon the place of humans in nature's cycles of death and life.

RICHARD SWINNEY is a residency-trained, board-certified emergency medicine physician practicing in rural Missouri. His articles on premodern combat trauma and medieval hunting have appeared in *SPADA 2: Anthology of Swordsmanship* (2010) and in *Acta Periodica Duellatorum*. Richard is a licensed master falconer and has been recognized as a master huntsman by St. Hubert's Rangers, an international brotherhood of medieval hunting enthusiasts. He is also the principal swordplay instructor of the Bramble Schoole of Defence.

GERALD T. THURMOND is a professor of sociology at Wofford College in Spartanburg, South Carolina, with a lifelong passion for animals, especially reptiles and birds. With John Lane, he is coeditor of *The Woods Stretched for Miles: New Nature Writing from the South* (1998) and has essays in *Pride of Place: A Contemporary Anthology of Texas Nature Writing* (2006), *Bartram's Living Legacy* (2010), and other publications. Six turtles live in his college office. He has a closet full of snakes and sometimes wonders why.

ANNETTE WATSON is associate professor of geography at the College of Charleston, where she teaches political science and environmental studies. Her research has appeared in policy and management journals, as well as journals on Indigenous studies; she is currently working in collaboration with Indigenous leaders on a study comparing the subsistence economies of Alaska Natives and the Gullah/Geechee of the U.S. Southeast.

J. B. WEIR is instructor of English at Guilford College in Greensboro, North Carolina, and a Ph.D. student in educational research methodology at the University of North Carolina at Greensboro. A graduate of the M.F.A. program in Creative Writing at UNCG, he has also taught at North Carolina A&T, St. Mary's College of Maryland, and Elon University. His recent research focuses on optimization algorithms in multistage test construction and on the role of data visualization in communicating quantitative information.

Index

hunters, general stereotypes of, 16, 19, 27, 29, 54, 58, 62–63, 67–68; academic stereotypes of: ix, 6, 14, 19, 24–25, 28–29, 31–32, 57, 152–55; academic administration view of, 32–33, 38–39, 46. *See also* antihunting sentiment

hunting, media representation of, 8, 18, 28, 38–39, 54, 62, 66, 155, 181

hunting, safety course, 46, 75

hunting, types of: boar, 97–107, 168; deer, 2, 18, 71–78, 100, 103, 121, 138, 146, 156, 162, 174; duck, ix, xi, 21, 30–33, 59, 66–67, 170; fox, 46–57; moose 21, 24, 26–27, 29, 169, 171; snakes, 79–96, 138; squirrel, 30, 63, 72, 109–116, 117–27. *See also* deer butchering

Hunting Act (U.K.), 54–58

ivory tower, ix, 16–17, 19, 22, 25, 29, 50, 55, 58, 67, 115

Jones, Allen, 187

Jones, Robert F., x

Kauffeld, Carl, 86–87

Lamb, Dana, 36

Larmouth, Donald, 141

Lea, Sydney, x

Leave No Trace program, 136–37

Le Guin, Ursula K., 146

Leibniz, Gottfried, 157

Leopold, Aldo, 34–35, 131–34, 136, 139, 143, 148, 170, 191

MacIntyre, Alistair, 134–35

McMurtry, Larry, 90

Monbiot, George, 179

National Sporting Library and Museum, 182

National Wildlife Federation, 20

Native Americans, 21–29, 74, 88, 140

Ortega y Gasset, José, 7, 9, 120, 152–65, 177, 188

Park, Robert, 47, 49

PETA (People for the Ethical Treatment of Animals), 145, 149

Petersen, David, 187, 190–91

Phoebus, Gaston, 99, 100–101, 103

Pollan, Michael, 18

Prescott, John, 54–55, 58

rednecks, 15–16, 22, 60, 62, 68, 73, 75, 78. *See also* Southerners

Roosevelt, Theodore, 15, 132–33, 135–36, 190–92

Rutledge, Archibald, 120

St. Hubert, 98–99

Salten, Felix. See *Bambi*

Schullery, Paul, 151

Scruton, Roger, 51, 53

Shepard, Paul, 64, 187

Singer, Peter, 124, 138

Smalley, Andrea, 183–84, 185

Southerners/Southern culture, 59–68, 82. *See also* rednecks

Thoreau, Henry David, 33, 113–15

Turner, Frederick Jackson, 132–33

United States Fish and Wildlife Service, 6

Valdene, Guy de la, xi

Varner, Gary, 138

vegetarianism/veganism, 14, 15, 39, 46, 74–75, 125, 132

White, T. H., vii

wildlife management, 34, 76–77, 133, 138

Wolf, Susan, 123–24

Wulff, Lee, 141, 143

Wyatt, Thomas, 121–22